DIMONA: THE THIRD TEMPLE?
The Story Behind the
Vanunu Revelation

Dimona: the third temple? The Story Behind the Vanunu Revelation

Mark Gaffney

Amana Books
Brattleboro, VT

Acknowledgements

Many people provided invaluable assistance in the writing of this book. Those deserving special thanks include William Arkin, Institute for Policy Studies; Dr. Alan Berman, Center for Naval Analysis; Noam Chomsky, Department of Linguistics and Philosophy, MIT, for pointing the way; Avner Cohen, Harvard Law School; Len Conley, Committee for a Nuclear-Free Berkeley; Jane Hunter, Editor, *Israeli Foreign Affairs* whose many suggestions were indispensable; Scott Kennedy, Resource Center for Non-violence (Santa Cruz), who read an early draft; Dr. Richard Muller and Dr. Charles Schwartz, Department of Physics, UC Berkeley; Taysir Nashif, author; John Pike, Federation of American Scientists; Daniel Rubinstein, Hebrew translator; Dr. Michel Roublev, International Jewish Peace Union; Doris Safie, for her keen editing skills; Alan Solomonow, American Friends Service Committee; Dr. Ronald Walters, Department of Political Science, Howard University; Jean Weininger, editor; Ann Wheybrow, editor-typist; and last, but not least, Judy Zimmet, Garrett Lambrev and Yani Herdes of the Mordechai Vanunu Defense Committee, for providing crucial source material on Mr. Vanunu.

I would also like to thank the visiting scholars to UC Berkeley's Palestine Class for their superb lectures on the Middle East, background material which helped frame the context. Much credit also to Jock Taft, class organizer.

This book is dedicated to Swami Chidvilasananda

Table of Contents

What happened in Hiroshima was not just another page in history, but a major landmark, pointing out the crossroads for mankind. . . . It is an illusion to believe that nuclear weapons can be defensive. Nuclear weapons are means of extermination, and cannot protect any country, including Israel. . . . In our region I took the first step to show that the danger is real and immediate. . . . This is why I am in prison, this is why many people are in prisons all over the world. We must arouse people and warn them. Ours is the role of the angry prophet. . . . Only peace between states can promise real security.

—Mordechai Vanunu, Ashkelon Prison
December 5, 1987

Introduction

It was the economist John Maynard Keynes who called war "the consumer of hope." That was in 1919, after the Treaty of Versailles had divided up the spoils of the Great War. Truly, it had been a bloodbath, a war-to-end-war, and in defining the new peace in its aftermath the victors sought to bolster a colonial order that was in rapid transition. Change was in the air. Cavalry had only recently been displaced by the first primitive but effective mechanized vehicles. The airplane had made its debut in battle. And the beginnings of a world communications network was shrinking the globe. Keynes' 1919 remark was a fitting epitaph not only for the war, but for a way of life passing forever into memory.

No less did it sum up the Treaty of Versailles itself which, if it accomplished anything, certainly did *not* bring lasting peace. Keynes was well aware that it was not *only* war which consumed men's hopes, but in this case the unjust settlement that followed it as well. Keynes knew – *The Economic Consequences of the Peace* was his exploration of the fact – that, potentially at least, the seeds for future conflicts were already being sown. They were being sown in Europe by the imposition of crushing reparations on Germany certain to breed distrust and enmity rather than heal the wounds of war. Soon the conditions would be created for a second even greater war involving more nations in an almost geometric progression of violence, including genocide.

But Versailles was sowing the seeds for upheavals elsewhere as well, particularly in the Middle East. True, the danger was not immediate. The rumblings were still far off. But the stage was being set by the western democracies' unworthy refusal to accommodate – or even recognize – Arab and Third World nationalism. To make matters worse, in the 1917 Balfour Declaration Britain had committed itself to support a Zionist settler colony in Palestine, veritably the bosom of the Arab world. In part, the decision expressed the sympathy of some British politicians with the idea of a Jewish state in the land of ancient Israel. Britain's primary concern, however, was self-interest: the declaration was calculated to shore up the Crown's own Middle East empire. Jewish settlements in Palestine, it was thought, would constitute a European-oriented and westward-looking population base that would secure British domination of the Suez Canal, Transjordan and Iraqi oilfields for many years to come.

However, given the understandable resistance of indigenous Palestinians to the expropriation of lands that had been Arab for more than a thousand years, Britain's logic of empire was ill-conceived, at best. At worst, it was folly within a few years London's Middle East policy had devolved into a nightmare. As more Jewish immigrants poured into Palestine, conflicts generated between Arabs and Jews over land and identity were exacerbated until a chronic state of hostility was born. Without winners and without apparent end, that tragic struggle ultimately threatened to drag the Great Powers into yet another cataclysm. All this must have been obvious to far-sighted men, even in 1919 – and much lamented.

But another development held profound implications which were *not* foreseeable in 1919. No one then, except perhaps a handful of physicists, could have guessed that all of humanity stood poised together in that moment on the threshold of a wholly unexpected universe of wonder and horror. Soon the revolution in Newtonian physics which was already well underway in 1919 would change everything "..except," as Albert Einstein phrased it, "the way men think." Soon theoretical physics would be hitched by technology to the production of weapons of inconceivable power. Along with the new weapons would also emerge new and unprecedented military technologies and a whole new class of men to match them, an elite, in effect, a new priesthood of scientists, engineers, military specialists and bureaucrats. The products of their overarching efforts – weapons systems suitable for gods, but not for men – would in less than a lifetime alter the balance of world history beyond recognition.

The following book, a study of Israel's nuclear weapons program, is the story of one small part of that greater drama.

2

In recent years a number of writers have attempted to assess Israel's nuclear agenda. However, most have limited the range of their discussion, intentionally neglecting or excluding pertinent historical, political, cultural and moral factors. A key reason for this shortfall has been a notable absence of consensus on crucial historical details. Indeed, the history of the Arab-Israeli conflict has been as bitterly contended as the conflict itself. Writers seeking to produce a dispassionate account in such an emotionally charged debate – once having dared venture where even angels fear to tread – not surprisingly have tended to keep their heads down.

A second explanation also accounts for the conservatism of previous accounts. For years writers have suffered a perennial shortage of 'hard' information concerning Israel's nuclear status, due to the Israeli government's commitment to absolute secrecy. Moreover, whatever scraps of evidence were available tended to be widely scattered or buried in scholarly journals. For all these reasons, the 'big picture' – the bird's-eye view – of Israel's nuclear agenda has remained elusive.

The result, unfortunately, has been an uninformed public. At the time of writing, September 1988, few Americans understood the pivotal role Israel's nuclear program has played in the unfolding conflict between Arabs and Jews in the Middle East, not to mention its growing implications for world peace.

Ironically, the level of ignorance and misinformation is even greater in Israel, where the honest dimensions of the nuclear peril have yet to penetrate the consciousness of the average citizen. In Israel nuclear weapons have a commonly perceived status unique among the Western democracies. In Israel political leaders have not been held accountable for public statements amounting to outright denials, even when *directly* contradicted by incontrovertible evidence – illustrating the prevailing atmosphere in the country with barometric accuracy.

Such statements have not been limited to the hawkish right. In early 1986 the well-known U.S. scientist Carl Sagan gave a moving address in Jerusalem in which he openly discussed the horrifying effects of nuclear war, including 'nuclear winter.' Sagan concluded that "if we take seriously our obligation to the tens of millions who perished in World War II, we must rid the planet of the blight of nuclear weapons." After Sagan finished speaking, the liberal Israeli Education Minister Yitzak Navon took the podium and quipped "Don't worry, according to the Bible, we have a pact with the Almighty which will protect us from such a dire end." Navon's little 'joke,' however cute, betrayed the absence in Israel of organized opposition on the nuclear question. No politician in the United States, nor in Western Europe, could have made such a comment without risking a public outcry and an immediate loss of credibility.

On the bright side, in the past few years a number of groundbreaking studies have appeared, including several by Israeli scholars,* finally bringing within reach a well-documented historical integration. As much as possible, the important conclusions of these studies have been incorporated in *Dimona the third temple?*

Of at least equal importance, revelations made in late 1986 by Mordechai Vanunu, a former Israeli nuclear technician, have swept aside part of the Israeli government's veil of secrecy, making a more comprehensive study possible for the first time. Drawing on many sources, therefore, and focusing as broadly as possible on historical antecedents as *well* as technological developments, *Dimona the third temple?* seeks to pull together as many pieces of the puzzle as possible in a multi-dimensional study in the hope of rendering the elusive whole more recognizable.

The book is divided into several sections. Chapter One chronicles the amazing story of Mr. Vanunu. Chapters Two and Three dive back in time to review the historical context which gave birth to Israel's nuclear program in the 1950s. Chapter Four surveys the available literature documenting the emergence of Israel's nuclear arsenal in the late 1960s. Chapter Five continues this review through the period of the 1970s, and includes a discussion of Israel's alliance with South Africa. Chapter Six focuses on Israeli nuclear strategies, and includes a discussion of the use of nuclear threats. Last but not least, Chapter Seven details the military build-up currently underway in the Middle East, outlining the increasing danger of another war, including a scenario for possible "first use" of nuclear weapons.

The reader should understand that this study is not offered without trepidation. Writing history is a risky and unforgiving business, unpalatable in my view because of the unavoidable need to rely on eyes which do not always obtain the clarity of a perfect lens. Moreover, large gaps in the record still remain. What is detailed here probably represents only a fraction of the true picture at best. For these reasons *Dimona the third temple?* makes no claim to be the final word

* Benny Morris, Simha Flapan, Tom Segev, Benjamin Beit Hallahmi and Avi Shlaim.

on the subject. Far from it. The book must be regarded as preliminary; the definitive study of the Israeli nuclear program remains to be written. Furthermore, some of the conclusions drawn herein, though plausible, should be regarded as speculative.

Even so, more than enough *is* known to warrant *Dimona the third temple?* Make no mistake this is a hard-hitting book, one that pulls no punches. The objective is to 'tell it like it is,' without mincing words, yet without being mean-spirited – no easy task. Because of the controversial subject matter, and the nature of the United States' ties to Israel, it is a book certain to be received with more than the usual degree of skepticism, to say the least. For these reasons I have spared no effort to document this case. In fact, I invite skepticism; and I urge the reader to use this study as a stepping stone for further research. In my view, the book's success will depend on whether it stimulates wider debate on these burning issues. Today such a debate is urgently needed.

3

In this context the term 'third temple' has two closely-related meanings. On the one hand it refers to the collective reality of the modern state of Israel, as Moshe Dayan himself used the term. But it also refers almost metaphorically to the proposed third reconstruction of the famous Temple of Jerusalem.

Two times in the ancient world that Temple was raised, first by King Solomon in the tenth century B.C.,* and then again after the

---

* Though the first Temple was erected during the reign of Solomon, the planning for it and associated government palaces was begun by Solomon's father and predecessor, King David, who in the tenth century B.C. unified the tribes of Israel and led them to battle against the Philistines and other neighboring tribes. After a series of impressive military victories, David established the first nation of Israel, ushering in the brief 'golden period' of Biblical Hebrew culture. According to the historian Orlinsky, the planning for a temple followed the creation of new administrative and military systems which consolidated political power in David's hands. A temple was the logical consequence of David's meteoric rise and the appearance of the new nation: "The centralization of political authority in the abode of the king called for a corresponding focus for religious jurisdiction, and David's ministers began to plan the erection of a royal chapel, a magnificent edifice which would represent the earthly dwelling of Israel's invisible God." Harry M. Orlinsky, 1960. *Ancient Israel,* Ithaca, Cornell University Press, p. 64.

release of the Hebrews from Babylonian captivity in 540 B.C. In each case the Temple was subsequently destroyed, the second and final occasion occuring in 70 A.D. at the hands of the Romans. As a result, today only a fragment of the original Temple remains – one foundational wall – along the western margin of the Dome of the Rock compound. Known as the 'Wailing Wall,' those remains continue to be a central devotional shrine for contemporary Israelis and Jews the world over. Recently, at least one article in the Israeli press has proposed a third reconstruction.

Given that contemporary Israel is a religious state where moral and political authority necessarily overlap – a reality consistent with the two meanings of 'third temple' – the reasoning behind the title of this book ought to be apparent. In such circumstances it is appropriate to ask whether a third temple has *already* risen, not in Jerusalem, as proposed, but in the Negev in the form of a nuclear weapons-producing reactor. That such a proposition is shocking – particularly in light of the spiritual richness of Judaism – I am only too aware; but it becomes inescapable once the facts are known. Hence the motivation for this book to evoke the fundamental moral question which spiritually aware Israelis and Diaspora Jews must now put to their political leaders and rabbis in no uncertain terms; namely, by what authority does democratic Israel deny its own citizens access to the facts regarding the government's expanding nuclear program?

I believe this was the issue that Mordechai Vanunu attempted to raise. Indeed, in the course of researching this study I have been struck repeatedly by the parallels between Mr. Vanunu and the prophets of the Old Testament. They, like Vanunu, sought to bring a greater truth before the people, even though doing so at times placed them in sharp conflict with the authority of the state. Here the parallels are nothing short of remarkable. Like Vanunu, more than a few of the Old Testament prophets paid a high price for speaking the truth. For condemning injustice or corruption where legitimate authority had been debased, prophets were outcast or persecuted. Like Vanunu, some experienced torture and/or imprisonment – even death. Yet on a number of occasions prophets correctly warned of impending calamities. Usually, because they were ignored, the people's suffering increased. Even so, their message could never be silenced for long. Ultimately, the prophets were visionaries who understood clearly that absolute security abides only in spiritual strength, not military power. In other words, in a world of nations real security means making peace with your neighbors, even if this implies painful compromise.

It is hoped that by illuminating facts which Israeli government spokesmen continue to deny, this study will bolster progressive Israelis in their efforts to save their country from modern-day zealots whose racism and intransigence – more than any Arab – now threaten the existence of Israel.

The reason why Israel's nuclear agenda should be a central concern for each and every American also needs to be clearly understood. As already noted, for better or worse Israel's fate is integrally linked with that of the Western powers, particularly the United States – and vice-versa. Unlike war-torn northern Ireland, the Falkland Islands, or Sri Lanka, Israel/Palestine, like Poland, lies very near to the geographic center-of-gravity of the modern world. As Israel/Palestine goes, so goes the Middle East and, very probably, most of humanity.

M.G.
Oakland
September, 1988

Chapter One

Mordechai Vanunu: Traitor, or Hero?

My brother is not a spy. He risked his life and his freedom to tell the little man in the street what was happening. He never tried to hurt anybody.
— Meir Vanunu [1]

For there is nothing hidden that shall not be uncovered; nor any secrets which shall not be revealed. So let them who have ears listen.
— Mark, 4; 22-23.

In late August 1986 a Colombian 'journalist' appeared in the Madrid offices of the London *Sunday Times* claiming he had inside information about an Israeli nuclear weapons program. The man's name was Oscar Guerrero. His story was far-fetched, to say the least.[2] Guerrero boasted he had helped a top Israeli scientist defect from Dimona, a nuclear reactor in Israel's Negev desert. Chased by the Mossad (the Israeli equivalent of the CIA), somehow they had escaped to Sydney, Australia, where they found haven in an Anglican Church.

On the other hand, Guerrero did present a handful of color photographs, some of which appeared authentic. After some checking, the *Sunday Times* realized that certain key structural features revealed in the photos jibed perfectly with the little that *was* known about Dimona. The photos were definitely 'inside' shots. The *Sunday Times* was intrigued enough to dispatch a member of its Insight Team who was trained in physics, Peter Hounam, back to Australia with Guerrero to interview the alleged scientist, and unmask the hoax. In a TV special produced later by the state-owned Australian Broadcasting

1

Corporation, Hounam described his first encounter with Mordechai Vanunu: "He was standing in Guerrero's bedroom, looking extremely frightened and shouting. Obviously he didn't know whether I could be trusted or whether I might be an Israeli agent come to grab him. So I had to first of all establish a good relationship with him. But pretty soon he agreed to tell me what he knew about the place [Dimona]. The most convincing thing that occurred early on was that he produced not only some more color prints of the plant but also a set of slides, about 22 slides, that he'd taken inside."[3]

It was then that a serious story first began to emerge. Vanunu quickly corrected Guerrero's false statements. He was not a scientist, but a nuclear technician. He had started work at Dimona in August 1977 as a *menahil,* a controller on the night shift. It was the start of an eight-year stint at the underground *Machon* II lab, Israel's top-secret plutonium separation plant. He had been laid off in October 1985.[4]

Vanunu's Personal Ordeal by Fire

Hounam quickly realized that for Vanunu, unlike Guerrero, the story of Dimona was political, not a money-making scam. Vanunu's primary motivation was moral.[5] For nearly nine years Mordechai Vanunu had worked – literally – in the bowels of the Israeli nuclear establishment, an experience that made his disenchantment and his activism all the more compelling. Engaged, Hounam could only listen as Vanunu poured out his story. He described how his alienation had grown from initial doubts, particularly after Menachem Begin's disastrous 1982 invasion of Lebanon. At that time Vanunu became involved with opponents of the war, helping to organize a solidarity campaign for Israeli soldiers imprisoned for refusing military service – the first *Yesh Gvul* movement. For Vanunu the Lebanon debacle had been a watershed, a turning point that shook his confidence in Israel's political leadership. Henceforth, Vanunu also began to question his own small role in producing weapons of mass destruction. By degrees he became convinced that the truth about the Israeli bomb – for so many years a closely guarded secret – needed to be told. The people of Israel and the world had to be warned of the awful peril awaiting them.

Vanunu also explained how he had come to sympathize with Palestinian nationalism. Two years before leaving Dimona, he had begun work on a Master's degree in philosophy at David Ben Gurion University in Beersheba, near his home. There he became involved in political meetings and demonstrations. At one point he was named chairperson of the student union court, and he also founded a branch of a student activist group known as 'Campus.'[6] These experiences brought Vanunu in contact with Bedouins and with Palestinian students from the West Bank. As he came to understand their situation – i.e., their oppression – he became increasingly supportive of their aspirations for self-determination. Vanunu's politics gravitated to the left. Such contacts also led to his interrogation by the *Shin Bet,* Israel's internal security police. He was warned to disassociate himself from Palestinians.[7] But the attempt to silence Vanunu failed in the sense that it only strengthened his determination to act.

Hounam listened in amazement as Vanunu told how he had smuggled a camera past security guards, and gathered, from within, an incontrovertible photographic record of Israel's secret nuclear agenda. Weeks later, in October 1985, Vanunu ended his career at Dimona, volunteering to be laid off during a fiscal cutback. Within two months he left Israel on a 'holiday vacation,' secreting the undeveloped film and other evidence out of the country in his backpack.

After touring through Southeast Asia – a solo journey that included several weeks in Thailand at a Buddhist monastery – Vanunu arrived in Sydney, Australia in the spring of 1985. One evening, while wandering the streets of King's Cross, Sydney's seedy entertainment district, Vanunu found himself at the entrance of a church-sponsored coffee shop. The lights were on, the doors were open. Later, the Anglican Vicar John McKnight recalled their first meeting: "I can remember the night quite distinctly. It was a Friday night. I was in the church with one other person, and Morde just walked in and started to look around...He explained that he was from Israel, on holiday in Australia. Over the months we got to know him as a very sincere person. He liked classical music. He was fairly intelligent."[8] Soon Vanunu became a regular visitor at the coffee shop and was drawn into the St. John's parish community.

Within two months Vanunu asked to be baptized as a Christian[9] – an act which, under the circumstances, surely illustrated the depths of his alienation. In fact, Vanunu's odyssey from Dimona across Asia to Sydney clearly had symbolic overtones, the renegade Vanunu having all the qualities of a complex character straight out of an existential plot worthy of a Camus or a Sartre. However, the difference between this man and the classical 'stranger' was that Vanunu had already stepped beyond philosophical nihilism and was moving toward personal redemption. Vanunu was a refugee, to be sure, but he was also a pilgrim. Moreover, because his eight-year up-close encounter with plutonium technology so clearly epitomized the radical central dilemma of the contemporary Western world, in a vital sense Vanunu's situation was also a case of 'Everyman.' The answers Vanunu sought but did not find in a Buddhist monastery he found, or thought he found, in a Christian community in Sydney. Later his girlfriend, Judy Zimmet, a nurse-midwife from Queens, New York, described him in terms of a Kierkegaard.[10] From an entirely different perspective – one more detached and analytical – Vanunu appeared to most resemble the simple fool of the Grail legend, the young Perceval, who became no less a hero despite his own naive innocence and lapses of judgement.[11] In any event Vanunu's rejection of narrow tribal loyalties was apparently an effort to embrace a wider humanity. Probably the complex sum of all these factors was responsible for his immediate appeal, outside Israel, as a rebel and a hero. Later, in solitary confinement, Vanunu would write of the struggle "to keep his soul alive."[12]

But to return to the story. Vanunu's involvement in the close-knit St John's Church community included participation in group discussions on issues such as poverty and the Christian commitment to peace. It was during one of these dialogues that Mordechai first discussed his job at Dimona helping to produce nuclear weapons from plutonium. According to Peter Couchman, an Australian journalist, at one point he offered to lead a session on peace and disarmament and to show some of the slides he had taken.[13] In the beginning, the group at St. John's, in their ignorance did not understand the significance of Vanunu's photographs. They were unaware of the international controversy surrounding the Dimona reactor. One member of the group, however, Oscar Guerrero, quickly recognized a potential windfall. Moved by the prospect of cashing in on Vanunu's 'state secrets,' Guerrero convinced his new Israeli friend of his own press connections, editors who would be interested in the story. So it happened that Guerrero contacted the *Times*.

The Plot Thickens

After several days of interrogating Vanunu, Hounam was convinced he had uncovered not only a great news story, but also a political bombshell of unimagined proportions. Vanunu was persuaded to fly back to London, whereupon the *Sunday Times* launched a systematic fact check to confirm the story. For two days the Israeli technician was debriefed by Dr. Frank Barnaby, a physicist formerly with Britain's bomb program. Barnaby was totally convinced: "It was clear to me that details he gave were scientifically accurate and clearly showed that he had not only worked on these processes but knew the details of the techniques. Also, the flow rates through the plant, which he quotes, exactly confirm the quantities of plutonium that were being made."[14]

The same photos and evidence were also presented to a group of British scientists whom the *Sunday Times* had approached earlier for consultation. One later summed up their views: "I knew in my bones [before] that the source was genuine, but now I am more convinced than ever." The expert confirmed that the photographs were entirely consistent with what a plutonium separation plant should look like. Moreover, he added: "I put this man in the category of a junior technician. All the things he says . . . fit with what would happen in a reprocessing plant . . . But there are gaps in his knowledge which he honestly says he does not know the answers to. If anyone was trying to con you I don't think he would have left such mysteries."[15]

The evidence was also reviewed by an American expert, Dr. Theodore Taylor, who once headed the Pentagon's atomic weapons test program. Taylor also was convinced: "There should no longer be any doubt that Israel is, and for at least a decade has been, a fully-fledged nuclear weapons state. The Israeli nuclear weapons program is considerably more advanced than indicated by any previous report or conjectures of which I am aware."[16]

Meanwhile, the *Sunday Times* background check confirmed Vanunu's identity. Inquiries made in Israel verified he had worked at Dimona. Finally, on September 23, the *Times* editors decided on a bold move: they presented some of the evidence, including Vanunu's passport, to the Israeli Ambassador in London, who categorically denied everything.[17] Two days later, however, Prime Minister Shimon Peres convened a meeting with leading editors of the Israeli press, instructing them to steer clear of the story – just the sort of indirect confirmation the *Sunday Times* was waiting for.[18] Peres' reflexive move to censor Israel's media prompted the editors' decision to publish the three-page exposé on Dimona.* It appeared ten days later on October 5, 1986.

* Hounam later explained: "Whenever a journalist here [in Israel] is getting close to an accurate story, someone from censorship calls him to confirm by telling the reporter to stay away from the story." Menachem Shalev, "Journalistic responsibility," *Jerusalem Post,* September 7, 1987.

During this period Vanunu could do nothing but wait for his story to appear. Day by day he became increasingly aware of the danger he faced, and more restive. To guarantee his personal safety, the *Sunday Times* staff had shuttled him from one safe house to another. After weeks of living on the run, however, Vanunu asked for a private hotel room. And despite the *Sunday Times* reassurances, he began to wonder if the story would ever be printed. Meanwhile he was free to wander the streets of London.

At about this time, the inimitable Oscar Guerrero re-appeared, demanding $300,000 in payoff money from the *Sunday Times* for his role as go-between. According to the *Sunday Times* account, before the matter of payment could be settled, Guerrero bolted with his version of the story to another newspaper, a tabloid, the *Sunday Mirror*. However, the *Mirror* was unconvinced. Instead of paying him off, the paper ran its own story on September 28, exposing Guerrero as "a liar and a hoax." The same article alluded to Vanunu's defection and even included his picture, which unfortunately became the source of much anxiety for Vanunu and no doubt contributed to the tragedy which ensued.

During a telephone conversation to Sydney on the morning of September 30, Vanunu worriedly told his friend Reverend McKnight that the *Sunday Mirror* article possibly had hurt his case by damaging his credibility. He feared the *Sunday Times* might not publish his story at all. He told McKnight he wanted to leave London "to get away from it all for a few days." Vanunu also called the *Sunday Times* with the news of his hastily planned departure. He told them he wanted to drop out of sight for a few days, to get lost in the crowd.[19] The editors tried to persuade him to remain in London. In particular, they warned him not to go abroad, since he could easily be picked up by Israeli agents.[20] Unfortunately, Vanunu ignored their advice. In what appears with hindsight to be a serious lapse of judgment, Vanunu checked out of the Mountbatten Hotel at 10 A.M. on September 30.[21] Instead of "getting lost in the crowd," he walked straight into the hands of the Mossad, and vanished from the face of the earth.

The disappearance itself – days before Vanunu's revelation in the *Sunday Times* stunned the world – generated a storm of international concern. Though Israeli diplomats denied any involvement in the incident, they began to come under mounting pressure from some members of the British Parliament to reveal the facts regarding Vanunu's unexplained disappearance.[22] At one point a television journalist and a reporter claimed they had seen Vanunu's name on a list in the Jerusalem District Court.[23] The list indicated a man named "Mordechai Vanunu" had appeared before the court on October 20. The rumors began to close in on the Israeli government. Finally on November 9, Israel verified the story. Vanunu was "under lawful detention in the wake of a court order which was issued following a hearing."[24] However, Israeli diplomats continued to deny that Vanunu left England against his will.[25] The official Israeli line was that he had been picked up by the Mossad off a yacht in the Mediterranean.[26] Rumors continued to circulate that a mysterious woman named 'Cindy' had been involved in the abduction. The woman, described as an attractive blonde, had been seen with Vanunu on the streets of London.

More details were revealed on December 23 by Vanunu himself as he was being taken into Jerusalem Court for a second hearing. As the prison van slowly passed a crowd of reporters, Vanunu pressed his hand firmly against the glass, displaying a message written on his palm:

Vanunu M. was highjacked in Rome, ItL.
30.9.86 2100. Came to Rome by BA fly 504.

Deciphered, the message read: "I'm Mordechai Vanunu. I was highjacked in Rome, Italy on September 30, 1986 at 9 P.M. I came to Rome via British Airways Flight 504."[27]

As the *Sunday Times* Insight Team later learned, Vanunu's cover had been blown even before he set foot in London. The Mossad had been tipped off about his whereabouts and his intentions days before he left Sydney.[28] Weeks later, the *Sunday Times* was able to verify from Israeli sources that the order to abduct Vanunu came from the very top – from Shimon Peres.[29] In fact, the order presented the Mossad with a very real dilemma, since Peres insisted that under no circumstances could the operation be allowed to embarrass Prime Minister Thatcher by overtly violating British laws. For years Britain – that is, Margaret Thatcher – had been one of Israel's staunchest backers in Europe, and her support must not be jeopardized. The order meant that Vanunu could not be kidnapped off the streets of London. Somehow he had to be lured outside the country before being picked up. Despite her record of support for Israel, according to one report, Thatcher later referred to the tactics used to entrap Vanunu as a "terrorist outrage."[30]

By means of surveillance, the Mossad had tracked Vanunu from the *Sunday Times* offices to his room at the Mountbatten Hotel,[31] at which point the mystery woman 'Cindy' made her first appearance. 'Cindy' was a Mossad agent with CIA connections.[32] Her job was to lure the mark to Italy where a prearranged plan for his abduction would be less easily discovered or thwarted. Vanunu fell into the trap.[33] On September 24 he 'met' Cindy for the first time on the sidewalk near his hotel. Somehow she managed to draw his attention without seeming to do so. They talked over coffee, met again, and began to strike up a friendship. Vanunu was taken in. She told him she was an American beauty school student visiting London. Later the *Sunday Times* learned that 'Cindy's' story was not entirely fabricated. The Mossad technique of constructing a false identity from an assortment of near-truths presented Vanunu with a highly convincing personality. According to the *Sunday Times*, 'Cindy' – in real life Cheryl Hanin, an American Jew from Orlando, Florida[34] – played on Vanunu's fear that the *Sunday Times* would never run his story.[35] She told him he was wasting his time with "that newspaper." She convinced him to fly to Rome with her for "a couple of days" where her sister had a flat. There, she would help him establish new press connections. Apparently she also enticed him with the prospect of sex – once they arrived in Rome.[36]

"Like an African slave"

After their arrival at Leonardo da Vinci airport, 'Cindy' and Vanunu cleared customs, and she hailed what Vanunu thought was a taxi. During the 25-minute drive on the *autostrada* toward Rome, the atmosphere in the car became tense. Vanunu began to grow suspicious, and thought of jumping from the car. But he reassured himself that his paranoia was only frayed nerves. The car pulled up to a shabby apartment building. As he entered, Vanunu was overpowered and knocked down by two Mossad agents and given an injection by 'Cindy.' Regaining consciousness several hours later, Vanunu found himself chained to a crate – "like an African slave," he later told his brother – aboard a cargo ship bound for Israel.[37]

International sympathy for Vanunu mounted. He later received the Swedish Right Livelihood Award[38] and the Danish Peace Prize, and was nominated for the Nobel Peace Prize for 1988.* Back in Israel, however, things were very different. There, he was charged with

---

* The letters nominating Vanunu for the Nobel Peace Prize are included as Appendix A of this book.

treason (assisting an enemy in wartime), aggravated espionage, and collecting secret information with intent to harm the state; to all of this he pleaded not guilty.[39] Among Israelis, Vanunu was widely perceived as a traitor. Former Knesset member and author Michael Bar-Zohar went so far as to call him "the greatest traitor of the 20th century."[40] Uzi Hasson, one of the state prosecutors in the case, probably came closest to summing up public sentiment when he claimed bitterly that Vanunu "had turned away from his family and his country."[41] The daily *Ma'ariv* echoed Hasson's remarks: "We are not moved by the fact . . . [that] someone took the trouble to bring Vanunu to Israel. . . . We say: 'well done'; and we don't give a hoot whether he was brought legally or by subterfuge, by sea or by air, alive or dead."[42] The Israeli government claimed that Vanunu had peddled state secrets to the highest bidder. Newspapers variously described him as sexually impotent, or of being a homosexual. One report claimed he was an exhibitionist.[43] Another suggested his girl friend was a lesbian. During a state television news report an unnamed 'expert' declared that Vanunu's handwriting showed signs of an "unbalanced" personality. Another attack cited his unfinished Master's degree as proof of general ineptitude. On one occasion sections of Vanunu's personal diary were read on state television without his permission.[44] He was widely portrayed as a 'loser'.

After the story broke, much of the early news coverage in Israel focused on the breach of security. *Ha'aretz* called it incomprehensible that someone like Vanunu had ever been allowed to go near Dimona, let alone be permitted to leave the country with state secrets. The paper suggested that "with respect to a person who worked eight years in Dimona, freedom to leave the country has to be restricted, made conditional, for example, on an additional security check."[45] Meanwhile, right-wing members of the Knesset called for a purging of 'leftists' from government and for a secret military trial. They also demanded the death sentence.[46]

Overnight Mordechai Vanunu became the most closely guarded prisoner in Israel. Though the whereabouts of his incarceration was never officially admitted, it was later discovered he was being held in Ashkelon prison near Tel Aviv. For the first month he was kept in solitary confinement and in total darkness in a tiny room – with only a mattress on the floor. During these first weeks the authorities attempted to conceal his identity. They forced him to grow a beard, to wear a kind of hat usually worn by mental patients, and – further mocking him – they even tried to change his name to David Enosh, that is, David 'human being.'[47] Vanunu was told that if he did not cooperate, his prison conditions would become worse. Later, he was moved to a windowless 3-by-6 meter cell with constant 24-hour fluorescent lighting, and a video camera was installed to watch his every move. When Vanunu protested this continual surveillance by smearing shaving cream on the camera lens, his radio and books were confiscated, and he was denied family visits.[48]

Eventually, Mordechai was allowed to see his immediate family for half-hour visits every two weeks, in the presence of security guards. Apart from his lawyer, he was allowed no other visitors – with one exception. His American girlfriend Judy Zimmet was to be allowed to see him, on condition that the two be separated by a soundproof glass screen and that they communicate only by means of handwritten notes.[49] Vanunu rejected the conditions as unacceptable, and petitioned the court, to no avail. There was no visit – nor any thereafter. To this day, the two remain separated.

For nearly a year Vanunu had no other contact with the outside world. Nor was he allowed to meet or talk with other prisoners. An outdoor prison yard which was provided for two hours of daily exercise was sealed off with burlap sacking to prevent Vanunu from even being seen by other inmates.[50] The prisoner continued to protest his treatment, staging hunger strikes on three different occasions, one of which lasted at least 35 days.[51]

Speaking at a press conference in Israel on March 4, 1987, Vanunu's brothers Meir and Asher described the inhuman conditions of his imprisonment, which they said were aimed at breaking him psychologically in order to support the impression fostered by the government that he was 'unbalanced'. The brothers, along with other Israeli activists, criticized the government's handling of the case. "The policy of utter secrecy adopted by the Israeli government in all aspects of the Vanunu affair is a direct outgrowth of the policy of secrecy and deception of the whole nuclear issue. The manner in which he was brought to Israel, his clandestine detention and arraignment in conditions of complete secrecy are all in direct contradiction to normal judicial process."[52] Meir Vanunu also denied allegations that his brother's revelation in the *Sunday Times* had been motivated by profit: "The claim that Motti was after money is ridiculous . . . . Motti was not materialistic and had few possessions. If he wanted money he could have tried to sell his information to another country interested in military secrets. On his way to Australia he stopped over in the U.S.S.R. Why didn't he just get off the plane and contact agents there?

Why didn't he try and contact foreign embassies? Instead he went to a free country with a free press and published his information openly."[53]

Speaking next, Ha'im Baram, a journalist from the *Kol Ha'ir* weekly, denounced the country's mass circulation newspapers, claiming that the media had capitulated to the pro-nuclear lobby headed by Shimon Peres by contributing to the government blackout on the issue.[54] Another speaker, Menny Barzilay, a personal acquaintance of Vanunu's, rejected as untrue the media portrayal of the accused as being mentally 'unbalanced.' Barzilay claimed that Vanunu had actually enhanced Israel's long-range security because he had exposed the perilous consequences of an all-too-possible miscalculation by Israel's leaders. He also stated that a recent poll conducted in Jerusalem showed that many Sephardic Jews believed Vanunu was being persecuted because of his Eastern origin.[55]

Family Under Siege

As to Vanunu's own roots, there is no doubt his personal encounters with ethnic prejudice in Israel had contributed to his political alienation from mainstream Zionism. Mordechai (Morde or Motti for short) Vanunu was born in Marrakesh, Morocco in 1952, one of eleven children. In 1963 his father Shlomo decided to move the family to Israel, partly because of growing anti-Israel feeling in the Arab world, and because Zionist agents had persuaded him to make the Return. In a 1987 interview, Mordechai's brother Meir recalled the family's earlier life: "We had a very good living in Marrakesh. My father had a store in the Jewish quarter. Zionist agents came to speak to my father about coming to Israel, and in 1963 we left."[56]

From the start the homecoming in Israel went badly, as it had for thousands of other Sephardic immigrants. "My brother said it felt like coming out of the Garden of Eden into the desert," Meir said.[57] In spite of Shlomo's requests to settle in Migdal Ha'emek, close to his relatives, Ashkenazi officials directed him to Beersheba, on the edge of the Negev. The family was put on trucks, and sent to a *ma'abara* [a temporary settlement of bare huts). Unhappy with the place – as only a man used to owning his own house can appreciate – Shlomo sought advice from his relatives. They suggested he bring the family to Migdal Ha'emek anyway, and take over an empty flat that was available. Shlomo took their advice, but several days later the authorities came and forcibly returned the family to Beersheba, where they had to remain.[58] Conditions were very difficult. In order to survive, Shlomo had to sell most of his possessions, and could only find work doing menial labor – to which he was unaccustomed and for which he was ill-suited.[59] Eventually he was able to start a small open-air shop in the market where he still sells religious artifacts. Even so, Shlomo's income today does not begin to match the prosperity he had known in Morocco.

In the face of their father's resignation and apparent helplessness in dealing with the state authorities, the sons rebelled. "Looking back," recalled Meir Vanunu, "we probably understood that there were Ashkenazim who were running the State, officers who were running the Army, and us 'piles of dust' filling the huts of the *ma'abrot* of Dimona and Beersheba. We all had a feeling of unrealized potential, a feeling of abilities repressed by the religious education system, which is strict and anachronistic...a feeling of deprivation and frustration because of our Oriental origins."[60] Meir's acidic remark, "piles of dust," alluded to a famous statement about Jewish immigrants made many years before by David Ben Gurion: "We converted the human dust which gathered here [in Israel] from all the corners of the earth, we converted them into a sovereign nation which occupies an honorable place in the family of nations."[61]

For Mordechai and his younger brothers, service in the army, though compulsory, seemed to offer a way out. Mordechai served three years in the Golan Heights as a trained sapper, rising to the rank of first sergeant. Afterward, he signed on for training to become a nuclear technician, going on the KMG payroll in late 1976. The following year he reported for work at Dimona. Later he resumed university studies, completing two Bachelor's degrees, in philosophy and geography, before starting the Master's program.

According to Judy Zimmet, Mordechai was "very serious, very quiet, a wonderful listener, very empathic, social and at the same time he loves his privacy. He wanted to try a lot of things. . . . I don't know everything he was thinking about. He was all the time sarcastic. It seems that all people here [in Israel] are sarcastic and angry. Motti said that when his father came from Morocco he cried because of the conditions in Israel. Motti felt that because of these conditions he did not achieve everything he could have achieved."[62]

Because of Vanunu's alleged treason, his family was suddenly thrust into an unhappy spotlight; on several occasions family members were harassed, even humiliated. For example, once when Shlomo was shopping for vegetables in a local market, the shopkeeper recognized

him as the father of "that traitor." Emptying Shlomo's bag of
vegetables, the shopkeeper refilled it with garbage and handed it
back.[63] Another time Shlomo was physically attacked, and he later had
to close his business for a time.[64] Through all this the parents remained
deeply devout, in sharp contrast to their sons.

When family members visited Mordechai in prison, security men
stood by listening to every word, and even interrupted the
conversation, apparently to prevent the prisoner from revealing
additional 'state secrets.' One family member described the
experience: "Until you go through it yourself you can't believe that
such things exist. They don't allow him to say a word, not even to us.
It seems they are preparing a trial that will be decided in advance. I
never knew the security services operate here in this way, but who am I
to tell them how to work?"[65] One brother stated: "If I were not his
brother I would probably have thought differently. I would have had
my information from the press."[66] A brother-in-law expressed a
somewhat different opinion: " I don't know if he did right or no, [sic]
let the court decide; but they must let him speak so we can hear his
arguments."[67]

The family was obviously torn. Judy Zimmet described their state
of siege: "We didn't talk much. This family are good people, people
who care. But most people here are cruel, brutal, thinking only of
themselves. They don't listen, they are angry all the time.
Aggressivity is considered here a virtue. These are not my values."[68]
Despite his misgivings, Shlomo Vanunu described his son as only a
father might: "Morde, there wasn't anyone like him. He was quiet,
very intelligent. He wasn't wayward. As a child he didn't say 'Buy me
this and that.' No, he was a thinker. People would listen to him."[69]

The Trial

Though hundreds of letters and petitions from around the world
protested Vanunu's illegal extradition and called for a fair and open
trial, the veil of state secrecy continued. The trial began in Jerusalem
behind closed doors on August 30, 1987.[70] The exceptional security
measures were described by Vanunu's attorney Avigdor Feldman:
"You'd think it was not Vanunu being brought to court, but the H-
bomb itself."[71] Not only was the press barred from the court and the
room's windows hermetically sealed,[72] but in addition, both local and
wire-service reporting were censored to eliminate virtually any news

reference to Vanunu's line of defense or to the testimony in the case. Both prosecution and defense were placed under legal gag orders. Defense witnesses were warned that they faced stiff prison terms if they revealed details of their testimony. Not even rumors or leaks could be published within Israel.[73] Vanunu's brothers, Meir and Asher, were threatened with criminal prosecution if they ever told how their brother Mordechai had been returned to Israel.[74] Meir later revealed the details anyway, despite the warning, leading to his own indictment and forced exile.[75]

The paranoia of the state authorities was illustrated by the manner in which Vanunu was taken to court. On the first morning of the trial, two identical prison vans with whitewashed windows left Ashkelon prison, taking different routes to Jerusalem. One contained the accused; the other was a decoy.[76] Not only was Vanunu prevented from making any statements to the press, but unprecedented security measures ensured he would not even be seen as he entered the court. A special wood, canvas and concrete tunnel had been erected at the court's rear entrance to conceal his passage. Those who did catch a glimpse reported that Vanunu was taken in handcuffed, with his head concealed by a motorcyclist's helmet. A police siren wailed as he was led in, apparently to prevent the prisoner from being heard if he tried to call out to newsmen.[77]

Despite the security measures, a few reporters managed to get a description of the courtroom interior. Reportedly, Vanunu was flanked by two *Shin Bet* security officers with orders to muzzle him physically if he attempted to discuss 'sensitive' material, that is, material which had been ruled inadmissible.[78] According to Vanunu's attorney and his brother Meir, the same two guards slapped him around and taunted him en route to court on September 2, the day he was scheduled to testify.[79] The abuse was an apparent attempt to 'shake him up,' to make Vanunu appear emotional and unstable before the court, lending credibility to the State's case. Nevertheless, defense attorney Feldman described Vanunu's three-and-a-half hour testimony as "calm".[80]

The first line of Vanunu's defense was to demand immediate dismissal of all charges because of the illegal way he had been brought to Israel. Defense attorney Feldman claimed that Vanunu's abduction – which was an obvious violation of Italian law, International law, and possibly British law as well – also violated the personal rights of the accused, invalidating the court's jurisdiction.[81] This argument was rejected by the court.

The second line of defense was an attempt to put nuclear weapons on trial instead of Vanunu.[82] The defense tacitly conceded Vanunu had committed the acts for which he was charged; there was no denying he had signed an agreement to maintain secrecy.[83] However, at issue was the legality of that document. Crucial to this approach was Feldman's petition to open the trial to the public and the press. Firstly, Feldman intended to subpoena people from inside the government to show that the decisions made by previous governments establishing the country's nuclear program had not been arrived at through democratic processes.[84] Feldman also hoped to summon key experts to argue that development of nuclear weapons outside international supervision – i.e., outside the nuclear safeguards and inspections established by the Non-Proliferation Treaty (NPT), which Israel has never signed – itself constituted a war crime against humanity. As Feldman put it: "Nuclear weapons have all the characteristics of an outlawed weapon. They do not differentiate between civilian populations and other [i.e., military] targets. The damage they cause far exceeds any political objective that might be achieved; and they cause irreversible damage to the climate and environment."[85] Feldman hoped to invoke the Nuremberg principles, which established that an individual must refuse to carry out illegal orders – that is, orders which might endanger humanity. The defense contended that Vanunu acted out of a higher moral authority. Weeks before the trial, Vanunu had unequivocally explained his motivation in an open letter from Ashkelon prison.

AN OPEN LETTER:

My principal message is in several spheres. The individual citizen, wherever he lives, has to find a way on the personal level to add his contribution to improve the quality of life on earth, to make everyday life pleasanter and more tolerable. Much can be accomplished, starting with what society offers. If, for example, a person can contribute in the sphere of social equality, by working against discrimination due to race, religion or sex, such a person can earn respect and is worthy of emulation. In my own case, I wanted to expand the awareness of the nuclear danger in my own country, Israel, and in the Middle East. And I believe my action contributed to the security and the brotherhood of nations.

I showed by my action that the individual still has power, regardless of the almost unlimited resources of the establishment. Indeed, individual action can be a mighty weapon. Through action the individual can hold the establishment accountable. By means of civil disobedience he can expose the dark machinations of any regime, for the sake of the general welfare. Because governments cannot operate without the cooperation of their citizens, I believe civil disobedience will eventually be discovered by many more people to be the mighty weapon it truly is. An action like mine teaches people to trust their own God-given intelligence. An action like mine demonstrates that people must not blindly follow their leaders on crucial issues involving nuclear weapons. Indeed, if there ever was a case which called for civil disobedience, it is this.

The nuclear threat is relatively new and has not yet been sufficiently comprehended in the world. Many people are simply unaware of the tremendous volcano under them. Should that volcano erupt, there will be no way back for mankind. It will be the end. And this threat, this holocaust, which hangs over us is all too possible, because of human frailty and error – as was shown by Chernobyl.

In the West people have grown accustomed to living with the nuclear menace, without realizing the magnitude of danger, and without conscious awareness of the real possibility the nightmare could actually happen. Not only have the superpowers sanctioned the intolerable presence of vast quantities of nuclear weapons, the fact is that many nations in the Third World are following in their footsteps, without regard to the dangers.

To do what I did I had to first overcome many personal obstacles. Most important among these was the exposure of my private life to slander, and the sacrifice of all my future plans. I had to overcome the force of general opinion around me, especially of those held up as wise. I also had to overcome the views of intellectuals and experts who worked with me [at Dimona]. I had to say to them "It is you who are mistaken. It is you who are on the wrong path. On this matter it is I who know better". And I remain certain my action was worth the sacrifices I had to make, since I was able to point out – consistent with my own philosophy – what must now be done in the name of mankind.

To act as I did undermines blind confidence in the leaders. We saw an example of this problem of blind trust during Israel's 1982 invasion of Lebanon. At that time a majority of Israelis supported the war without doubting it – yet today the situation is exactly reversed. Today most people know it was not a defensive war – but folly. Today most people know it was simply a bloodletting to bring about by force the so called "new order" in Lebanon. Yet, because Israelis followed their leaders blindly in that war, many civilians and even children were executed in cold blood. I knew the truth from the war's first day. I knew it was going to be one more example of slaughter. I don't know how I knew, but I did. I simply would not believe the stories and announcements of the Israeli government. Because of those events, I began to take another more critical look at Israel's nuclear program.

Today I am convinced of the great danger posed by Israel's nuclear policies. Today the government still does not even admit the existence of nuclear arms in the country. They hint at their existence, yet they refuse to allow international inspection of the Dimona reactor. Because the citizenry here is not informed, people are unable to work in a coordinated way to prevent the disaster which may lie ahead. The danger is that in a future crisis Israel's leaders will be influenced by unreliable information, or will mistake a false threat for a real one, and so will trigger off a nuclear holocaust.

Today nuclear weapons are principally designed for use against civilian populations. A single bomb exploded over a modern city can kill hundreds of thousands of its citizens. Nor does the tragedy end there. Long afterward, contaminating fallout radiation can make whole regions uninhabitable for many years. In addition, as was demonstrated at Hiroshima and Nagasaki, thousands of people will continue to die from cancer for years after the explosion. Moreover, it must be understood that since Hiroshima the dangers have increased because the destructive power of today's bombs is many times greater. The numbers of these weapons have reached terrifying levels. It is no wonder the Soviets and Americans are seeking to eliminate some missiles from the European theater. Yet, from the standpoint of the individual, the best way to effect protection is to study the problem. Only by learning more about the danger can one hope to organize effective prevention.

A society unable to recognize the nuclear danger, a society that fails to take the steps necessary for survival, is a sick society. Indeed, the best evidence of this fact is the dark cloud, the menace, the warning signs which continue to hang over us. But there are other risks as well. A people that chooses to go on living in daily ignorance of such a threat develops other social and psychological problems which are greatly damaging in and of themselves – without a bomb ever going off. Hence it is not just the deployment of nuclear weapons, but their very existence, which threatens mankind.

Mordechai Vanunu
Ashkelon Prison, Jerusalem
July, 1987

On March 24, 1988, news of Mordechai Vanunu's conviction was announced to the world. The guilty verdict was not unexpected. Those who had followed the proceedings, such as *Sunday Times* correspondent Peter Hounam, predicted the outcome well in advance: "I liken it to a murder case in which the court decides it is not necessary to prove that the victim is dead."[86] Again the press was barred from the courtroom. When the decision was announced, the only line made public from the 60-page verdict stated that "the defendant is guilty on all three counts."[87] Several days later Vanunu was sentenced to 18 years in prison, a ruling he has appealed.[88]

Despite the verdict and harsh sentence, in the view of some observers the trial of Mordechai Vanunu succeeded just the same by bringing Israel's moral predicament into sharp focus. This was described recently by Reverend McKnight: "Israel [today] is in a moral bind. They executed Eichmann because he obeyed the directions of his superiors, and *not* the dictates of his conscience, when he killed thousands of Jews. Now they want to punish Vanunu for doing what Eichmann did *not* do."[89] In Britain, Ken Coates, spokesman for the Bertrand Russell Peace Foundation – one of the groups that nominated Vanunu for the Nobel Peace Prize – was even more direct: "All he has done is to refuse to obey orders to participate in genocide."[90]

For these reasons, anti-nuclear activists concluded that Vanunu had won a decisive moral victory. Indeed, the world at large, and humanity, had won. The verdict implied that Vanunu's revelations were accurate. Facts which had been kept secret because they could not stand the light of day had been exposed. Even more important, the verdict ensured that Israeli state denials would not go unchallenged in the future. Credibility being a scarce commodity, once lost it could never fully be regained. Nor would Vanunu soon be forgotten. His stiff sentence guaranteed that his name would haunt state censors for years to come, just as it would continue to inspire others working for nuclear disarmament. Indeed, henceforth there would be ever greater numbers who, impressed – even awed – by the dimensions of one man's self-sacrifice, would continue in Mordechai's footsteps.

The case of Mordechai Vanunu also exposed the absence of public debate in Israel on the key matter of nuclear proliferation. According to Uri Avnery, a magazine editor and former Knesset member, "Most Israelis automatically assume that Israel needs a weapon of last resort."[91] Yet, as this book will show, no solid basis exists for such a conclusion. In fact, thanks in part to Vanunu, we now know Israeli weapons development has advanced well beyond the limits of what arguably could be called defensive weaponry, even taking into account Israel's legitimate security needs.

Today most Israelis assume that the principal danger they face comes from outside – an external Arab or Soviet threat. The assumption rests on a narrow tribal perspective which Vanunu himself described: "Those who founded this state think only about the holocaust of the Jewish people in Europe. But you can't cause a world holocaust because of that."[92] In a nation where many believe that "all the world is against us, and we must take care of ourselves,"[93] as Meir Vanunu expressed it, few will have eyes or ears to recognize a more insidious internal danger.

But having said this, in all honesty one must admit that very few Israelis have had a real opportunity to know the facts concerning their country's nuclear program. Quite simply, there has been no free-flow of information in Israel on nuclear-related matters. Nor has the case of Mordechai Vanunu altered this basic equation. Israeli state censorship continues to stymie the efforts of those few who are trying to raise the real issues in a public forum. Debate *has* occurred – as we shall learn in a later chapter – but only behind closed doors *within* the defense establishment.[94] As Vanunu's lawyer Avigdor Feldman expressed it, "There must be some sort of equilibrium between state security and the citizen's right to know. We are told that the citizen participates in the decision-making process when he votes. But how can he vote if he does not know [the facts]?"[95] In Israel, the equation Feldman referred to continues to be overwhelmingly one-sided, amounting to what Vanunu called a "dictatorship of state security."[96] In such a climate, it is not surprising so few Israelis recognize the dangers.

Fortunately, a few clear-thinking individuals *have* spoken out. Reserve Colonel Meir Pa'il, a leading Israeli military historian, warned recently that the day is soon coming when the nuclear threat will overwhelm all other issues facing Israel.[97] This book will argue that such a day is already upon us.

Notes to Chapter One

1. David Winner, "My brother is not a spy," *Jewish Chronicle,* August 14, 1987.

2. This assessment of Guerrero has been widely reported. For example, see Peter Couchman, "Four Corners," transcript from the one hour documentary produced by the Australian Broadcasting Company, Parliamentary Library of the Commonwealth of Australia, August 31, 1987, conversation by Couchman, p. 8.

3. *Ibid,* p. 9.

4. Spokesman, The Bertrand Russell Peace Foundation, 1988. *Israel's Bomb. The First Victim,* Nottingham, Russell Press Ltd., p. 42.

5. Menachem Shalev, "Journalistic responsibility," *Jerusalem Post,* September 7, 1987; also see Couchman, op cit, p. 9.

6. Rayna Moss, "Imprisoned Israeli anti-nuclear activist nominated for the Nobel Peace Prize," International Foundation for Development Alternatives (IFDA) Dossier 61, September- October, 1987, p. 52.

7. Ian Black, "Israel to remain silent on 'spy'," *The Guardian,* November 12, 1986.

8. Couchman op cit, p. 6.

9. "Background Details on Mordechai Vanunu," a statement prepared by Rev. John McKnight, Rector, Parish of King's Cross, 120 Darlinghurst Rd., Darlinghurst, New South Wales, Australia 2010; phone in Sydney: 357-6844.

10. In a note written to the author.

11. Conversation with author Stephen Green, April 6, 1989.

12. Letter from Vanunu to Father Stephen Gray, June 26, 1987. For a reprinted version, in part, see Harding, Mark, "A prisoner of conscience tries to get it write," [sic] *The Herald* (London), September 3, 1987. Reverend Gray is Reverend McKnight's associate minister at the parish of King's Cross and became close to Mordechai during his stay in Sydney.

13. Couchman, op cit, pp. 6-7.

14. "Revealed: the secrets of Israel's nuclear arsenal,"; "How the experts were convinced," London *Sunday Times,* October 5, 1986.

15. *Ibid*

16. *Ibid*

17. According to the *Sunday Times* (London), the official

response was: "It is not the first time that stories of this kind have appeared in the press. They have no basis whatsoever in reality and hence any further comment on our part is superfluous", "How the experts were convinced," October 5, 1968; also see John Bullock and John Eisenhammer, "Mystery over whereabouts of Israeli nuclear 'spy'," *The Independent,* November 8, 1986.

18. Ian Black, "Israelis turn deaf ear to N-weapons controversy," *The Guardian,* November 17, 1986.

19. Bullock and Eisenhammer, op cit.

20. Couchman, op cit, p. 16.

21. Martin Bailey and Robin Lustig, "Cindy's role in Israeli 'kidnap'," The Observer (London), November 16, 1986.

22. Andrew Whitley, "Israel cool on Vanunu affair," Financial Times, November 12, 1986; Black, "Israel to remain silent...," op cit; David Horovitz, "UK wants to know how Vanunu came to Israel, Jerusalem Post, November 20, 1986.

23. Bullock and Eisenhammer, op cit.

24. Thomas Friedman, "Israel Holds Technician Who Sold Atom Secrets," *The New York Times,* November 10, 1986, p. A-10.

25. Bailey and Lustig, op cit; also see Ian Murray, "Shamir refuses to give Vanunu mystery details," *The Times,* November 13, 1986; also see Charles Richards, "Israel promises to reply on Vanunu," *The Independent,* November 14, 1986.

26. Thomas Friedman, "Israel Said to Abduct Seller of A-Bomb Secrets," *The New York Times,* October 27, 1986.

27. Thomas Friedman, "Israeli Suspect Flashes a Hint He Was Abducted," *The New York Times,* December 23, 1986.

28. Couchman, op cit, p. 11.

29. Bullock and Eisenhammer, op cit.

30. Martin Mann, "Talkative Israeli Technician," *The Spotlight,* August 24, 1987, p. l.

31. Bullock and Eisenhammer, op cit.

32. *Ibid*

33. Bailey and Lustig, op cit.

34. *Jerusalem Post,* November 30, 1987.

35. "How Israeli agents snatched Vanunu," Insight Team, *The Sunday Times,* (London), August 9, 1987.

36. Mann, op cit.

37. Mann, op cit; also see "Riddle of Vanunu ship," Insight Team, *The Sunday Times,* August 16, 1987; also see "Cindy the spy faces summons," *The Observer* (London), August 30, 1987.

38. "Israeli who told nuclear secrets to receive award," *Philadelphian*, October 10, 1987.

39. "Israeli Technician Pleads Not Guilty," *The New York Times*, December 29, 1986; also see "Charge sheet against Vanunu," *Jerusalem Post*, September 4, 1987.

40. Hillel Schenker, "Vanunu affair sparks protests...," *In These Times*, February 25-March 10, 1987.

41. Peter Hounam, "Witness to the secret trial of Israel's whistle blower," *The Sunday Times*, December 13, 1987.

42. Cited in *The Times* (London), November 20, 1986.

43. Zvi Gilat, "A family under siege," *Hadashot*, February 13, 1987, (trans. by Israel Shahak).

44. Moss, op cit, p. 53.

45. Cited in *The Times*, (London), November 20, 1986.

46. Moss, op cit.

47. Leviticus, "From Victim to Symbol," *Israel & Palestine*, September 1987, p. 19.

48. David Rose, "Brother pleads for action on Israeli kidnap," *The Guardian*, August 10, 1987.

49. Menachem Shalev, "Vanunu can speak--but only by note," September 9, 1987; also see Menachem Shalev, "Vanunu's petitions bemuse prosecutor," *Jerusalem Post*, September 10, 1987.

50. "How Israeli agents snatched Vanunu," op cit.

51. Moss, op cit, p. 53; also see Menachem Shalev, "Vanunu plans to begin hunger strike to mark year since 'kidnapping'," *Jerusalem Post*, September 29, 1987; also see Hugh Orgel, "Vanunu in a war of nerves with his jailers," *The Sentinel*, January 27, 1987.

52. *News From Within*, March 31, 1987, p. 12; also see Jeanne Butterfield, "Nuclear Veil Penetrated by Vanunu Trial," *The Guardian*, March 18, 1987.

53. Moss, op cit, p. 52.

54. *News From Within*, op cit.

55. *Ibid*

56. Seumas Milne, "The world wakes up to Vanunu," *The Guardian*, October 23, 1987.

57. *Ibid*

58. Gilat, op cit.

59. *Ibid*

60. *Ibid*

61. Cited in Amos Elon, 1971. *The Israelis: Founders and Sons*, New York, Holt, Rinehart and Winston, p. 310.

62. Nahum Bamea, "I love him, I don't care," *Koteret Rashit*, January 28, 1987, (trans. by Israel Shahak).

63. Winner, op cit.

64. Benny Morris, "Vanunu being held here to face trial," *Jerusalem Post*, November 10, 1986.

65. Gilat, op cit.

66. *Ibid*

67. *Ibid*

68. Barnea, op cit.

69. Couchman, op cit, p. 5.

70. "Espionage Trial Over Nuclear Secrets Begins in Israel," *The New York Times*, August 31, 1987.

71. *New York Times*, August 31, 1987, p. A-8.

72. Ian Black, "Vanunu defense wants less court secrecy," *Guardian* (London), August 8, 1987.

73. Peter Hounam, "Sympathy grows for Vanunu as trial opens," *The Sunday Times* (London), August 30, 1987.

74. Glenn Frankel, "Israel's Secret Treason Trial," *Washington Post*, December 11, 1987.

75. David Horovitz and Menachem Shalev, "Israel warrant out against Meir Vanunu," *Jerusalem Post* August 24, 1987; also see *Boston Globe*, September 2, 1987; also see David Rose, "Brother pleads for action on Israeli kidnap," *The Guardian*, August 10, 1987.

76. Couchman, op cit, p. 3.

77. Ian Black, "Vanunu goes on trial," *Jerusalem Post*, August 31, 1987; also see Eric Silver, "Israelis ban the bomb debate," *The Observer* (London), September 6, 1987.

78. Ian Black, "Vanunu tells of kidnap," *The Guardian*, September 3, 1987.

79. Glenn Frankel, "Israel's Secret Treason Trial," *Washington Post*, December 11, 1987; also see *Christian Science Monitor*, September 1, 1987.

80. Menachem Shalev, "Vanunu has his say," *Jerusalem Post*, September 3, 1987.

81. Black, "Vanunu tells of kidnap," op cit.

82. Hounam, "Sympathy grows for Vanunu..." op cit.

83. Glenn Frankel, "Israel's Secret Treason Trial," *Washington Post*, December 11, 1987.

84. Charles Richards, "Taking the stand as hero or traitor," *The Independent*, August 26, 1987.

85. Menachem Shalev, "Vanunu's defense," *Jerusalem Post,* August 28, 1987.

86. Hounam, "Witness to the secret trial of Israel's whistle blower," op cit; also see "A Right to Disobedience?," *Newsweek,* September 7, 1987.

87. Glenn Frankel. "Israel Convicts Vanunu of Treason...," *Washington Post* March 25, 1988.

88. *New York Times,* March 28, 1988.

89. McGee, op cit.

90. David Rose, "Brother pleads for action on Israeli kidnap," *The Guardian,* August 10, 1987.

91. Ethan Bronner, "Report on nuclear status fuels debate...." *Boston Globe,* February 4, 1987.

92. Moss, op cit, p. 52.

93. Milne, op cit.

94. Richards, "Taking the stand as hero or traitor," op cit.

95. Shalev, "Vanunu's defense," op cit.

96. Jeanne Butterfield, "Vanunu trial opens, but is cloaked in secrecy," *Guardian,* September 16, 1987.

97. Schenker, op cit.

Chapter Two

"Given that this fear exists..."

To get an overall picture of Israel's current nuclear agenda, its doctrines and direction, it is helpful – even necessary – to review some essential history. Israel's commitment to the development of nuclear weapons can be traced to key decisions made in the 1950s. But to elucidate those origins one must also understand the context in which the decisions were made, namely, the intense political struggle waged in Israel in the 1950s and '60s for control of foreign policy vis-a-vis the surrounding Arab states. The following three chapters will attempt to sketch out the framework of that drama.

The Legacy of the Lavon Affair

In 1963 Levi Eshkol became Prime Minister of Israel as a direct consequence of a scandal that first rocked Israel during the mid-1950s. Perhaps because the guilty were never prosecuted, the imbroglio festered for years, erupting again in 1961 when new facts in the case emerged. At that time, those implicated in a previous cover-up involving falsification of documents and outright lies included Moshe Dayan, Shimon Peres, and others at the highest level of the government. Nor did the belated revelations of abuse lead to legal prosecutions or a court settlement. Instead, the country was convulsed by a second round of poisonous recriminations and controversy, a public outcry that ultimately brought about the ignominious resignation of Prime Minister David Ben Gurion in June 1963, heralding his political decline.

It is interesting that Israeli accounts of the scandal, known as the Lavon Affair, referred to it at the time as a "security misfortune"[1] or a "security mishap,"[2] much as the present-day Iran-Contra arms scandal and the Pollard spy case have been described in Israel as a "sensitive issue for the government," or as a "rogue operation." It is a phraseology which has the effect, probably intended, of leading an uninformed reader *away from* the central facts in the case.

Indeed, most of the literature on the Lavon Affair succeeds in obfuscating the central part played by Ben Gurion and his allies in undermining Prime Minister Sharett's historic 1954 peace initiative. Fortunately, at least two well-documented accounts exist, one by Stephen Green based in part on recently declassified U.S. Government documents, and another by Livia Rokach, based on Moshe Sharett's personal diary.[3] In the context of an investigation into the Israeli nuclear program, the Lavon Affair offers an apt starting point, because it vividly illustrates how Israeli moderates have been frustrated over the years in their efforts to find diplomatic rather than military alternatives to conflicts born with the creation of the Jewish State.

Moshe Sharett and David Ben Gurion

Moshe Sharett was a Zionist who for many years had admired and supported David Ben Gurion. The two men, though very different, had worked side by side in the Jewish Agency to bring the nation of Israel into being.[4] But their smooth working relationship ended by early 1953 because of Ben Gurion's growing reliance on maximum military force as the main tool of his foreign policy. In a word, Ben Gurion believed in military rather than political solutions. Sharett, who in the fall of 1953 served as Foreign Minister in Ben Gurion's cabinet, knew that diplomatic efforts to achieve an accommodation with the Arab states would have a chance to succeed only if the Defense Ministry could be persuaded to halt the large-scale attacks that had become Ben Gurion's trademark. Ben Gurion served in a dual capacity, both as Prime Minister and Defense Minister.

After repeatedly confronting the militarists in party councils, Sharett eventually secured such an agreement after Ben Gurion's October 12 reprisal attack on a small Jordanian village called Kibya. The raid, in which 53 Arabs were massacred, created a stir of outrage within Israel and abroad. In the face of widespread protests Ben Gurion retreated, resigning his dual portfolio. The 'architect of the Jewish state' asserted his wish to "retire" from politics for a year to live on a kibbutz.

Sharett's 1954 Peace Initiative

No sooner had Sharett become Prime Minister than he inaugurated what may well be the only genuine peace initiative in Israeli history. First he sought and received the Knesset's formal endorsement of his new policy, whereupon peace talks were begun with Egypt's President Abdel Nasser.[5] To everyone's surprise, the negotiations progressed rapidly, even to the stage of drafting a formal peace treaty between Egypt and Israel on areas of agreement, namely, refugee resettlement and the future status of Jerusalem.[6]

Though the talks remained deadlocked on other key issues, even this modest success was too much for the hawks still remaining in the government, specifically Chief-of-Staff Moshe Dayan, the new Defense Minister Pinhas Lavon, Military Intelligence Chief Benjamin Gibli, and Director General Shimon Peres, all of whom favored Ben Gurion's hard line.

Taking their cue from Sharett, the hawks launched their own initiative: secret military operations aimed at disrupting the ongoing peace talks. Without the Prime Minister's knowledge or approval, secret raids were mounted on Syria and Jordan and along the Egyptian frontier. Some of the raids were conducted by Ariel Sharon's elite 101 unit, the Israeli equivalent to the U.S. Special Forces. Other provocations included the planting of bombs in Cairo by Israeli agents.

The considerable scandal surrounding this latter fiasco, which became known as the Lavon Affair, first broke in 1954. While an inquiry was launched by Sharett's government, because of a cover-up the investigation was unable to determine the facts in the case. As a result, the affair simmered for years until finally boiling over again in 1961 when Lavon, the principal defendant, presented fresh evidence that Dayan, Peres and Gibli had perjured themselves before the investigative commission by falsifying documents which made it appear that he, Lavon, had ordered the Cairo operation.[7]

The affair probably involved an internal power struggle within the Israeli intelligence community. As reported by Green, one of its consequences was the disgrace of Gibli's Military Intelligence (Modiin), and the shifting of control over foreign intelligence operations to Mossad, the Israeli equivalent of the CIA.[8] In his study, Yoram Peri described the affair not simply as a conflict between the hawks and Sharett, but also as a power struggle between Lavon and Ben Gurion's surrogate, Dayan.[9] In other words, though there was near consensus among the hawks in opposition to Sharett's policy of conciliation, there were also deep divisions among the hawks themselves.

During Sharett's inquiry, it was revealed that several of the bombs planted in Cairo had been aimed at selected British and American targets. As a result, it was concluded that the affair's main objective had been to undermine Egyptian-British and Egyptian-American relations. At the time, negotiations were under way between Egypt and Britain for the removal of British troops and the transfer of the Suez Canal to Egyptian control. Also, for months Nasser had been seeking an arms agreement with the United States. Obviously, these were negotiations which Israel's Defense Ministry had an interest in foiling, along with the peace talks with Egypt. In fact, Sharett's peace initiative was effectively destroyed long before the incriminating details of the Lavon Affair ever emerged.[10]

While the unauthorized policy of raids and sabotage had the immediate effect of undermining Sharett's negotiations with Nasser, it did not torpedo them outright. Talks between representatives of the two leaders continued in Paris, probably because of Nasser's high regard for Sharett's statesmanship. In other words, as long as Nasser believed that a peace settlement, or at least a *modus vivendi,* was possible, talks continued.[11]

In the early days of 1955, as part of the initial fallout from the scandal, Prime Minister Sharett reshuffled his cabinet. The accused, Defense Minister Lavon, was fired, even though his guilt had never been proven. Then, incredibly, Ben Gurion, the very man who despite his 'retirement' had counseled the *actual* perpetrators from his kibbutz retreat, was reinstated as Defense Minister. The reappointment proved to be the biggest mistake of Sharett's political life, as it foreshadowed not only the final undoing of his peace initiative, but his own political career as well. Possibly the lapse was an example of Sharett's occasional tendency, described in many accounts, of wavering under intense pressure. Another factor may have been the peculiar nature of Israeli democracy; apparently Prime Minister Sharett came under tremendous pressure from within his own party to readmit Ben Gurion – by this time his political opponent – to the cabinet.[12]

Ben Gurion's first move as Defense Minister amounted to a public repudiation of Sharett's peaceful diplomacy: announcement of a return to the former policy of massive reprisals. It was Ben Gurion's way of telling Sharett he would run the army his own way. In fact, according to Donald Neff's version of events, Ben Gurion openly challenged Sharett "to take over the Defense Portfolio from me or appoint someone else in my place" if he did not like it.[13] Sharett backed down. Within days the Israeli Defense Forces (IDF) launched a large-scale raid on Gaza which, according to various historical accounts, signaled a turning point in Middle East history.[14]

The Gaza Raid: Turning Point

The attack embarrassed Nasser at a time when the new Egyptian leader was attempting to foster in his own country an atmosphere amenable to peaceful diplomacy. Nasser had good reasons for wishing to avoid hostilities with the new Jewish state, namely, a host of domestic problems crying out for solutions.[15]

Until this point, as evidenced later by Israel's capture of Egyptian intelligence records during the Sinai campaign, the Egyptian government had, despite Israeli accusations to the contrary, maintained a firm policy of curbing infiltration into Israel by Palestinian guerrillas.[16] True, the policy was not 100% effective, given the indigenous nature of the guerrilla movement. Realistically, a complete sealing off of Egypt's border with Israel was probably beyond Nasser's reach at the time. In any event, those Palestinian raids which did occur were in almost every case attacks by lone individuals or a handful of men and, while troublesome, at no time posed a serious military threat to Israel's existence;[17] nor for that matter did the surrounding Arab governments, either alone or collectively, as Dayan himself admitted on May 26, 1955 in a meeting of Israeli Ambassadors.[18] According to field reports filed by senior UN officials, until this point the Egyptian armed forces exercised remarkable restraint despite Israeli provocations.[19]

The February 28, 1955 Gaza raid changed all this, however. The raid was an unmistakable signal to Nasser that Sharett's peaceful diplomacy had been eclipsed by Ben Gurion. Judging he had been betrayed, Nasser broke off the Paris talks. Even so, he was sufficiently committed to peace to continue searching privately for a settlement, or at least for a curtailment of hostilities. In early spring of 1955, without fanfare, Nasser launched his own peace initiative, quietly enlisting the help of U.S. Quaker intermediaries. Through them secret contacts continued with Sharett and Ben Gurion. A recent account by the principal mediator, Elmore Jackson, argues persuasively for Nasser's continuing desire for a negotiated settlement.[20] By this time, however, a complex cauldron of events was working against peace. The fragile window of opportunity for an agreement was closing rapidly.

The Israeli Challenge to Nasser

For its part, the Egyptian army under King Farouk's corrupt regime had never been a force to contend with. Poorly equipped, poorly trained and, with a few notable exceptions, poorly led, it had been defeated by Israel during the 1948 war with apparent ease. Depleted by the war, it had never been rebuilt. In fact, had Farouk's army been a real force, it is doubtful the near-bloodless officers' revolution led by Nasser in 1952 could have succeeded. As Nasser put it: "Our revolution was stimulated in the army by a lack of equipment."[21]

Through the winter of 1955 Israeli warplanes flew over Cairo at will, dramatically revealing Egypt's military backwardness. The flagrant violations of Egyptian airspace were made all the more humiliating by Nasser's powerlessness to prevent them.[22] Moreover, by March 1955 Nasser was receiving intelligence reports of a major Israeli military buildup. The reports were accurate.[23] The arms were coming from France, the result of a secret arms deal concluded the previous year (1954) between Shimon Peres and French Defense Minister Pierre-Marie Koenig. The deal was a harbinger of even bigger things in the offing, namely, a nuclear alliance.*

In the meantime, however, the Israeli buildup of French Mystère IV fighter-bombers, tanks and artillery was itself a clear violation of the Anglo-French-American Tripartite Agreement of 1950. The Western democracies had drawn up the agreement to prohibit the movement of arms into the region; in other words, for the express purpose of *preventing* just such trade in arms.[24] Soon Nasser was under tremendous pressure from his own generals to at least match the Israeli buildup.[25]

Against such a backdrop, it is not surprising Nasser's peace initiative ground to a halt. The talks were going nowhere, yielding to the inevitability of an arms race. Nasser was quite correct in sensing a growing challenge from Israel. As early as February 8, 1955 – even before the Gaza raid – Lewis Jones, an American embassy aide in Cairo, concluded on the basis of previous Israeli attacks that "Sharett does not have control, if such mad actions can be carried out."[26]

---

* The French connection began as early as 1949, when Francis Perrin, France's High Commissioner of Atomic Energy, first visited Israel. Contacts continued and a formal nuclear cooperation agreement was signed in early 1953. At this time France acquired the patent of an Israeli-chemical process for the production of heavy water. In exchange, Israeli scientists were allowed to study at France's Institute of Nuclear Science and Techniques at Saclay, near Paris. Israel also gained access to French nuclear installations and technical data. Cooperation led to French involvement at Dimona. Fuad Jabber, *Israel and Nuclear Weapons,* pp. 20-24.

The Gaza raid also triggered massive demonstrations by Palestinians in the Gaza Strip aimed *not* at Israel but at Egypt, in reaction to Nasser's policy of curbing infiltration. Clashes occurred between Palestinians and Egyptian troops. Under the circumstances, Nasser had little choice but to rescind the policy; henceforth he began to organize and equip the Palestinian rebels, later known as *fedayeen* (self-sacrifice).[27] Soon border incidents by both sides threatened still further escalations. In August 1955 another large Israeli attack occurred at Khan Yunis in southern Gaza.[28]

Nasser's Soviet Arms Deal

Increasingly desperate to arrange an arms deal of his own, the Egyptian leader found all channels in the West blocked by the same Tripartite Agreement which France and Israel were busily flouting. Frustrated repeatedly in Washington, and without clear alternatives, Nasser eventually made good his warning to seek arms elsewhere, even from the U.S.S.R. For this impertinence – some would call it pluck – he would soon be roasted in the Western media as an agent of 'Soviet expansionism.'

Brokered through Czechoslovakia, the famous arms deal with the Soviet Union which was announced on September 27, 1955 sent shock waves through the capitals of the West. Several days later during a press conference, Nasser was asked whether he planned to use the new military hardware to attack Israel. The query afforded the Egyptian leader an opportunity to vent his frustrations:

> *War is not an easy decision for anybody, especially for me. No Arab is saying now that we must destroy Israel. The Arabs are asking only that refugees [from Palestine] receive their natural right to life and their lost property which was promised them by United Nations resolutions seven years ago. No, we are not aggressive. The threat is from the other side. I have said many times that I want to build up my country. Now I am obliged to give defense priority over development. It was the other way around before Ben Gurion's vicious attack on Gaza February 28. I cannot defend Egypt with schools and hospitals and factories, and what will be the use of them if they are destroyed?*

Nasser followed with a statement unambiguously acknowledging the crucial role America would have to play in order to achieve a Middle East peace settlement:

> *The initiative for development of future relations is completely with the United States. The Arabs do not insist on better treatment than that accorded Israel. Equal treatment will come about if the United States acts purely in its own interests and does not pay special attention to interests favored by a small minority of Americans.*[29]

Nasser's invitation to America to assume the crucial leadership role in resolving the conflict could hardly have been more explicit. Unfortunately, Washington was not listening. Or if it was listening, it was not hearing. The thought that Gamal Abdel Nasser, a Third World leader, could independently pursue a genuine non-aligned policy was as unacceptable to Washington in 1956 as Daniel Ortega's non-alignment of Nicaragua in 1985. Then as now, instead of opportunities Washington, because of its own ideological rigidity, saw only impossibilities. Within days of the announced arms deal, the CIA gave Israel the green light to attack Egypt.[30]

Word of Nasser's new Soviet arms deal also sent a tremor through Israeli society and galvanized the country. Alexis Ladas, the UN political officer in the Jerusalem mission, probably came closest to capturing the nation's mood in his report to UN headquarters:

> *A state of mind has developed in Israel which at times approaches hysteria and which permeates the population from top to bottom. It affects not only the whispering in the marketplace but also the councils of the mighty. It is a conviction that Israel, a peace-loving nation of fugitives from persecution desiring nothing but to live in concord with her neighbors, is surrounded by increasingly powerful and savage enemies whose only purpose is to crush her out of existence. Once given the fact that this fear exists, everything else follows quite logically. It is quite understandable that the supply of arms to Egypt should put the fear of God into the Israelis. It is quite understandable that Gaza should be viewed by them not as what it is in fact:*

> *a death trap for the Egyptian Army and a concentration*
> *camp for a quarter of a million refugees; but as what it*
> *might become in the future: a dagger pointed at the heart of*
> *Israel.*[31]

At the time, of course, very few Israelis were aware that it had been Israel and not Egypt which had precipitated the new arms race. Few realized that plans for a major Israeli buildup were already well under way. As already noted, word of the French-Israeli arms negotiations had leaked out in March 1955, a full six months *before* Nasser's announcement of a Soviet arms deal.[32] Few Israelis knew all this at the time and Ben Gurion was not about to inform them. In fact, the public excoriation of Nasser that followed in the Israeli press, though based on a general ignorance, nevertheless suited Ben Gurion's objectives perfectly.*

And what were those objectives? In cabinet meetings earlier in the year Ben Gurion had proposed the occupation of Gaza by the IDF and the unilateral abrogation of the Egypt-Israel Armistice Agreement signed after the 1948-49 War.[33] Now all this and much more seemed within reach. Later, Ben Gurion stunned the French with a plan to divide up the entire Middle East. This plan called for the elimination of Nasser, the partition of Jordan, and the Israeli occupation of Lebanon up to the Litani River. The rest of Lebanon would become a Christian state, a pro-Western stooge would be installed in Syria, and Israel would occupy the Sinai.[34]

Because Sharett energetically opposed these policies, Ben Gurion, now Prime Minister, demanded his resignation in June 1956, thereby silencing the last eloquent voice of opposition in the cabinet. Immediately thereafter, Ben Gurion launched the final preparations for Israel's part in the planned Anglo-French invasion of Suez: the fabled Sinai campaign.[35]

---

* Zionist accounts of this period typically date the start of the Middle East arms race with Nasser's Czech arms deal. Golda Meir's memoirs are a prime example. Her gross mis-quoting of Nasser is also typical. In her view, Nasser made no bones of his intention to "reconquer Palestine" —despite the explicit record, already noted, to the contrary. Golda Meir, *My Life,* p. 294.

Birth of the Nuclear Option

It was during this period, in the highly charged days and months preceding the 1956 Suez War, that David Ben Gurion and his protégés, Moshe Dayan and Shimon Peres, gestated their decision to develop the nuclear option. Had they foreseen the profound implications that decision held for Israel and the world, one must wonder if they would have reconsidered taking the first fateful step.

All this is doubly ironic in light of the shift that occurred later in U.S. foreign policy toward viewing Israel as Washington's strategic watchdog in the region. The consequent vast increase in U.S. military aid to Israel during the 1970s – which continues today – paralleled and no doubt in many ways supported Israel's own secret nuclear weapons program. Indeed, as we shall see, that nuclear program was possible *only because* of calculated deception on the part of Israel, and willing complicity on the part of the United States. Regrettably, successive U.S. Presidents have failed to recognize that U.S. and Israeli interests are not the same.

The other irony is that Soviet influence in the region today is to a large degree traceable to the very events which have just been described, that is, the secret French arms pipeline to Israel which all but destroyed the Tripartite Agreement. It was Nasser's understandable response to *that* unequivocal challenge which introduced Soviet arms to Egypt and later to Syria, where the Soviet Union has maintained a presence ever since – a presence, it must be admitted, which at times has been at least as uncomfortable for Moscow as for Israel.[36]

The fact is that the very same treaty Ben Gurion so readily flouted, the Tripartite Agreement, held the potential for effecting a measure of real security for Israel. Had Israel's leaders endorsed and honored it instead of undermining it, the Tripartite Agreement could have become a basis for demilitarization of the region – so crucial for Arab acceptance of Israel in return for peace. First, of course, Ben Gurion would have had to accept the concept of fixed and final borders for Israel. And, as we now know, this he was adamantly unwilling to do.[37]

Instead of seeking compromise, Ben Gurion shaped a foreign policy of active engagement which his successors would further evolve and broaden on many fronts. As we shall see, Israeli nuclear proliferation was destined to play a pivotal role in those developments.

Notes to Chapter Two

1. Amos Perlmutter, 1969. *Military and Politics in Israel,* New York, Praeger, p. 87.

2. See Document #5. Memorandum for Brig. General Chester V. Clifton, cited in Stephen Green, 1984. *Taking Sides: America's Secret Relations With a Militant Israel,* New York, William Morrow and Co., Appendix, pp. 302-303.

3. *Ibid,* pp. 94-122; also see Livia Rokach, 1980. *Israel's Sacred Terrorism,* Belmont, Mass., Association of Arab-American Graduates, Inc.

4. In his carefully researched and brilliantly executed final book, the late Simha Flapan argued that Sharett, no less that Ben Gurion, was implicated in the many Zionist schemes and deceptions of the formative post World War II years. Far from representing a second viable alternative to Ben Gurion's policies, Flapan concluded that Sharett always agreed with Ben Gurion on objectives, only occasionally differing over tactics. Flapan is probably correct. The fact remains that by 1954 those tactical differences had become the difference between war and peace. Simha Flapan, 1987. *The Birth of Israel,* New York, Pantheon Books, pp. 51-52.

5. *New York Times,* September 2, 1954.

6. *New Outlook,* January 1965; also see *New York Times,* March 30, 1953, p. 5.

7. Sharett's diary suggests he was aware of the facts much earlier. For example, in one harrowing entry on January 9, 1954 Sharett wrote: "Teddy [Kolleck] painted a horrifying picture of the relations at the top of the security establishment. The Minister of Defense is completely isolated--none of his collaborators speaks to him. During the inquiry, these collaborators [e.g., Peres, Dayan, and a number of senior Ministry officials and army officers] plotted to blacken his name and trap him. They captured the man who came from abroad, [the commander of the unit in Egypt, Avraham Zweidenberg, also known as "Paul Frank"], who escaped . . . instructed him in detail how to answer, including how to lie to the investigators, and coordinated the testimonies so as to close the trap on Lavon. Teddy is convinced that Lavon must go immediately. Gibli too must be dismissed, but Dayan, however, should not be touched for the time being."

As we now know, neither Dayan nor Peres was ever "touched." Rokach attributes much responsibility for the subsequent tragedies of Middle East history to Sharett's failure to blow the lid off the security establishment by revealing the sordid facts of the Lavon affair to Israeli society. It is hard to quarrel with Rokach's analysis. Such a move would have asserted civilian control at a pivotal moment of history. As it was, because no house-cleaning occurred, the intelligence community became more entrenched. Rokach also suggests, probably accurately, that because Sharett did not talk he became ended in the intrigue himself and, as a consequence, self-destructed politically. Livia Rokach, op cit, p. 37; also see Green, op cit, pp. 94-122; Avi Slaim, "Israel's Relations with the Arabs: Ben Gurion and Sharett, " *The Middle East Journal* Vol. 37, No. 2, Spring 1983. pp. 180-201. For source material in Hebrew see: Moshe Sharett, 1980. *Yoman Ishi* (personal diary), Tel Aviv, Sifriyat *Ma'ariv,* 8 vols; also see Avri El-Ad with James Creech III, 1976. *Decline of Honor,* Chicago, Henry Regnery Company; Perlmutter, *Military and Politics in Israel* (1969), op cit, pp. 119-126.

8. Also see Donald Neff, 1981. *Warriors at Suez,* New York, The Linden Press, p. 62.

9. Yoram Peri, 1982. *Between Battles and Ballots,* London, Cambridge University Press, pp. 232-240.

10. The scholar Benjamin Beit-Hallahmi takes the view that the Lavon operation was aimed at preventing the withdrawal of British troops from Suez. It certainly sounds plausible. Israel probably regarded the troops as a buffer between themselves and Nasser. Benjamin Beit-Hallahmi, 1987. *The Israeli Connection: Who Israel Arms and Why,* New York, Pantheon Books, p. 6; also see Peri, op cit, pp. 232-240.

11. Elmore Jackson, 1983. *Middle East Mission. The Story of a Major Bid for Peace in the Time of Nasser and Ben Gurion,* New York, W.W. Norton and Co., p. 41.

12. Neff, op cit. A similar situation appears to have occurred in 1966, when Prime Minister Levi Eshkol, a moderate and a foe of nuclear proliferation, came under intense political pressure to reappoint Moshe Dayan as Defense Minister, even though Eshkol had already fired him from the cabinet. The move later proved fatal to Eshkol's anti-nuclear policy.

13. Michael Bar-Zohar, 1977. *Ben Gurion: A Biography,* New York, Delacorte Press, cited in Neff, op cit, p. 63.

14. Fuad Jabber, 1971. *Israel and Nuclear Weapons,* London, Chatto and Windus, p. 114; also see Shlaim, op cit, p. 188. For an excellent account of the raid see Neff, op cit, pp. 29-36; also see Jackson, op cit, pp. 41 and 66.

15. Numerous diplomats and news reporters who met Nasser after the 1952 Officer's Revolution confirmed his pragmatism and his interest in peace with Israel. These diplomats included various UN officials such as General E. L. M. Bums, Chief-of-Staff of the UN Truce Supervision Organization (UNTSO), the highest ranking UN official in the region. Bums spoke with Nasser in November 1954:

"He told me it was his desire that there should be no trouble on the northeastern border of Egypt, no disturbances . . . no military adventures." Neff, op cit, p. 33; also see David Hirst, 1977. *The Gun and the Olive Branch*, London, Futura/Macdonald and Co., p. 198.

16. Ehud Ya'ari, 1975. *Mitzrayim ve-Ha Fedayeen, 1953-1956* [Egypt and the Fedayeen, 1953-1956], Givat Haviva, Center for Arabic and Afro-Asian Studies.

Another more recent account by Abu Iyad, one of the leading figures of Fatah, describes firsthand the Egyptian government's repression of efforts by Palestinians to organize cells of resistance. Abu Iyad, 1979, *Palestinien sans patrie*, Paris, N.P. This view was corroborated by former BBC reporter Alan Hart in interviews with two other PLO leaders, Yasser Arafat and, Khalil al-Wazir (Abu Jihad, recently assassinated by Israeli agents. Alan Hart, 1984. *Arafat: Terrorist or Peacemaker?*, London, Sidgwick and Jackson, pp. 97.

17. A memorandum to President Eisenhower by U.S. National Security Council member James Lay affirms that U.S. intelligence had no evidence of organized *fedayeen* raiding during this period. Lay wrote: On the Arab side, small scale infiltration persists on the part of individuals and small groups acting on their own responsibility. There is no evidence of organized military activity by the Arab states acting in concert or by any individual Arab state. On the other hand, the Israeli government . . . appears to be following a deliberate policy of reprisals based on the theory that matters will have to be made worse before they become better." Cited in Green, op cit, p. 119. That this view was shared by U.S. diplomats across the board is indicated by Sharett's entry in his diary on April 14, 1955: "Reports by U.S. embassies in Arab capitals, studied in Washington, have produced in the [U.S.] State Department the conviction that an Israeli plan of retaliations, to be realized according to a pre-fixed timetable, exists, and that the goal is that of a steady escalation of the tension in the area in order to bring about a war." Cited in Rokach, op cit, p. 31.

18. The ambassadors were Abba Eban (Washington), Ya'acov Tsur (Paris) and Eliahu Eilat (London). Dayan stated: " . . . we face no danger at all of an Arab advantage of force for the next 8-10 years. Even if they receive massive military aid from the West, we shall maintain our military superiority thanks to our infinitely greater capacity to assimilate new armaments." Entry in Moshe Sharett's personal diary dated May 26, 1955 quoted in Rokach, op cit, p. 41.

19. See field reports filed by UNTSO Chiefs-of-Staff Vagn Bennike and Bums, as well as by Israeli-Jordanian Mixed Armistice Commission Chairman Hutchinson. Cited in Green, op cit, p. 99; also see the following books by the latter two officials, *Between Arab and Israeli* and *Violent Truce*.

20. Elmore Jackson's book *Middle East Mission* offers a detailed account of Nasser's peace initiative, together with an analysis of why it failed. See Note 11.

21. Neff, op cit, p. 67.

22. *Ibid,* pp. 67 and 83.

23. Several months later the early reports were confirmed to Nasser by British Intelligence, which had its own reasons for leaking the facts on the secret French arms deal. Britain at this time had a defense treaty with Jordan, and feared that new French arms might tempt Ben Gurion to move militarily against the young King Hussein, bringing Israel into direct confrontation with British troops. Exposure of the secret arms pipeline was intended as a warning to Ben Gurion. Neff, op cit, p. 83; also see Jackson, op cit, p. 70-71.

According to Neff, "French transfers of conventional weapons to Israel began slowly in the early 1950's with battle tanks, cannon, and surplus World War II planes. By the end of 1954 France became more generous largely as a result of the rebellion that started that year in Algeria; the Jewish state was seen as a counterbalance to the Arab rebels. There was considerable support in France for Israel, especially in the military, which admired Israel's tough tactics, and among Paris' leading politicians. Many French politicians shared socialist ideals with Israel's leaders and had fought alongside Jewish fighters in the Resistance." According to Neff, in 1954 the flow of French arms increased significantly. By early 1955, Israel received the first of at least 60 French Mystère IV fighter-bombers, the most advanced aircraft in the Middle East at that time. Neff, op cit, pp. 83, 160-162, and 325.

24. Green, op cit, pp. 123-147; also see Jackson, op cit, pp. 58-75.

25. Neff, op cit, p. 67; also see Jackson, op cit, p.17.

26. Entry in Sharett's diary, February 8, 1955, p. 712. Cited in Rokach, op cit, p. 38.

27. Neff, op cit, p. 35; also see Hart, op cit, pp. 97-109.

28. Neff, op cit, p. 86.

29. Abdel Nasser's Press Conference of October 5, 1955. Cited in Jackson, op cit, pp. 66-67.

30. On October 1, 1955 Sharett wrote: "Teddy [Kolleck] brought in a classified cable from Washington. Our 'partner' named [code] 'Ben' [Kermit Roosevelt of the CIA] . . . describes the terrible confusion prevailing in the State Department under the shock of the Nasser-Czech, i.e. 'Russian' deal. [Henry] Byroade and all the others who were in favor of U.S. support to Egypt lost their say completely. He adds: 'We are surprised at your silence.' When our man asked for the meaning of these words and whether we are expected to go to war, the answer was, 'If, when the Soviet arms arrive, you will hit Egypt – no one will protest.'" Sharett, *Personal Diary*, p. 1182, cited in

Rokach, op cit, p. 47.

31. Ladas to P. Bang-Jensen, January 6, 1956. Cited in Neff, op cit, p. 120.

32. Neff, op cit, p. 86.

33. Green, op cit, p. 120.

34. In fact these plans had been hatched as early as May, 1948, and discussed on numerous occasions since. Notice that insofar as Ben Gurion's plan involved Lebanon, this implied that plans for its destabilization and partition existed long before the PLO established a base there, indeed, long before the PLO even existed. Sharett, *Personal Diary,* October 26, 1953 p. 81 and February 27, 1954, p. 377, cited in Rokach, op cit, pp. 15 and 22; also see Noam Chomsky, 1983. *The Fateful Triangle,* Boston South End Press, pp. 161-163.

Sharett also noted in his diary that Moshe Dayan solidly backed Ben Gurion: "In his view all we need to do is to find a [Lebanese Christian] officer, even just a major. We should either win his heart or buy him with money, to make him agree to declare himself the savior of the Maronite population. Then the Israeli army will enter Lebanon, occupy the necessary territory, and will create a Christian regime which will ally itself with Israel." Sharett, *Personal Diary,* May 16, 1954, cited in Rokach, op cit, p. 26. A later account by Dayan himself confirmed the plan's existence. See Moshe Dayan, 1976. *Milestones* (Hebrew), Tel Aviv, Idanim, p. 255; also see Neff, op cit, p. 342; Simha Flapan, *The Birth of Israel,* op cit, pp. 15-53.

35. Of his resignation, Sharett later wrote: "I have learned that the state of Israel cannot be ruled in our generation without deceit and adventurism. These are historical facts that cannot be altered. In the end history will justify both the stratagems of deceit and the acts of adventurism. All I know is that I, Moshe Sharett, am not capable of them, and I am therefore unsuited to lead the country." The following April, after the Sinai War, Sharett bemoaned his own inability to set aside mere personal ethics in the interests of state-building: "I go on repeating to myself: nowadays admit that you are the loser! They showed much more daring and dynamism. . . . They played with fire and they won. Admit that the balance sheet of the Sinai War is positive. Moral evaluations apart, Israel's political importance in the world has grown enormously... You remain alone. Only your son Coby is with you. The public, even your own public, does not share your position. On the contrary . . . the public now turns even against its 'masters,' and its bitterness against the retreat [from Sinai and Gaza forced by U.S. President Eisenhower] is developing into a tendency to change the political balance in this country in favor of [Menachem] Begin." Sharett, *Personal Diaries,* Nov, 16, 1956 and April 4, 1957, cited in Rokach, op cit, p. 49; also see Hirst, op cit p. 201; also see Green, op cit, p. 130; David Ben Gurion. *War Diaries,* (unpublished),

Oct, 22, 1956; Bar-Zohar, op cit, pp. 1234-1235; Moshe Dayan, 1976. *The Story of My Life,* New York, William Morrow and Co., p. 228.

36. Years later, Israeli deep-penetration bombing raids on the Egyptian heartland – coming at a time when Israel could have negotiated from strength instead of escalating the level of conflict – again forced Nasser into the arms of the U.S.S.R. For a detailed study of the 1968-1970 War of Attrition which led to the introduction of thousands of Soviet troops and advisers to Egypt see Stephen Green, 1988. *Living by the Sword,* Brattleboro, Vt., Amana Books, pp. 45- 60.

37. In the early 1950s Israel sought a formal defense agreement with the United States. At the time, this was rejected because of the perception in Washington that U.S. policy in the region should be balanced, that is, not weighted in favor of Israel. At the time the Arab states were regarded as vital to U.S. interests. This perception was abandoned – along with the policy – in the late 1960s. M.T. Klare, 1984. *American Arms Supermarket,* Austin, University of Texas Press, p. 140; also see M. Zak, "Aid to the Kurds – Without a Defense Treaty, " *Ma'ariv,* October 1, 1980.

In 1955 Washington produced a counter-offer, a U.S./Israeli security pact. The proposed agreement was rejected because it would have required Israel to accept declared and fixed borders. See entry in Sharett's diary, February 14, 1955, cited in Rokach, op cit, p. 38; also see Flapan, op cit, pp. 15- 53; Neff, op cit, p. 105. For extensive other documentation on this point see Chomsky, op cit, pp. 161-163. Ben Gurion's position on Israel's borders will be discussed at greater length in subsequent chapters.

Chapter Three

Creating "facts," not flowers

The wisdom of Israel is now the wisdom of war,
nothing else.

David Ben Gurion,
January 8, 1948[1]

Long before word of an Israeli nuclear program began to leak out in the late 1950s, two fundamentally different ways of thinking had emerged among Zionists on the question of how to deal with the surrounding Arab nations.[2] The first approach was personified in the figure of David Ben Gurion, the architect of the Jewish state, and Israel's first Prime Minister. His approach has been described by a number of writers, including former Israeli Prime Minister Moshe Sharett:

> *The one approach says that the only language the Arabs*
> *understand is force. The state of Israel is so tiny and isolated*
> *that if it does not increase its actual strength by a very high*
> *coefficient of demonstrated action, it will run into trouble.*
> *From time to time the state of Israel must give unmistakable*
> *proof of its strength and show that it is able to use force in a*
> *crushing and highly effective manner. If it does not give such*
> *proof it will be engulfed and may even disappear from the*
> *face of the earth.[3]*

The idea was to humiliate the Arabs in battle so completely they would be forced to sue for peace on terms Israel could then impose.

In the early 1950s Ben Gurion and his close supporters believed that the Arabs – even in defeat – had not been sufficiently intimidated

41

to justify serious diplomatic efforts towards a final political settlement. Their thinking may be summarized as follows. By relying on superior military force and by manipulating Arab disunity, Israel had gained new lands and new strength. Even though the Arab armies had been decisively beaten in the field, the Arab states had demonstrated the potential to rebound and fight again. Though Palestinian guerrillas were poorly armed and ill-organized, border infiltration and sporadic acts of terrorism continued, and with them the prospect of a protracted military struggle. It was believed that over the long run such a war of attrition would be more costly to Israel than to the Arabs. If the Israelis were ever to transform stalemate into permanent peace, it would first be necessary to convince the Arabs once and for all of the futility of attempting to defeat Israel militarily.

Given such an attitude of unqualified pessimism at the precise moment when the 'ultimate weapon' had appeared on the horizon, it should not be surprising that some of Israel's leaders would consider a bomb program. The nuclear option afforded, or so it was thought, the tempting possibility of a deterrent, an ace-in-the-hole so powerful as to be far beyond anything the Arab nations would be able to match in the foreseeable future.

This bleak pessimism of Ben Gurion and his MAPAI party allies concerning the very possibility of peace with the Arabs was described by author/editor Simha Flapan in his first book, *Zionism and the Palestinians:*

> *Ben Gurion's attitude toward the Arabs was apocalyptic, expecting and preparing for the worst. . . . This admonition, which had all the elements of a self-fulfilling prophecy, was not the result of a careful and rational analysis of trends and developments; rather, it grew out of his temperament and his penchant for viewing reality through the prism of the traumatic experiences in Jewish history.*[4]

Flapan's perspective has been confirmed in other recent accounts, as, for example, by the writer Michael Bar-Zohar, whose 1978 political biography of Ben Gurion documented the leader's deep pessimism in numerous conversations with his closest aides and with foreign leaders who had known him.[5] Avi Slaim's 1983 study of Ben Gurion produced a similar impression:

> *Ben Gurion had surprisingly little knowledge or understanding of the Arabs and their culture and no empathy whatever for them. His image of the Arabs as an implacable enemy, fanatically bent on the frustration of the national aspiration of the Jews, became more and more rigid with the passage of time, along with the belief that it was beyond the capacity of the Jews to overcome by peaceful means this inherent Arab hostility. Only by the repeated and vigorous application of force, he concluded, could Israel demonstrate its invincibility and, in the long run, compel the Arabs to come to terms with her existence.[6]*

As we now know, persuasive evidence repudiates the view of inherent Arab hostility and demonstrates that in fact the surrounding Arab states were prepared to accept Israel's existence under certain conditions. On numerous occasions before, during and after the 1948-49 War of Independence, various Arab leaders expressed willingness to negotiate a solution to the conflict which included recognition of Israel.

Some of this evidence was presented recently by the late Simha Flapan in a powerful book, *The Birth of Israel,* which grew out of Flapan's examination of thousands of newly declassified Israeli government archives, including the release of David Ben Gurion's *War Diaries.* Flapan was also able to review unpublished material from various Arab sources. His findings undermine prevailing notions about the 1948 war and demolish conventional wisdom as to the real intentions of Israel's leaders, particularly Ben Gurion's. *

Flapan's brilliant recapitulation of the chronology of that tumultuous period demonstrates that, far from seeking to 'drive the Jews into the sea,' the Arab nations in 1948 were neither militarily prepared nor otherwise disposed to fight the emerging Jewish state. In

---

* Simha Flapan's credentials are impeccable. A lifelong Zionist, he emigrated to Palestine from Poland in 1930. His long and distinguished career included work as a writer, publisher, peace activist, and educator. For twenty-six years he served as National Secretary of Israel's MAPAM party and Director of its Arab Affairs Department. He also founded and for many years served as editor of Israel's foremost progressive magazine, *New Outlook.* This chapter attempts to convey the substance of Flapan's thinking and his conclusions. However, it is no substitute for a careful review of his important book *The Birth of Israel.*

fact, according to Flapan, at that time Arab nationalists in Saudia Arabia, Egypt and Syria were more concerned with preventing the establishment of an expanded Hashemite Kingdom by Jordan's King Abdallah than in battling Jews in Palestine.

Abdallah's dream of an Arab kingdom embracing parts of Lebanon, Syria and Trans-Jordan (Palestine) was a carryover, a revival of the old promise of a united Arab kingdom kindled years earlier by T.E. Lawrence (Lawrence of Arabia) and the British. In 1915 that promise, subsequently cruelly betrayed at Versailles, had been Britain's means during World War I of rallying the Arabs to its cause: the defeat of the Ottoman Turks.* Though Abdallah strove mightily to resurrect it, by 1948 the dream was an anachronism, in direct conflict with the new emerging wave of anti-colonial Arab nationalism exemplified by younger Arab leaders such as Nasser. In the nationalists' view, Abdallah's grand design was fatally flawed because it relied on British support. In other words, a Hashemite kingdom amounted to perpetuating in another form the same colonial rule Arabs had long opposed and were now committed to overturn. From the Arab nationalist viewpoint, the principal enemy was colonialism – in whatever form. As for Zionism, it also was regarded as an extension of British rule, and for good reason. Instead of making good their promise to liberate Palestine after the ouster of the Turks in World War I, the British themselves had occupied the region militarily while presiding over its colonization by a new wave of foreign immigrants, European Jews. From the Arab standpoint, one form of colonization had simply been replaced by another.[7]

Ben Gurion's Collusion with Abdallah

David Ben Gurion was well aware of these deep divisions in the Arab world, and shrewdly used them to his advantage by playing one side off against the other. Ben Gurion realized that, for a variety of reasons, a collusion with Abdallah served Zionist interests. First, since a Hashemite kingdom and a Palestinian homeland were irreconcilable alternatives, by supporting Abdallah, Israel could effectively block

---

* Even as they made promises to the Arabs, the British were making other plans with the French to subdivide the Arab world into colonies, and exploit the region's principle resource: oil. For a retelling of the British campaign to unite the Arabs against the Turks, see T.E. Lawrence's classic account, *The Seven Pillars of Wisdom.*

implementation of the UN partition plan for a Palestinian state without visibly seeming to do so. Zionists need not appear as the villains. By occupying the UN-designated Arab sector of Palestine (part of which later became known as the West Bank) Abdallah would do the job for them. And second, a non-aggression pact with Abdallah neutralized Jordan's British-trained army, at the time the best Arab force in the Middle East, the crack Arab Legion. This reduced, if it did not entirely eliminate, the chances of an attack on Israel's vulnerable eastern flank. In a scrap with Egypt and Syria this meant a two-front rather than a three-front war – regarded as essential for a *Haganah* victory. Later, as the situation on the ground shifted, Ben Gurion's tactics changed accordingly. When the alliance with Abdallah ceased being useful, it was abandoned.[8] And, in fact, Israel's abandonment of Abdallah led to his assassination soon thereafter. The collusion was an early example of a strategy – 'the enemy of my enemy is my friend' – that Israel employed more recently in the Iran-Contra arms scandal.[9]

The Truce that Failed

Flapan was able to substantially document claims made by the Zionist elder statesman Nahum Goldmann that the 1948 war could have been averted in the first place. As president of the World Zionist Organization and the World Jewish Congress, Goldmann had charged over many years that the war might have been averted – saving 6000 Jewish lives – had Ben Gurion been willing to accept a compromise solution along the lines of the 1947 UN Partition Plan.[10]

At that time, in early 1948, feverish efforts were under way on the diplomatic front to head off an Israeli proclamation of independence, widely viewed as tantamount to an open declaration of war.[11] At the eleventh hour the UN Security Council proposed a U.S.-backed truce. Significantly, the idea was supported by Egypt and Syria, the Arab states principally involved.[12] Obviously, had they sought war those Arab states would have rejected the proposal outright. In fact it was Ben Gurion and his co-conspirator Abdallah who rejected the UN truce proposal. And in retrospect, their parallel logic in doing so is obvious: a truce meant new delays and the possible frustration of their expansionist plans.

On the other hand, Nahum Goldmann's perspective of the truce proposal was quite different. Goldmann believed that the truce proposal presented the Zionist leadership with an important opportunity to win formal Arab recognition through the diplomatic gesture of temporarily delaying a proclamation of independence. Goldmann believed that by this time the creation of a Jewish state was not in doubt; its emergence had already been accepted by many Arab leaders as inevitable. Of course, support for a truce also would have implied Zionist support for the UN partition plan mandating a Palestinian homeland alongside Israel, as well as support for the concept of fixed borders. Hence the deeper logic of Ben Gurion's rejection of the truce proposal: it was the acid test proving that his previous support for the 1947 UN Partition Plan had been strictly tactical. The bottom line was simply that Ben Gurion was not interested in a compromise solution.[13]

According to Flapan, it was Abdallah's refusal to support a truce which led to the Arab nationalists' invasion of Palestine. Initially, it was intended *not* to destroy Israel, but to prevent the first step in the implementation of Abdallah's grand design, a Hashemite kingdom, since it was feared the collapse of the UN truce proposal would tempt Abdallah to annex Arab Palestine. The fact that the Arab forces were *not* aimed at the annihilation of Jews is proven by the manner in which they were initially deployed. The best Arab units, comprised of almost half the invading Arab army, did not even engage Israel. They were dispatched to the Arab cities of Beersheba, Hebron and Jerusalem to forestall Jordanian occupation of those areas. Other Egyptian units moved up the Gaza seacoast toward Tel-Aviv, areas which also had been designated for the Palestinian state. Significantly, it was in those same areas – the Arab quarter of Palestine – where nearly all of the subsequent fighting occurred during Israel's War of Independence.[14]

This bird's-eye account summarizes Flapan's interpretation of the complex events leading up to and immediately following Israel's proclamation of independence on May 14, 1948:

> *In summing up the complicated developments during this fateful period in the Jewish-Arab conflict, one reaches the paradoxical conclusion that, although militarily this was a war between Arabs and Jews, politically it was a war between Arabs and Arabs. The issue was not the existence of the Jewish state, because both Arab camps were ready, under certain conditions, to recognize the new reality. Rather, the central issue at stake was the relationship of the Arab world to the great powers outside the Middle East. One side sought the establishment of an Arab Kingdom, under the aegis of the British Empire; the other sought the economic*

and political independence of the Arab countries as a
prerequisite of Arab unity and progress. Both were ready to
consider an alliance with Israel to further their aspirations.[15]

Within the first weeks of fighting both Egypt and Syria realized they could not defeat Israel militarily.[16] By November 1948 all the Arab states, including Iraq and even Jordan, desired to end the war, and from then on sought ways to end the fighting.[17] On this point Flapan's book corroborates the findings of a previous study by Tom Segev, also based primarily on Israeli government documents. Segev showed that Ben Gurion and his associates squandered clear opportunities to negotiate peace with the defeated Arab nations following the war. On one such occasion the Syrian leader Husnei Zaim proposed a meeting with Ben Gurion for the purpose of concluding a peace agreement. Zaim also indicated his willingness to absorb permanently as many as 350,000 Palestinian refugees – a remarkable concession. Yet Ben Gurion set impossible preconditions, effectively killing the talks before they even began. Other negotiations with Egypt broke down for similar reasons during the first day of talks.[18]

Later in 1949, under the auspices of a UN Conciliation Commission, the Arab states formally agreed to an agenda known as the Lausanne Protocols, which called for Arab recognition of Israel on the basis of the 1947 partition plan. Incredibly, nothing came of the opening. By this stage Ben Gurion was unwilling even to consider a return to the UN boundaries which formerly Israel had supposedly accepted.[19] Ben Gurion was not in a conciliatory mood:

Before the founding of the state, on the eve of its
creation, our main interest was self-defense. To a large
extent, the creation of the state was an act of self-
defense....Many think that we're still at the same stage. But
now the issue at hand is conquest, not self-defense. As for
setting the borders, it's an open-ended matter....In the Bible
as well as in our history there are all kinds of definitions of
the country's borders, so there's no real limit. No border is
absolute. If it's a desert – it could just as well be on the other
side. If it's a sea – it could be across the sea. The world has
always been this way. Only the terms have changed. If they
should find a way of reaching the stars, well then, perhaps
the whole earth will no longer suffice.[20]

Israel's intransigence led Mark Ethridge, the U.S. delegate to the Lausanne Conference, to tell President Truman that Israel's apparent decision to base her future security on military strength while foregoing the chance to make peace seemed "unbelievable", considering Israel's tiny size.[21]

Perhaps this was because of the decisive way the war had ended, or because of the maximalist political tide then running in Israel. Whatever the reason, it was Ben Gurion's refusal to seek lasting peace after the war which prompted an American diplomat in Damascus to comment that Israel had "won the war, but lost the peace."[22] Ben Gurion's unwillingness to respond to genuine peace overtures eventually transformed a serious conflict into bitter stalemate.

The Palestinians

While not all of Israel's leaders shared Ben Gurion's attitude toward the Arab states, with regard to the indigenous Palestinians there was near unanimity. In fact Flapan argues that the question of Palestinian rights was never adequately addressed by Zionism. Period. As Flapan put it: "From the beginnings of Zionist settlement in Palestine, the attitudes of the majority of the Zionist parties toward the local Arab population ranged from total obliviousness to their presence ('the land without a people for the people without a land') to patronizing paternalism and indifference to outright denial of their national rights."[23] Though many Israelis could see that the seizure of Arab homes and lands was sowing the seeds for future conflict, only a brave few called for the obvious solution – recognition of Palestinian rights. In fact, the few who did speak out represented only one of the many Zionist parties, or rather, a faction within one party. This was the Hashomers Hatzair element of the left-wing MAPAM party (the United Worker's Party). Hashomer Hatzair was a youth and kibbutz movement that supported the idea of a bi-national secular state. According to Flapan, of the other two Jewish groups that supported Palestinian nationalism, one, Brit Shalom, was not a party but an association of intellectuals and the other, the Communist Party, was non-Zionist.[24]

The reasons why Zionists failed to address the Palestinian question are complex, but all derived from self-interest. It was assumed that the destiny of Palestinians must not interfere with the work of building the Zionist enterprise. Palestinian nationalism, it was decided (incidentally, without consulting Palestinians) was merely an expression of a broader pan-Arab movement, a view consistent with Ben Gurion's secret alliance with Abdallah. The Zionist view was that the future of the Palestinians lay elsewhere within the larger Arab community; it lay anywhere, in fact, save within the region of Greater Israel. This explains Ben Gurion's policy of driving Palestinians from their homes and villages into exile.* Moreover, the natural consequence of this logic was the political/economic suppression of those Palestinians who remained. To the extent their culture was proof of a unique Palestinian Arab identity, it was unwanted. If it could not be eliminated through forced exile, it would be suppressed.

It should be added that the Palestinian issue was relatively easy for Zionists to ignore in the 1950s. The Palestinian nationalist movement had been crushed years earlier by the British in the Arab rebellion of 1936-39, during which most Palestinian leaders had been either killed, exiled or imprisoned. And with the catastrophic dispersal of the Palestinian population during and after the 1948-49 war, Palestinian society had not recovered sufficiently by the 1950s to be a factor in the conflict.** Its re-emergence as a force in the Middle East equation only occurred years later in the 1960s, with the rise of Yasser Arafat's Fatah.

The Nuclear Debate in Israel

But if there was near-unanimity regarding the Palestinians, there was none on the question of nuclear development, which was regarded primarily as a foreign policy issue vis-à-vis the surrounding Arab states. The controversy began in 1957 when word leaked out that a secret nuclear reactor was under construction near Dimona in the

* Flapan's research, based on old IDF intelligence estimates, documented that the vast majority – 84% – of the 370,000 Arabs who fled Palestine before June 1, 1948 did so as a result of Zionist military actions. Only 5% left on orders from Arab leaders. Another 11% may have left voluntarily. The first wave accounted for roughly half of the total exodus. *The Birth of Israel*, pp. 83-118. Flapan's conclusions have been confirmed in an even more recent study by Benny Morris. *Benny Morris, 1988. The Birth of the Palestinian Refugee Problem*, 1947-49, New York, Cambridge University Press.

** Flapan calculates the Palestinian refugee population at somewhere between 530,000 – reported by the Israeli Commission – and 770,000, the figure quoted by the UN's Palestine Conciliation Commission (UNPCC). *The Birth of Israel*, p. 216.

Negev desert. The news generated immediate protests. Dr. Ernst David Bergmann, chairman of Israel's Atomic Energy Commission (IAEC) at the time, later admitted in a lecture in Tel Aviv how widespread the opposition had been: "With two or three exceptions," he said, "the leaders of the country opposed the new nuclear policy which they regarded as irresponsible." Bergmann, who was a former pupil of Albert Einstein's and a strong supporter of Prime Minister Ben Gurion, added that the project was only executed "...thanks to Ben Gurion's visionary genius;" in other words, only because Ben Gurion succeeded in ramming it down the country's throat.[25]

Shimon Peres, one of Ben Gurion's young protégés, stated that many had criticized the Dimona project as "an act of political adventurism that would unite the world against us."[26] One prominent member of Ben Gurion's own MAPAI party (the Palestine Worker's Party, later the core of the Labor coalition) referred to it as a "political, economic and military catastrophe."[27]

Even the country's military leaders – with the important exception of Moshe Dayan – opposed the decision to go nuclear. For example, Yigal Allon, the commander of the elite commando force, the *Palmach,* and the principal hero of 1948, argued forcefully against the nuclear program. Allon's views carried much weight, as he was considered to be one of Israel's brightest military strategists.[28] Yitzhak Rabin, who later became Chief-of-Staff in 1964, also opposed the nuclear option.[29] Even the quintessential hawk Ariel Sharon went on record with the opposition.[30] These individuals, along with most of the country's top military brass, favored reliance on conventional military strength.

Meanwhile, the cream of Israel's intellectual community favored a second, more moderate, approach. These men, whose ranks included the theologian Martin Buber,[31] believed that the peace option must at all costs be kept alive. They felt that Israel should make every effort to coexist peacefully with its Arab neighbors. Their arguments were strategic, but also embraced moral, political and economic considerations. Their starting point was the conviction that the same Jewish people who recently had experienced the horrors of Hitler's Third Reich had a basic interest in preventing a drift toward another holocaust – a nuclear one. Above all, they argued for a non-provocative defense policy because they were convinced that a posture of belligerence ran counter to Israel's best long-term interests, since it would make new enemies and tend to isolate Zionism in the world community.

Among intellectuals, the reasons for opposing a nuclear development program, even a 'peaceful' program, were only too obvious. It was commonly understood that the civilian IAEC's role was strictly advisory. The big decisions over policy were being made in the Defense Ministry.[32] And since Prime Minister Ben Gurion also held the Defense Ministry portfolio, this meant it was none other than he, Ben Gurion, the 'prophet of fire,' who personally controlled nuclear research and development.

Viewed with hindsight, the extraordinary political power wielded during this period by Ben Gurion is amazing, considering that Israel was a democracy. The plain fact is – democracy or no democracy – Ben Gurion was never held accountable for his nuclear agenda. When six of the seven members of the IAEC resigned in 1957 to protest Ben Gurion's secret decision to build the Dimona reactor, no government inquiry was held into the reasons for the resignations.[33] Nor was a new commission appointed. Bergmann, the sole remaining member, continued as chairman as though nothing had changed, even though henceforth there was no commission over which to preside – a sure sign that the body had been a rubber-stamp for what in reality was a military program.[34] With 20-20 hindsight, the conclusion is inescapable that no democratic check existed over one man's personal control of what would soon become a nuclear weapons program.

The Ben Gurion Cabinet

Numerous accounts have called the Dimona reactor a child of the 1956 Suez War. However, recently declassified CIA documents indicate U.S. intelligence believed that the decision to begin construction had been made by Ben Gurion and his close associates in early 1956, even *before* the Suez campaign.[35] Moreover, statements made years later by Shimon Peres indicate the project had been proposed as early as 1955.[36]

In her autobiography Golda Meir claimed that, despite Ben Gurion's firm grip on the helm of the ship of state, democratic process was nevertheless maintained throughout; that issues facing the country were as a rule discussed and voted on in cabinet meetings. Because Meir herself served during this period in several cabinet posts (as Minister of Labor and as Foreign Minister), her account certainly offers important insights into the day-to-day workings of Ben Gurion's government. It is interesting, nonetheless, that Meir's memoirs, which amount to some 400 pages, include not a single reference to an Israeli nuclear program – not even to a civilian program for power production – despite its obvious importance as an issue at that time.[37] Such a conspicuous omission suggests Meir's account was highly selective, to say the least. And in fact, this blanket omission of the nuclear question – as if it never even happened – is typical of Israeli histories of this period.

It is well known that Golda Meir hardly ever differed with Ben Gurion on policy matters. Nor is it unreasonable to suggest this as the reason why it was *she* who was chosen to fill Moshe Sharett's vacant post. The cabinet in-fighting was a recent painful memory, so it does not require a great leap of imagination to speculate that, by this time, Ben Gurion preferred a team player who would defer to him when it came to making policy. Yoram Peri, former advisor to Yitzhak Rabin, and a specialist on civilian-military relations, offered a perspective of Ben Gurion in his 1983 study, *Between Battles and Ballots,* consistent with this view:

> *He, Prime Minister and Defense Minister, was the only conduit connecting the two sub-systems, the military and the political. He made all possible efforts to prevent contacts between the military and civil-political echelons and saw himself as solely responsible to the Cabinet and the Knesset in security matters....He prohibited military men fro m appearing before the Cabinet and from addressing the Knesset and other government bodies, thereby blocking formal information-channels...except the one that he controlled. He deflected all attempts to introduce a legal definition of the Cabinet's authority over the army's day-to-day activities, so limiting the Cabinet's practical control over the military....At Cabinet meetings he would raise pre - formulated proposals that the Cabinet was expected to approve. On many foreign and defense affairs, even when they touched on the most fundamental strategic principles, he did not consult ministers....And he used to say: "The information I give you is correct, but that does not mean it is all the available information."[38]*

Today we know that parliamentary democracy played no role whatsoever in the decision to launch construction of Dimona. Recently declassified documents indicate the CIA believed that Ben Gurion had not consulted with his cabinet;[39] nor that he informed the Knesset of the reactor until the U.S. State Department forced his hand years later by independently breaking the story to the press. State had learned from the CIA that Dimona was not a "textile plant," nor a "pumping station," as Ben Gurion had claimed on different occasions.[40] Presumably the CIA had detected the reactor by means of high altitude U-2 reconnaissance.

On December 21, 1960, the Prime Minister went before the Knesset and admitted to the world that the Dimona Project was a nuclear reactor. Even so, Ben Gurion categorically denied that the country was producing an atomic bomb. He labeled reports that Israel was constructing an atomic device as "either a deliberate or unconscious untruth."[41] He declared the reactor was intended for "peaceful purposes only," insisting the design stopped short of weapons production. Elaborating further, and stretching the limits of credibility in the process, he described Dimona as a "scientific institute for research into the problems of arid zones and desert flora and fauna...." "The Dimona reactor," he said, "will serve the needs of industry, agriculture and health, and will train scientists and technicians for the future construction of nuclear power stations."[42] Soon after, he was quoted as insisting that any plutonium produced by the reactor would be returned to the country supplying the uranium.[43]

Israel's First Peace Movement

After the announcement a new round of protest and debate erupted, followed by the appearance of Israel's first peace movement. In 1961, a Committee for the Denuclearization of the Arab-Israeli Conflict was formed by 17 prominent scholars and scientists, including two former IAEC commissioners. The Committee declared the adoption of a nuclear option to be a fundamental mistake and demanded that Israel seek the denuclearization of the Middle East. In April 1962 the Committee published the following demands:

1. That the Middle East countries refrain from military nuclear production; if possible, by mutual agreement;
2. That the UN be requested to supervise the region in order to prevent military nuclear production;

3. That the countries of the Middle East avoid obtaining nuclear arms from other countries.[44]

The Committee's views immediately drew wide support across the entire spectrum of political opinion in Israel at that time. In the ensuing Knesset debate, Zalman S. Abramov, leader of the Gahal party, criticized the Israeli government's rejection of a proposal made by Swedish Prime Minister Tage Erlander that non-nuclear countries abstain from producing nuclear weapons.[45] The government rejection also prompted M.K. Hasan, leader of MAPAM, to propose an Israeli initiative to prevent the introduction of nuclear weapons into the region. However, government spokesmen denounced Hasan's proposal as irrelevant to the real threat originating from the conventional arms race, insisting at the same time that "there are no nuclear weapons in the Middle East and Israel will never be the first to introduce them."[46] This would remain the official government position over many years, even after Mordechai Vanunu's stunning revelations appeared a quarter century later.[47]

A Garden in the Negev?

As late as January 1963, Deputy Defense Minister Peres was still declaring that the Defense Ministry was harnessing Dimona to desalinate a billion cubic meters of seawater annually, in order to turn the Negev into a garden. By this time, however, the story was wearing a bit thin. Peres' remarks prompted Aharon Weiner, the Director of Tahal, Israel's Water Company, to state flatly that the story was simply "unfounded."[48]

It is true a desalination plant had been considered for the Negev. For years the U.S. State Department had entertained the idea, perhaps naively, that by introducing almost unlimited fresh water into the dry region, new agricultural and economic opportunities would be created which would alleviate sources of conflict between Arabs and Israelis, thereby stabilizing the region politically. It was also seen as a way to nudge Israel toward voluntary compliance with international regulation of nuclear power development. The proposal was to give Israel $40 million for a nuclear desalination plant, contingent on Israel's submitting the Dimona reactor to international regulations and inspections.[49] Even though the proposal held great promise for Israel's economy, Ben Gurion rejected it out of hand. General D.K. Palit and

P.K.S. Namboodiri commented on the decision in their book *Pakistan's Islamic Bomb:* "The fact that the Israelis rejected the plant, which...could have been highly beneficial to the country's economy, is indicative of *what* they proposed to do with their atomic energy establishments at Dimona."[50]

As we now know, Peres, the ramrod behind Israel's massive arms purchases from France during the buildup for the Suez campaign,[51] had something in mind other than 'making the desert bloom.' Various sources place him squarely at ground zero with respect to the Dimona project, in other words, at the very epicenter of the circle of men committed to creating "facts" rather than flowers in the Negev.[52]

Notes to Chapter Three

1. *War Diaries* (unpublished).

2. This fundamental point is supported by widely disparate opinions on both sides of the issue. For a dissenter's view, see Mist, op cit, pp. 172-202; also see Simha Flapan, "Wonderful Logic – All Wrong," *New Outlook,* September, 1963, p. 26; Simha Flapan, "Nuclear Power in the Middle East," in *New Outlook,* July, 1974. p. 49. For a different Zionist view, see Yehoshafat Harkabi, 1983. *The Bar Kokhba Syndrome,* Chappaqua, New York, Russell Books. p. 136; also see Shlaim, op cit, p. 180.

3. Moshe Sharett, "Yisrael ve-Arav: Milchama ve-Shalom (Israel and the Arabs: War and Peace)," *Ot,* September, 1966. Note: the English translation appeared in *The Jerusalem Post,* October 18, 1966.

4. Simha Flapan, 1978. *Zionism and the Palestinians,* New York, Harper and Row. p. 140.

5. Michael Bar-Zohar, 1978. *Ben Gurion: A Political Biography,* Part III, Tel Aviv, Am Oved. pp. 1365, 1379 and 1399.

6. Shlaim, op cit, p. 182.

7. Flapan, *Birth of Israel,* op cit, pp. 57-79.

8. *Ibid,* pp. 121-152; for a detailed study of the collusion with Abdallah see Avi Shlaim, 1988. *Collusion Across the Jordan: King Abdallah, the Zionist Movement, and the Partition of Palestine,* Oxford, Clarendon Press.

9. Jonathan Marshall, Peter Dale Scott and Jane Hunter, 1987. *The Iran-Contra Connection,* Boston, South End Press, pp. 83-124.

10. Flapan, *Birth of Israel,* op cit, pp. 6-7, and chapters 2, 5 and 7. This body of material should be reviewed together.

11. *Ibid*; Note: some argue that the war began immediately following the Partition Plan Resolution in 1947. However, the fighting previous to May, 1948 was exclusively between Zionists and Palestinian nationals, and did not involve the surrounding Arab states.

12. *Ibid,* pp. 155-199.

13. *Ibid,* pp. 20-53, p. 76, p. 185.

14. *Ibid,* pp. 150-152.

15. *Ibid,* p. 150.

16. *Ibid,* pp. 201-232.

17. *Ibid,* p. 48.

18. *Ibid,* pp. 208-212; also see Tom Segev, 1986. 1949: *The First Israelis,* New York, Macmillan. pp. 3-42.

19. Segev, op cit, pp. 3-42.

20. Political Consultation, 4. 12.49, State Archives, Foreign Ministry, 2447/3, cited in Segev, op cit, p. 6.

21. Ethridge to Truman, 4. 11. 49, Foreign Relations of the U.S., 1949, p. 905. Cited in Segev, op cit, p. 35.

22. Segev, op cit, p. 37.

23. Flapan, Birth of Israel, op cit, p. 36.

24. *Ibid*, pp 42, and 109-113.

25. Yoram Nimrod, "L'eau l'atome et le conflit," *Les Temps Modernes* (Paris), XXII, 1967, No. 253 Bis. pp. 902-903; also see Amos Perlmutter, Michael Handel and Uri Bar-Joseph, 1982. *Two Minutes Over Baghdad*, Cornwall, Great Britain, Vallentine, Mitchell & Co., Ltd. p. 27.

26. *Jewish Observer and Middle East Review*, July 9, 1965.

27. Nimrod, op cit, p. 903.

28. Yigal Allon, 1969. *Massach Shel Chol* (A Curtain of Sand), Hakibbutz Hame' uchad Publishers.

29. Perlmutter, *Two Minutes*, op cit, pp. 27 and 42.

30. Efraim Inbar, "Israel and Nuclear Weapons Since 1973," in Louis René Berès, ed., 1986. *Security or Armageddon*, Lexington, Mass., Lexington Books. pp. 65 and 75.

31. "Symposium: The Atom Bomb in Israel," *New Outlook*, March-April 1961; also see Maurice Friedman, 1983. *Martin Buber's Life and Work: The Later Years*, 1945-1965, New York, E.P. Dutton, Inc. pp. 332-371, "Buber Versus Ben Gurion."

32. Jabber, op cit, p. 18.

33. *Ibid*, pp. 18-19, 33 and 34.

34. Aubrey Hodes, 1968. *Dialogue With Ishmael: Israel's Future in the Middle East*, New York, Funk and Wagnells. p. 230.

35. Green, *Taking Sides*, op cit, p. 312.

36. Jabber, op cit, p. 26.

37. Golda Meir, 1975. *My Life*, New York, G. P. Putnam's Sons, pp. 153-155.

38. Peri, op cit, pp. 158-159.

39. Green, *Taking Sides*, op cit, p. 312.

40. *Ibid*, pp. 153-154; also see Sylvia Crosbie, 1974. *A Tacit Alliance: France and Israel from Suez to the Six Day War*, Princeton, N.J., Princeton University Press. p. 162; also see Bar-Zohar, op cit, p. 1401.

41. *Ma'ariv*, February 24, 1963.

42. Flapan, "Nuclear Power," op cit, p. 50.

43. Cited in Perlmutter, *Two Minutes*, op cit, p. 27; also see Steve Weissman, and Herbert Krosney, 1981. *The Islamic Bomb*, New York, Times Books, p. 17.

44. Flapan, *New Outlook*, July, 1974, p. 50.

45. *New Outlook*, vol. 5, no. 9, November-December 1962.

46. Roger F. Pajak, 1982. *Nuclear Proliferation in the Middle East*, Chapter 4: "Nuclear Status and Policies of the Middle East

Countries," National Security Affairs Monograph Series 82-1, Ft. Lesley McNair, National Defense University Press, p. 33; also see Flapan, "Nuclear Power in the Middle East," Parts One and Two, in *New Outlook*, July and October, 1974.

47. "Peres Attacks Report on Israeli A-Arms," *New York Times*, October 7, 1986.

48. *Davar*, January 3, 1963.

49. According to Zdenek Cervenka and Barbara Rogers' study, as late as March 7, 1966, the U.S. State Department published a report confirming the feasibility of a 1,250 megawatt nuclear reactor for generating electricity both for sale and to power a desalination plant capable of producing 100,000,000 gallons of fresh water a day. The report declared that the system could be in operation by 1972 at a total cost of some $200 million. Though Shimon Peres reportedly favored French financing – undoubtedly because he believed it could be acquired without nuclear regulatory conditions – in early April 1966 Prime Minister Eshkol began negotiations with the United States to implement the project, which never materialized. Zdenek Cervenka and Barbara Rogers, 1978. *The Nuclear Axis: The Secret Collaboration Between West Germany and South Africa*, New York, New York Times Book Co., p. 317; also see *Yediot Aharonot*, (Tel Aviv), April 4, 1966.

50. D.K. Palit, and P.K.S. Namboodiri, 1979. *Pakistan's Islamic Bomb*, New Delhi, Vikas, p. 49.

51. Neff, op cit, pp. 26-27; also see Perlmutter, *Two Minutes*, op cit, pp. 23-24; Green, *Taking Sides*, op cit, pp. 123-147; Neff, op cit, pp. 162-163, 234-236, and 241.

Chapter Four

Dimona: The third temple?

*It is not important what the goyim are saying
but what Jews are doing.*
– David Ben Gurion[1]

*Lately, the curtains have been drawn from the
Secret Services and we had a view of the methods of
dealing with spying in the U.S.A. The abandoning of
Jonathan Pollard and the love affair with the
Iranian murderers. We hear and read but fail to get
an answer to the question: where was all this born,
who decided, and why?*

*In the last two years we discovered an ugly side
of the General Security Service to such an extent
that it seems as if Ministers were subject to
blackmail by heads of the service. In such a political
reality it is scary to discover that attitudes to the
nuclear policy reach the public only via Moscow's
responses to the Jericho II rocket and the strange
manner of capturing Mr. Vanunu. The anxiety
increases due to the attempt, which has failed, so
far, to prevent Vanunu from testifying at his own
trial even though it takes place behind closed
doors.*

*Who are these mysterious people who spend the
research and development budgets and maneuver
our fate, and our children's fate, in such secrecy that
even experienced judges sitting behind closed doors
are forbidden to know about their actions? How do
we know they are sane and responsible? How do we
know that they act according to government's
wishes? After all, in every one of the affairs which
came to light recently, it turned out that the Prime
Minister knew nothing.*
– Shulamit Aloni MK[2]

Over the years, because of a combination of ultra-tight security and state censorship, the Israeli bomb program remained one of the century's best kept secrets. In early 1980, a book on the subject was about to appear in print in Israel but was banned by the government for security reasons. The manuscript, titled *None Will Survive Us: The Story of the Israeli A Bomb,* was the work of two Israeli journalists, Eli Teicher and his colleague, Ami Dor-On, the former managing editor of the daily *Ha'aretz.* The book had been submitted to the government censors as required by Israeli security regulations.

On March 30 the *New York Times* reported that in addition to the ban, the authors had been warned by the chief censor they would face 15 years to life in prison if they ever revealed the contents of the book. Later Mr. Teicher said, "I felt like I was in Moscow – not Tel Aviv...." Mr Dor-On was quoted as saying that he had no plans to defy the ban. "If we want to live in Israel we can't do it, " he said.[3]

More daring was shown by another Israeli, Mordechai Vanunu, who fled the country to reveal many of the secrets of the Dimona project, where he had worked for almost nine years as a nuclear technician. Vanunu's story appeared on October 5, 1986 as a feature exposé in the London *Sunday Times.* Thanks to his courage, it is now possible to complete with fair accuracy a broad sketch of the Israeli bomb program.

With French assistance, construction of the silver-domed 26-megawatt Dimona reactor (modeled on France's EL-3 heavy water reactor at Brest, in Brittany) was completed in December 1963. We may assume that soon thereafter it began producing a steady supply of radioactive waste, i.e., plutonium. The Dimona project was more extensive than just a reactor, however. The reactor was merely one important component, perhaps the hub, of a large research complex spread out over ten production units (*Machons*) and employing as many as 2700 scientists and technicians. The name of the complex, the Nuclear Research Center of the Negev (NRCN), is also known by its Hebrew acronym KMG *Kirya-le-Mehekar Gariny.*

The secret plutonium separation/reprocessing plant, *Machon II,* the existence of which was verified by Mr. Vanunu, was also part of the 1957 reactor deal made with French Premier Guy Mollet. Blueprints for the plant were provided by the French company Saint Gobain Nuclear (SGN). Work on the underground lab began soon after construction of the reactor, when French engineers bulldozed an 80-foot deep trench in the desert near the reactor. In it they buried the six-level concrete bunker which was to house the secret facility. Later

Machon II was outfitted with French extraction/reprocessing technology shipped clandestinely as 'textile machinery.'[4] Aboveground, the 80 by 200 foot windowless concrete building appeared innocuous enough, resembling an ordinary two-story warehouse. Only one detail suggested otherwise: an incongruous elevator tower on the roof.

After the election of Charles de Gaulle as President in 1959, a reassessment of French involvement apparently occurred. In his autobiographical *Memoirs of Hope,* de Gaulle claimed that French assistance had ended in 1960.[5] However, on October 12, 1986, a week after the Vanunu cover story, the London *Sunday Times* carried a follow-up report challenging de Gaulle's version of events. The report included an interview with Francis Perrin, the chief of the French nuclear program from 1951-1970. Perrin admitted that despite thirty years of official denials, de Gaulle had lied: though other nuclear ties were terminated following his election, de Gaulle had allowed construction of the separation plant to proceed with French assistance.[6]

Once operational, the reprocessing plant removed the final obstacle to A-bomb assembly via the plutonium path, namely, the production of weapons-grade plutonium fuel. However, the plant's completion date remains one of the unresolved mysteries of the Israeli program. One detailed 1982 study by French journalist Pierre Péan claimed the plant had been completed by 1966.[7] Other evidence suggests its completion was delayed until after the 1967 Six-Day War. French advisors remained in Israel as late as 1969.[8]

"Israel will not be the first..."

After replacing Ben Gurion as Prime Minister in 1963, Levi Eshkol introduced a new policy amounting to a nearer convergence of American and Israeli interests. The new policy stressed increased Israeli reliance on conventional military superiority at the expense of the nuclear program, but did not eliminate nuclear research entirely. It was to continue at a lesser level, keeping alive the nuclear option should it ever be needed.* Even so, there is reason to believe Eshkol's

* "Eshkol . . . reserved the right to continue research and training activities at the Dimona reactor and to re-examine the situation and the possibility of exercising the 'nuclear option' . . . if and when conventional arms supplies would fall below the quantity and quality required to successfully confront Egypt in the arms race or in an eventual military confrontation." Simha Flapan, "Nuclear Power in the Middle East," *New Outlook,* July 1974, p. 51.

new policy did succeed, at least initially, in frustrating the completion of the separation plant. In June 1963, shortly after Eshkol became Prime Minister, the Scientific Director of the Defense Ministry's development program, Shimon Yiftah, stated in a news conference that Israel would not erect a chemical separation plant to reprocess the plutonium produced by the Dimona reactor.[9] In fact, Eshkol had demonstrated his opposition to the nuclear agenda as early as 1961, while serving as David Ben Gurion's Finance Minister. According to one account, at that time he had refused to fund Dimona from the national budget, forcing Ben Gurion to raise the needed money covertly from Israeli industrialists and Diaspora Jews.[10]

On May 18, 1966, in a speech to the Knesset, Eshkol declared that "Israel will not be the first to introduce nuclear weapons into the region." In succeeding years the expression would be repeated so often by Israeli diplomats – in the face of evidence to the contrary – that it became almost meaningless. At that time, however, in the context of Eshkol's 1966 speech, the remark was widely hailed as the signal of a new Israeli restraint, and a welcome departure from the former hawkish policies of David Ben Gurion.

In his 1984 book *Taking Sides,* Stephen Green offered a more cynical interpretation based on his own investigation into the Israeli nuclear program. Green claimed Israel had already fabricated its first bombs – probably made with enriched uranium – by the date of Eshkol's public disavowal:

> *Looking at the first twenty years of Israel's history there is simply no factual basis upon which to presume discretion or restraint in matters of military development. None. Within about twenty-five minutes of the time Israel could have developed an atomic weapon Israel did develop an atomic weapon.* [11]

In Green's view, Eshkol's shifting of defense priorities, including a dramatic increase in spending for conventional arms at the expense of nuclear, simply indicated the bomb program had already come of age, that the bomb-in-the-basement had been achieved. Indeed, what better time to announce a halt? Israel would lose nothing in terms of security and would gain respect internationally for showing, or seeming to show, restraint.

Green's interpretation hews close to the facts of the case.* Increasing evidence suggests that by the early 1960s Israel was moving rapidly toward exploding its first A-Bomb, or at least had the capability of doing so. An article in *Commentary* magazine in February 1961 reported Israel had both the laboratory facilities and the technical know-how to detonate a nuclear device.[12] If, during this early period, there were no documented Israeli blasts, it was only because Israel's nuclear scientists were already involved with the French team conducting tests in the Sahara. We know that between 1960 and 1964 a total of 17 French atomic tests occurred at Ekker and Raggan in Algeria.[13] In their book, *The Islamic Bomb,* Steve Weissman and Herbert Krosney claimed that Israel had access to French nuclear test data as a *quid pro quo* for contributions to the French program, a view shared by various other sources.[14] When the French moved their operations to the Pacific in 1964, the stage was set for Israel to initiate its own test program.

By this time Arab governments and analysts were also convinced an Israeli bomb was imminent. In August 1965 the prominent Egyptian journalist, Muhammad H. Heikal, published an extensive article in *Al-Ahram* in which he stated that "Israel is close to the capacity to explode

---

* Fuad Jabber reached a similar conclusion as early as 1971, when he wrote: "Declaratory policy aside, Israel has gone steadily ahead in the development of the capacity to build atomic bombs, though the active nuclear course set by Ben Gurion in the 1950's was ostensibly frozen by Eshkol. ... In actual practice, available evidence indicates that no efforts have been spared to equip the establishment scientifically and technologically with all it would require to produce nuclear weapons at short notice." *Israel and Nuclear Weapons,* p. 123.

Professor Beit-Hallahmi also expressed an informed cynicism in his recent critical study of a related issue, namely, Israel's worldwide network of military alliances: "What the past teaches us is quite clear. First, there is a pattern of serious and deep Israeli involvement in supporting certain regimes in the Third World. Second, most of the details of these involvements are not known while they take place, so that reliance on open sources will inevitably lead us to underestimate the extent of these involvements. Consequently, present Israeli activities are probably much wider and deeper than we have been told in public forums or the media ... Many years from now it will become clear that this book *The Israeli Connection* has erred on the side of caution, that Israeli complicity in Third World repression was much greater than currently appreciated." Mr. Vanunu's revelations have demonstrated the validity of Beit-Hallahmi's analysis at least as regards Israel's nuclear agenda. *The Israeli Connection,* pp. XIV and 243.

an atomic device...."[15] In December 1965 the Secretary General of the Arab League alerted all members of the organization with a memorandum warning that nuclear weapons might be used by Israel in a new war.[16] Moreover, in his speeches during the first months of 1966, President Nasser himself referred repeatedly to the increasing danger of an Israeli nuclear capability.[17]

During these same months prominent Americans also expressed concern over the prospect of an Israeli nuclear capability. On June 5, 1965, the *New York Times* announced the release of a report by a special committee selected to study the spread of nuclear weapons to the Middle East. In the report the committee Chairman, Roswell I. Gilpatric, announced that Israel had reached and was about to cross the nuclear threshold.[18] Several days later Senator Robert Kennedy told the U.S. Senate that "the need to halt the spread of nuclear weapons must be the central priority of American policy." Kennedy pointed out that both Israel and India already possessed supplies of "weapons-grade fissionable material and [had the capability to] fabricate an atomic device within a few months." Kennedy proposed an immediate U.S./Soviet initiative to obtain a pledge from Israel and other nations that they would neither acquire nor develop nuclear weapons in return for security guarantees.[19] Unfortunately, nothing came of Kennedy's proposal. An editorial in the London *Jewish Observer* summarized the negative Israeli government response:

> The...attempt to restrict proliferation in the Middle East may increase rather than lessen the danger of war....The threat comes from the acknowledged aim of Nasser...to destroy Israel....The halting of such nuclear development as exists would not change this situation for the better. It might, on the contrary, encourage aggression by conventional weapons.[20]

In December 1965 Edward Teller, the father of the American H-Bomb, announced after a visit to Israel that no obstacles remained to producing atomic bombs, inasmuch as Israel had everything needed.[21] Within weeks the *New York Times* carried a story detailing a secret Israeli contract with France to acquire medium-range ballistic missiles capable of targeting Egypt. The revelation was regarded as proof of Israel's nuclear aspirations – and capabilities.[22]

Both Paths to the Bomb

Solid evidence demonstrates that Israel sought both plutonium *and* uranium paths to the bomb. Ben Gurion's earlier claim that unreprocessed plutonium-bearing waste from Dimona would be returned to the supplier (i.e., France) told only half the story. Ben Gurion did not mention the key point of the agreement: France would reprocess the plutonium and *return it* to Israel. The mutual agreement was another facet of the *quid pro quo* for Israeli technical assistance in the French bomb program. According to researcher Steve Weissman, existence of the agreement was confirmed by "two extremely well-placed sources in Paris and Jerusalem." The French source claimed the Israelis sent France a total of forty tons of unreprocessed plutonium, half of which was reprocessed and returned. The Israeli source verified the agreement but claimed that France broke the contract and never returned any plutonium. Whether or not Israel did receive French reprocessed plutonium is difficult to ascertain, since these events converge with de Gaulle's aid cut-off following the 1967 war.[23]

Even if plutonium was not yet available by 1966, there was still uranium. Strong evidence indicates that at least 200 pounds, and perhaps much more, of highly enriched uranium (HEU 235) – enough for at least five to ten bombs – as well as classified documents detailing secret military research and development programs, had been smuggled into Israel over a period of years by a Pennsylvania-based firm, the Nuclear Materials and Equipment Corporation (NUMEC), in violation of various U.S. laws.[24] U.S. intelligence officials believed the diversion began soon after the company was founded in 1957. Later FBI investigations disclosed criminal negligence, with strong evidence of fraud, in the company's bookkeeping. Furthermore, the FBI discovered probable intent when it was learned that the company's President, Dr. Zalman Shapiro, a self-proclaimed Zionist, had traveled around the U.S. openly recruiting American Jewish scientists to work for Israel. It was learned that Shapiro had direct links to the Israeli embassy. In fact, Shapiro even formed a NUMEC subsidiary in half-partnership with the Israeli government. Despite a powerful case, no Federal indictments were ever handed down. On the contrary, in the spring of 1966 the U.S. Atomic Energy Commission (AEC) selected

NUMEC – even as a U.S. General Accounting Office (GAO) investigation into the company was under way – for the largest plutonium fuel-processing contract ever awarded a private U.S. firm.[25]

According to a December 1977 exposé in *Rolling Stone* based on well-placed U.S. government sources (which included a highly placed Pentagon consultant, a former National Security Agency official, a former CIA official, a former White House aide, as well as other government officials), a cover-up of the whole messy NUMEC affair was ordered by none other than President Lyndon Johnson in February 1966 – just as the Justice Department began preparing a case against Shapiro. Presumably Johnson had decided that a public airing of the facts would embarrass White House support for Israel, which had dramatically increased in the mid-1960s, to say nothing of damaging the public's confidence in the American AEC. Indeed, not only would the case have exposed obvious differences between U.S. and Israeli security interests, it would also have revealed the AEC's utter ineptness in handling this "most tightly controlled substance in the world."[26] Finally, a court case might also have clarified inherent ambiguities between 'atoms for peace' and atoms for war. Unfortunately, these questions would have to wait.[27]

Incredible as it sounds, diversion of enriched uranium to Israel continued for some months *even after* the Johnson initiated cover-up began, despite increased AEC scrutiny. In fact, according to *Rolling Stone's* sources, the diversion continued until Zalman Shapiro sold NUMEC to the Atlantic Richfield Company in 1967.[28]

Moshe Dayan's Nuclear Legacy

Various press reports have exposed a number of other related intrigues which also occurred in the 1960s. In June 1976, *Wehrtechnik,* the semi-official West German Army monthly, declared, in an unconfirmed report, that as early as 1963 Israel had staged its first underground test in the Negev. *Wehrtechnik* also reported that soon after this Prime Minister Eshkol discovered Defense Minister Moshe Dayan secretly ordering the assembly of nuclear warheads.[29]

In a 1973 account, writer Shabtai Teveth claimed that the ongoing dispute between Dayan and a coalition of Eshkol supporters in the cabinet centered on defense policies, a debate in which the issue of nuclear proliferation must have figured prominently. We know Eshkol's coalition favored strict limits on the nuclear program, while

Dayan had supported Ben Gurion's agenda from the beginning. According to Teveth, at about this time the Eshkol coalition began clamoring for assurances that Dayan would not be given influence over defense matters above and beyond that of other ministers. This is curious since at the time Dayan was serving as Minister of Agriculture. Taken together, these events, plus Dayan's forced resignation from the cabinet by Eshkol in November 1964 under less than clear circumstances, lend credibility to the *Wehrtechnik* report that Dayan had been caught exceeding his authority.[30]

On April 12, 1976 *Time* magazine reported a similar incident which supposedly occurred in 1968. This report claimed that Dayan, who had been reappointed Defense Minister at the time of the June 1967 War, secretly gave the order to proceed with the construction of the controversial Dimona plutonium separation plant, even though the Prime Minister and most of the cabinet opposed the plan, and even though the Israeli equivalent of the U.S. National Security Council had vetoed the idea.[31]

While the *Time* report was essentially correct, recent testimony by Mr. Vanunu suggests it seriously understated the facts. Strong – overwhelming – evidence points to even bigger changes under way at Dimona by this time. Dayan's alleged decision to complete the separation plant was only one part, though a key part, of a concerted effort to bring Israel's nuclear program to full maturity. Also involved was a closely related decision to enlarge the Dimona reactor in order to expand production of plutonium. The reason? Probably the bottleneck in the nuclear weapons production line was the reactor itself. Rated at only 26 megawatts, the Dimona reactor was initially classified as a research reactor; its capacity to produce plutonium was rather limited. Expanding the reactor brought it into sync with Dayan's accelerated timetable for building up Israel's nuclear arsenal.

It is interesting that in this regard Vanunu's testimony was not unprecedented; it merely confirmed claims made several years earlier by journalist Pierre Péan in his 1982 study of French-Israeli cooperation, *Les deux bombes* (The Two Bombs). Péan quoted French sources who acknowledged the Dimona complex had been "far larger than admitted and cleverly disguised."[32] On the basis of information provided by Vanunu, British nuclear experts confirmed that boosting Dimona's output by at least a factor of five could have been accomplished without entirely rebuilding the reactor, since expansion had been factored into the original design. Thus, after 1967 the reactor was upgraded with relative ease from the original 26 megawatts to the current 150 megawatts. Vanunu described how the reactor's cooling system had been ingeniously camouflaged to conceal its true capacity.[33]

The expansion ordered by Dayan increased the reactor's output of unprocessed plutonium five-fold to around 40 kilograms a year, enough to build eight to ten Hiroshima-size warheads a year, implying a nuclear arsenal ten times larger than previously estimated. In other words, in 1987 Israel's nuclear arsenal probably numbered between 100 and 200 warheads, making Israel the world's sixth-rated nuclear power.

Other Pieces of the Puzzle

Finally, several other events occurred in the late 1960s, related pieces of the puzzle which also support this interpretation. First, in 1968 the Mossad masterminded the illegal diversion from West Germany of 200 tons of potential reactor fuel in the form of yellowcake, a partially processed uranium ore concentrate. The details of this remarkable secret operation, later known as the Plumbatt Affair, came to light only by chance seven years after the fact in July 1975, when a Mossad 'hit' team was dispatched to Norway to assassinate a senior PLO official. The Mossad believed that the PLO official, Ali Hassan Salameh, had been one of the men responsible for the massacre of Israeli athletes at the 1972 Munich Olympics. As it happened, the vaunted Mossad murdered the wrong man – a Moroccan Arab – by mistake. Soon after, Dan Aerbel, one of the Israeli agents picked up by Norwegian police, broke down under interrogation – apparently because of a predisposition to fits of claustrophobia due to a psychological trauma suffered earlier in life. At one point Aerbel reportedly blurted out: "I owned the Scheersburg A. It carried the uranium to Israel...." Though initially dumfounded, Norwegian authorities eventually pieced together the evidence, reconstructing the diversion scheme, with Aerbel filling in the details. The Mossad had purchased the yellowcake in Europe through a phony Italian company. Once en route to Italy aboard a Liberian registered tramp freighter, the Scheersburg A, the cargo was simply diverted to Israel. The heist accounts for the extra fuel requirements of an expanded reactor.[34]

Nor was the Plumbatt Affair a lone aberration. *Rolling Stone's* sources confirmed that the seizure was only one part of a far broader Mossad operation which began soon after the NUMEC pipeline dried up in 1967. Informants told *Rolling Stone* that sometime in 1967-68,

Mossad set up a special commando unit for the sole purpose of hijacking uranium from the Western nuclear powers. In addition to the Plumbatt heist, on at least three other occasions in 1968-69, Mossad hit teams made forays into France and England to seize shipments of weapons-grade fuel or, alternatively, yellowcake. Probably the most shocking detail uncovered by *Rolling Stone* was the revelation that at least two of the raids were secretly arranged with the complicity of the French and, in the case of the Plumbatt heist, the West German governments. Apparently France and West Germany were more than willing to deal in uranium secretly with Israel in exchange for cash and/or technical secrets.[35]

One last fragment completes the puzzle. A few months after the Plumbatt Affair, Israeli technicians deliberately provoked an American inspection team on its arrival at Dimona. In fact, they harassed the inspectors persistently enough that the men called off the visit, permanently ending the inspection effort begun in the early 1960s – part of a special agreement between John F. Kennedy and David Ben Gurion. The provocation was consistent with Israel's desire for utmost secrecy, on the assumption that a decision had been made to expand the facilities.[36] Vanunu's testimony also explained why the U.S. inspection team never discovered – or even suspected – the existence of the underground *Machon II* lab during previous inspections. The corridors leading to the elevator shafts – which would have exposed the six secret underground floors of the bunker – were bricked off and plastered over for each visit. Apparently, the inspections always occurred by a prearranged schedule, so the Israelis always had plenty of lead time to conceal embarrassing facts.[37]

Pierre Péan's 1982 account went further, revealing an even more shocking scheme. According to Péan, the Israelis secretly operated the reactor at the higher levels required to maximize plutonium production (under the noses of the American inspectors) without ever being detected. The deception was carried out with the usual Israeli attention to detail. A dummy control room was constructed for the sole purpose of fooling the inspection team. During their years of inspections, the inspectors apparently never once saw the real control room. Fake data from simulators were fed in to create the impression the reactor was operating at low power producing electricity for peaceful uses, when in fact it was geared up all the time, producing maximum quantities of plutonium.[38] If Péan is correct – and his claims certainly are consistent with Vanunu's confirmations on a number of points – the case is undoubtedly a prime example of Israeli deception.

On the basis of the available evidence, it seems reasonable to conclude that following the 1967 war a decision was made in the Defense Ministry to move forward with the manufacture of a second-generation plutonium bomb, [39] the work of the country's most brilliant scientist, Yuval Ne'eman.[40] Israel had just achieved a stunning victory in the Six-Day War, adding new territories while humiliating the Arab armies again. Despite the triumph, President Charles de Gaulle angrily cut off the French arms pipeline as a result of the Israeli attack on Sharm El Sheikh – the shot which launched the war. And despite South African aid to fill the gap, Moshe Dayan was haunted by the prospect of increasing military isolation.[41]

The Defense Minister was aware that over the long run Israel could not rely on the Mossad to supply enriched uranium in the quantities required for a full-scale nuclear buildup. Similarly, Dayan was in a position to know that Israel's development of uranium enrichment was still years away. As the infrastructure at Dimona began to come on line, therefore, Dayan must have been eager to set it to work producing an advanced plutonium warhead that Israel could "deploy with confidence", laying the groundwork at the same time for greater military independence.

Undercutting Eshkol

More or less feeble efforts to gain some civilian control over the Israeli nuclear establishment continued through the 1960s right up until the cabinet's final capitulation in 1968, when it was presented with the 'facts' of a full nuclear build-up.[42] For example, in 1961 a Ministerial Security Committee – the equivalent of the U.S. National Security Council – was set up by a new coalition government to oversee the Defense Ministry. Incredibly, the chairmanship of the new watchdog committee was given to none other than the Defense Minister himself.[43]

A more serious reform – which has already been mentioned – was attempted in April-May 1966 by Prime Minister Eshkol. At that time the IAEC's hawkish chairman, Ernst Bergmann, was forced to resign. New commissioners were appointed to reflect civilian priorities. Then Eshkol attached the chair to his own office, and made U.S. President Lyndon Johnson an offer to freeze weapons research at the Dimona complex in exchange for new U.S. conventional arms shipments. The offer is interesting since it clearly implied a much more ambitious nuclear agenda at Dimona than had been previously admitted.[44]

Nor did Johnson refuse Eshkol's requests. For years Washington had been pressing for a shift in Israeli defense priorities – away from nuclear development. When the offer came, Johnson leapt at the opportunity. During 1966, the United States provided Israel with an unprecedented $90 million in military aid, by far the largest yearly amount given through the decade of the 1960s.[45] Delivery of M-48 Patton tanks and A-4 Skyhawk fighter planes coincided with a massive Israeli military buildup already under way. By this time tensions were mounting toward the storm which would break the following year, the Six-Day War of June 1967.

Meanwhile, at about this same time, as reported by Taysir Nashif in his 1977 book *Nuclear Warfare in the Middle East,* the Israeli Defense Ministry sent a group of eleven nuclear engineers to the U.S. for training in the technology of underground testing. On their return to Israel, these same scientists reportedly started work at an Israeli test site in the Negev.[46] Furthermore, according to evidence compiled by Nashif, in late September or early October 1966, just a few months *after* the Prime Minister's promise to halt the bomb program, Israel went ahead with an underground nuclear test.

The evidence was produced by two separate teams of American and West German scientists engaged in marine research in the region. One team detected a sudden rise in the level of radioactive tritium in Mediterranean seawater, a finding corroborated by the second team working in the Gulf of Aqaba. The scientists concluded that the rise in tritium was due to an underground nuclear explosion.[47]

It does not necessarily follow that Prime Minister Eshkol deliberately deceived President Johnson by secretly ordering an Israeli nuclear test. Given Eshkol's vocal opposition to proliferation, and his reform record (he was responsible for Israel's signing of the Atmospheric Test Ban Treaty in 1963), his commitment to nonproliferation seemed real enough. The more likely explanation is that Eshkol himself was deceived by the Defense Ministry – an already familiar pattern, as we have seen.

But the full story of Moshe Dayan's intrigues during this crucial period of Israel's history remains to be told. We do know that Eshkol and Dayan agreed on almost nothing. Polar opposites, the two men had been brought back together only in the rarefied atmosphere of national unity preceding the Six-Day War. On the eve of that conflict the nation demanded a military hero to lead the army into battle. Prime Minister Eshkol, who must have been keenly aware of the potential threat to his nonproliferation policy represented by a man like Dayan, understandably resisted the appointment until the political pressures became insurmountable.[48] And true to form, Dayan later proved to be the undoing of Eshkol's administration.

No sooner had the war ended than a power struggle resumed between the two men for control of defense/nuclear policy. Recall that the precedent for control over the nuclear program had already been set years before by Ben Gurion for the express purpose of insulating the nuclear agenda from civilian oversight. To date, little has been told of how the aging Prime Minister was outmaneuvered by Dayan. About those machinations we can only guess. Clearly, however, with the cabinet's capitulation in 1968, Dayan and the nuclear advocates had won. That same year Dayan established an Advisory Committee on General Research, appointing as its coordinator none other than Professor Ernst Bergmann, the very man Eshkol had fired two years before. Bergmann was later identified by the West German magazine *Der Spiegel* as the supervisor of the secret plutonium separation plant. No doubt his reappointment symbolized the totality of Dayan's victory.[49]

The National Security Sector

Taken together, these events reveal the inherent weakness of Israeli democracy – a notable lack of structural integrity – which any serious future peace negotiations must take into account. And while it is undeniable that the problem of integrity is hardly unique to Israeli politics, in what other Western democracy – banana republics aside – would a prime minister be compelled to readmit to his cabinet a minister he had already forced from office? In what other democracy could a defense minister flout the authority of the prime minister, and get away with it by overturning a resignation ordered by the prime minister himself? In what other democracy could an individual cabinet minister effectively veto official government policy without being reprimanded? Such situations have occurred repeatedly in the three-ring-circus atmosphere of Israeli politics.[50]

At issue is the power of the Israeli Defense Ministry – specifically, the security sector. Israel has no constitution and no bill of rights. Israeli law was inherited from the British Mandate, including Defense (Emergency) Regulations promulgated in 1945 (some as early as 1936) which provided sweeping emergency powers for the military and administrative authorities. Technically, Israel has lived in a 'state of emergency' from its inception.* As a result, "the Israeli Defense Force (IDF) grew into the single most autonomous bureaucratic instrument of the newly established state. Zahal [IDF] is jealous and proud of its traditions, successes and reputation and tolerates no intervention from internal and especially external sources."[51]

While Israelis have routinely denied the military's interest in politics, their arguments seem weak, given their narrow meaning of 'politics.' Amos Perlmutter's early views are perhaps typical: "The maturity of Israeli political structures... especially the political parties, the kibbutzim and the Histadrut, would present a formidable challenge to the army if it were to choose to play independent politics." Perlmutter goes on to list the factors opposing military domination: the rapid turnover of officers, the economic and social integration of veterans, the nation's dependence on the reserve system, the identity of political goals, the army's professionalism, the legitimacy of civilian political structures, etc.[52]

Clearly, one of the key phrases here is 'identity of goals.' In other words, as long as Israel's political and military leaders share the same 'social-democratic values, ' the fusion of civilian and military structures runs smoothly. Significantly, Perlmutter's early essay never even speculated on the one case which in this context matters most: the exception which proves the rule. This study has already explored one such occasion – the 1954 peace initiative of Moshe Sharett. That was an initiative truly modest in scope, much more so than the kind of

---

* "In May 1951 the First Knesset, in a resolution carried almost unanimously, ruled that these regulations were incompatible with a democratic state and instructed the Constitution, Law and Judicial Committee to submit a bill to the Knesset within a fortnight for the annulment of these regulations and their replacement by a State Security Law. However, for reasons that are not clear, this instruction has not to date been implemented and the regulations have therefore remained in force. .... They provide the legal basis for most of the security measures enforced by the Israeli authorities since the Six-Day War. The manner of application of the regulations has come under frequent scrutiny in the press and periodical scrutiny by the High Court of Justice; nevertheless, the failure to give the regulations a thorough scrutiny by the legislative authority and the retention of an emergency act promulgated thirty years ago by a nonrepresentative government under vastly different circumstances is a severe blemish in Israel's democratic and libertarian record, especially since, as the First Knesset suggested, Israel's security concerns could have been taken care of by more appropriate legislation." Nadav Safran, *Israel: The Embattled Ally*, p. 134; also see Simha Flapan, *The Birth of Israel*, p. 102.

comprehensive political settlement which will be necessary to bring lasting peace to the region. Even so, the response of the military – that is, the security sector – in *that* circumstance was anything but supportive of civilian authority. Indeed, given the facts in that sorry case – the undercutting of official government policy – Perlmutter's 'smooth fusion' of civilian and military structures can hardly be taken seriously. What is worse, whatever 'identity of goals' may have existed before 1967 has steadily deteriorated in the intervening years. Today Israel is more deeply divided than ever.

In Israel the military does not just carry out policy. In the broad area of security, which it defines, the military *makes* policy. In a system which invites abuses, one is likely to find them. Thus a Prime Minister like Yitzhak Shamir can wash his hands of 'rogue operations' should they become public scandals. In effect he is saying: "I'm not responsible; it was the guys in the security sector who did it." For sake of clarification, the Prime Minister should also add: "This is the way we *always* do business here. My authority does not extend to them in the first place." Of course, as we shall see, in the case of Shamir and all other Israeli political leaders in recent memory, no significant political differences *do* exist between the two foci of power, at least on the central issue of the Palestinians. The question still remains: in the absence of structural integrity, what hope is there for a future moderate leadership, even *if* elected, to effect a political settlement embracing a genuine and painful compromise? The problem is not simply a matter of the right hand not knowing what the left is doing. The appropriate analogy more nearly approximates the case of a split brain; i.e., the Iron Fist is an autonomous hand, unregulated and uncontrolled. *

---

* According to Yoram Peri, a former advisor to Prime Minister Yitzhak Rabin, the creation of an autonomous "security sphere" was exactly what Ben Gurion intended. Peri states: "[Ben Gurion] worked vigorously to create a national consensus in the security sphere and to immunize defense issues from political disputes, by transferring them to the military for professional decisions."

Peri relates that in the late 1970's one Israeli writer, Dan Horowitz, described the problem of autonomy in terms of an underlying split in society: "a 'schizophrenic society' has developed, one in which there is a clear delineation between the security sphere and all the other civil spheres, the two areas being subjected to two different 'rules of the game.' " Now quoting Peri: "The dividing line is therefore not between institutions – military on the one hand, civil on the other – but between spheres, the security sphere and all other spheres ... This explains why the army can influence Israeli policy-making in

In 1987 the combined sphere of the IDF and national defense sector represented a whopping 30-50% of the Israeli annual budget, accounting for 25% of the national workforce. Nor do figures lie. As early as August 1980 one writer, quoted by Yoram Peri, had warned "that instead of a State which has an army, Israel is liable to become an Army which has a government...."[53] The writer was referring to Israel's enormous military-industrial complex. But as bad as entrenched bureaucracy may be, the problem is deeper still: as long as Israeli democracy permits the Defense Ministry to legally outflank and even supersede the other branches of government, Israel cannot honestly lay claim to democratic checks and balances – the heart and soul of representative government.* The reason for this, we are told, is national security – which only begs the question. Indeed, the national security state lies very near the root of the problem. Given all this, the diminishment of the Knesset's role in creating and carrying out policy should not be surprising.

In 1988 the dominance of the security sector has never been greater. Nor have Israel's high courts challenged the military's authority

---

the security field above and beyond the level usually acceptable in similar democracies ... However, the generals reciprocate by agreeing to abide by the civil rules of the game in all spheres of domestic politics. Thus although Israel's foreign policy is affected by images emanating from 'the military mind,' there is no penetration of military values into other civil sub-systems ... It is this dividing line between the two spheres, that 'enables Israel to function as a democratic society.' " Peri went on to argue that this state of affairs may no longer be operable since Likud's 1977 electoral victory, with IDF policy becoming increasingly ideological and more openly political. Yoram Peri, *Between Battles and Ballots,* pp. 8, 41-44, 48, 59, and 264. Peri articulated this view even more forcefully after the 1982 Lebanon invasion. Yoram Peri, "From Coexistence to Hegemony," *Davar,* October 1, 1982.

* According to J.C. Hurewitz: "Under the law, the Defense Minister need not consult his cabinet colleagues or procure Knesset endorsement before making major decisions, even the decision to mobilize the reserve brigades. He must, it is true, bring such a mobilization order to the attention of the Knesset Committee on Foreign Affairs and Security, which may confirm the order, or modify it, or withhold confirmation, or refer it to the Plenary Knesset. However, in the event of a situation that seems to demand mobilization, is the Knesset likely to reverse the order of the Defense Minister?," J.C. Hurewitz, 1968. "The Role of the Military in Society and Government," in *The Military in the Middle East,* N. Fisher, ed., Columbus, Ohio, Ohio State University Press. p. 100; also see Jabber, *Israel and Nuclear Weapons,* p. 55; Flapan, *The Birth of Israel,* p. 102.

to censor Israel's press – the very lifeblood of a democracy – in cases where 'national security interests' have been invoked. *

The problem is that, as Israel's military power has expanded, so also, like a self-fulfilling prophecy, have the frontiers of 'national security.'

---

* Nor has the complicity of Israel's courts been limited to "first amendment" issues. Recently a former senior security executive confessed publicly that "secret security officials routinely lied in court when trying to obtain convictions in security cases and that dozens of courts routinely accepted their lies because they came from official *Shabaq* operatives," a fascinating bit of circular logic – or rather, illogic. Its meaning: that untold thousands of Palestinians were convicted and sent to jail over the past 16 years because of false testimony, or on the basis of confessions extracted by means of torture. Leviticus, "From Victim to Symbol," *Israel and Palestine,* September 1987, p. 20; also see Menachem Shalev, "Shin Bet Lied for 16 Years," *Jerusalem Post,* November 1, 1987, p. A-1.

Notes to Chapter Four

1. Cited by Elon, op cit, p. 214.

2. *Yediot Aharonot,* August 30, 1987.

3. David Shipler, "Israel Bans a Book on Atomic 'Arsenal, '" *New York Times,* March 30, 1980, p. 5.

4. London *Sunday Times,* October 5, 1986, pp. 1, 4 and 5; also see Spokesman, op cit, pp. 39-51.

5. "I put a stop to irregular dealings which had developed between Tel Aviv and Paris on the military plane since the Suez expedition. In particular French cooperation in the construction of a factory near Beersheba [Dimona] for the transformation of uranium into plutonium – from which, one fine day, atomic bombs might emerge – was brought to an end." Charles de Gaulle, 1971. *Memoirs of Hope: Renewal and Endeavor,* New York, Simon and Schuster, p. 266.

6. Insight Team Report, "France Admits it Gave Israel A-Bomb, " London *Sunday Times,* October 12, 1986.

7. Pierre Péan, 1982. *Les deux bombes* (The Two Bombs), Paris, Fayard, p. 120.

8. London *Sunday Times,* October 5, 1986.

9. Jabber, op cit, p. 122.

10. Bar-Zohar, *A Political Biography,* (1978), op cit, pp. 1522-23, cited in Efraim Inbar, "The Israeli Basement – With Bombs or Without?, " *Crossroads,* 8 (Winter/Spring), p. 88.

11. Green, *Taking Sides,* op cit, pp. 175-176.

12. Gideon Gottlieb, "Israel and the Atom Bomb, " *Commentary,* February 1961, p. 94.

13. 1973. *White Paper on the French Tests* France, Ministère des affaires etrangères.

14. Weissman and Krosney, op cit, pp. 113-114; also see Taysir N. Nashif, 1977. *Nuclear Warfare in the Middle East: Dimensions and Responsibilities,* Princeton, The Kingston Press, Inc. p. 24; also see Peter Pry, 1984. *Israel's Nuclear Arsenal,* Boulder, Westview Press, pp. 16-17; *New York Times,* July 18, 1970, p. 8; Green, *Taking Sides,* op cit, p. 152; Elaine Davenport, 1978. *The Plumbatt Affair,* Philadelphia, Lippencott, p. 174.

15. Pajak, op cit, p. 34; also see Flapan, *New Outlook,* October 1974, p. 39.

16. Flapan, *New Outlook,* op cit, October 1974, p. 39.

17. *New York Times,* February 21, 1966, p. 8, February 23, p. 2, April 18, p. 6, May 9, p. 8.

18. *New York Times,* June 5, 1965.

19. Kennedy quoted by Simha Flapan, "Israel's attitude toward the NPT, " Nuclear Proliferation Problems, Stockholm, SIPRI, 1974.

20. The (London) *Jewish Observer,* July 2, 1965.

21. Yusuf Mruwwih 1969. *Al-Abhath Al-Dhariyah Al-Isra'Iliyah,* Beirut, Markaz al-abbath, p. 64.

22. *New York Times,* January 7, 1966.

23. Weissman and Krosney, op cit, pp. 117-118.

24. The figure of 200 pounds is conservative. The actual diversion may have been as much as 572 pounds – or more. John F. Fialka, "How Israel Got the Bomb, " *The Washington Monthly,* January 1979, p. 54; also see Howard Kohn and Barbara Newman, "How Israel got the Nuclear Bomb, " *Rolling Stone,* December 1, 1977, p. 38; Green, *Taking Sides,* op cit, pp. 157, 162 and 169.

25. Fialka, op cit.

26. In 1976, at the request of a Congressional subcommittee, the Nuclear Regulatory Commission (NRC) inventoried the records of all commercially-run nuclear reactor plants in the country. In August 1977 the NRC disclosed the results of the study: that a staggering 8000 pounds of enriched uranium and/or plutonium could not be accounted for. Howard Kohn, "widening gaps in nuclear safety, " *Rolling Stone,* December 1, 1977, p. 40.

27. Fialka, op cit; also see Kohn and Newman, op cit; Green, *Taking Sides,* op cit.

28. Kohn and Newman, op cit.

29. In part, the report stated: "Western experts believe that by 1963 Israel had staged a subterranean test in the Negev and that soon afterwards preparations of A-bomb materials started. In 1969 everything was settled but production of the bomb did not start right away. Israel's scientists concentrated on the development of new methods to cut production time of the bomb. Dimona in the Negev is not only guarded by troops, but also has a highly developed electronic system and radar screens, working round the clock. It is strictly forbidden to all planes, including Israeli war-planes, to fly over the area. During the Six-Day War an Israeli Mirage III went astray in the area. The plane was ruthlessly shot down by an anti-aircraft missile fired by their own people. When in 1973 a Libyan civilian aircraft inadvertently approached the area, Israeli fighters tried to force the plane to change course. When this proved to be of no effect the plane was shot down.

108 of the 113 passengers were killed." *Wehrtechnik,* June 1976.

30. Shabtai Teveth, 1973. Moshe Dayan: *The Soldier, The Man, The Legend.* Boston, Houghton Mifflin Co., pp. 308-310. Note: Writer Amos Perlmutter claimed Dayan resigned in May 1964 in solidarity with Ben Gurion's continuing protests over the still-simmering Lavon fiasco. However, this first instance appears to have been a feint. In fact, Dayan stayed on until November, when he resigned under increasing pressure. In his own words: "I knew that I would not be allowed to remain for long in the same line with the other MAPAI members of the government. I would be jostled and shoved and eventually pushed until I stumbled. It was better to get out while I still stood on my feet." Dayan, *Milestones,* op cit, p. 272. Perlmutter did admit that "The clashes in the political arena were actually surface demonstrations of similar struggles going on within the fabric of Israeli society as the processes of integration conflicted with the rapid modernization and growth of scientific and nuclear enterprises." Perlmutter, *Military and Politics in Israel* (1969), op it, pp. 102-105.

31. *Time,* April 12, 1976, p. 39; also see Perlmutter, *Two Minutes,* op cit, p. 43.

32. Péan, op cit, p. 96.

33. The London *Sunday Times,* October 5, 1986.

34. For an account of the Plumbatt Affair see Davenport, op cit; also see Steve Weissman, "How Israel got the Bomb, " *Inquiry,* November 13, 1978, pp. 20-23; also see Peter D. Jones, "Uncovering the Israeli-South African Connection, " *Win* Magazine, May 1, 1980, p. 15; also see Kohn and Newman, op cit.

35. Kohn and Newman, op cit, p. 38.

36. Weissman and Krosney, op cit; also see Davenport, op cit, pp. 11-92; also see Jones, op cit.

37. Couchman, "Four Corners", op cit, p. 13.

38. This account also supports the view that the *Machon II* separation plant was completed earlier than previous reports had indicated. Péan, op cit, pp. 104-105.

39. Yoram Peri, "Mushroom Over the Middle East, " *New Outlook,* May 1982, p. 42; also see Leonard S. Spector, 1984. *Nuclear Proliferation Today,* New York, Vintage Books, pp. 124-125.

40. Note: Ne'eman now heads the far-right Tehiya party, formed by former Likud members who broke away after Camp David because of dissatisfaction with Begin's return of the Sinai to Egypt. Tehiya represents a pure 'unadulterated' version of *Herut.* Pry, op cit, pp. 53-59; also see Davenport, op cit, p. 173; The Insight Team of the London

Sunday Times, 1974. *The Yom Kippur War*, Garden City, New York, Doubleday and Co., Inc. p. 283.

41. Raphael Medoff and Mordechai Haller, "South Africa in the Mind of Israel, " *National Review*, April 15, 1988, p. 38; also see Beit Hallahmi op cit, p. 117.

42. *Time*, April 1976, p. 39; also see *New York Times*, July 18, 1970, p. A-1

43. Jabber, op cit, p. 55.

44. Pajak, op cit, p. 33; also see Jabber, op cit, p. 48.

45. Mohamed El-Khawas and Samir Abed-Rabbo, 1984. *American Aid to Israel: Nature and Impact*, Brattleboro, Vermont, Amana Books, p. 34 and Table 2, p. 35.

46. Yusuf Mruwwih, 1967. *Akhtar Al-Tagaddum Al-'ilmi Fi Isra'il*, Beirut, Markaz al-Abhath, pp. 83-84, cited in Nashif, op cit, pp. 24-25.

47. According to Nashif, underground nuclear explosions can be conducted in such a way as to minimize detection. In fact, one such test was conducted by the U.S. on December 3, 1966 without being discovered. It was accomplished by suspending the bomb at a depth of 1100 meters in an excavated air chamber. Apparently the air cavity absorbed the main shocks of the explosion. Mahmud 'Azmi, "Al-Khayar al-Nawawi, al-Isra'ili Darurah Istyatijiyah, " *Shu'un Filastiniyah*, No. 43, March, 197S, p. 95. Cited in Nashif, op cit, pp. 24-25.

48. Donald Neff, 1984. *Warriors for Jerusalem*, New York, Linden Press, p. 183; also see Rokach, op cit, p. 61.

49. Jabber, op cit, p. 48, 51; also see *Der Spiegel*, May 5, 1969.

50. Other examples exist in addition to those already cited. In his memoirs Yitzhak Rabin accused fellow cabinet minister Shimon Peres of similar machinations; specifically, he accused Peres of publicly encouraging defiance of cabinet policy opposing West Bank settlements. Other examples are cited by Yoram Peri in his remarkably candid study. Peri, *Between Battles*, op cit, p. 6; also see Yitzhak Rabin, 1979. *The Rabin Memoirs*, Boston, Little, Brown and Co., pp. 307-308.

51. Amos Perlmutter, 1978. *Politics and the Military in Israel 1967-1977*, London, Frank Cass, p. 174.

52. Perlmutter, *Military and Politics in Israel*, (1969) op cit, pp. 119-126; also see Peri, *Between Battles*, op cit.

53. Peri, *Between Battles*, op cit, pp. 213-231 and 264.

Chapter Five

Is the Talking Over?

*I don't understand this comparison between us
and South Africa. What is similar here and there is
that both they and we must prevent others fro m
taking us over. Anyone who says that the Blacks are
oppressed in South Africa is a liar. The Blacks there
want to gain control of the White minority just like
the Arabs here want to gain control over us. And we
too, like the White minority in South Africa, must
act to prevent them....I was in a gold mine there and
I saw what excellent conditions the Black
workers...have. So there are separate elevators for
Whites and Blacks, so what? That's the way they
like it.*

—Raphael Eitan, former Chief-of-Staff, IDF[1]

*Israel and South Africa have much in common.
Both are engaged in a struggle for existence, and
both are in constant clash with the decisive
majorities in the United Nations. Both are reliable
foci of strength within the region, which would,
without them, fall into anti-Western anarchy. It is in
South Africa's interest that Israel is successful in
containing her enemies, who are among our own
most vicious enemies; and Israel would have all the
world against it if the navigation route around the
Cape of Good Hope should be out of operation
because South Africa's control is undermined. The
anti-Western powers have driven Israel and South
Africa into a community of interests which should
be utilized rather than denied.*

— Die Burger, May 29, 1968.[2]

> *The fact of the matter is that the government
> and its security forces are...ruled by fear...in spite of
> their immense power. Like anyone living in mortal
> fear, they occasionally resort to irrational means in
> the hope that a show of strength...might scare the
> resistors satisfactorily....This is the basis of security
> operations in South Africa most of the time.*
>
> — *Steve Biko*[3]

By the 1970s the political views of David Ben Gurion had become institutionalized. Public opinion had also shifted to the political right. In one of the great ironies of history, Israelis no longer debated the existence of a nuclear arsenal – which, in any case, had become a fact – since it was widely credited with staving off a military disaster in the first days of the 1973 Yom Kippur War, when Syrian tanks threatened to overrun Israeli positions on the Golan Heights.

Though the complex web of events leading up to and including the Yom Kippur War is far from a simple task to unravel – the problem being analogous to the old puzzle of identifying which came first, the chicken or the egg – the irony here is that an equally strong case could be made to show that the Israeli nuclear arsenal not only did *not* deter the war but actually helped bring it about. It is well documented, though not widely recalled in the U.S., that in February 1971, soon after coming to power, Egypt's President Anwar Sadat attempted a major peace initiative with Israel, which Israel flatly rejected.[4] A few days after Sadat's offer was announced, Jordan's Foreign Minister Abdullah Sallah stated that Jordan too was prepared to recognize Israel if it returned to the pre-1967 borders. There was no Israeli response.[5] In 1972, to demonstrate the seriousness of his commitment to a compromise settlement, Sadat expelled the Soviet advisors who were in Egypt – only to be ignored in Jerusalem, as well as in Washington.[6]

Also in 1972, Israel's Labor government rejected a proposal by King Hussein to establish a confederation of Jordan and the West Bank, a proposal that was anything but radical. According to Noam Chomsky, in rejecting this latest Jordanian peace plan, the Israeli Knesset announced "that the historic right of the Jewish people to the Land of Israel is beyond challenge." It was the first time the Knesset had officially endorsed the concept of 'Greater Israel'.[7]

In a scenario of events which is admittedly complex, it is worth examining why Israel ignored or rejected these initiatives by Sadat and Jordan in the early 1970s.[8] By this time Israel was anything but weak and vulnerable. Superiority in conventional arms, coupled with a nuclear arsenal, held in reserve, gave Israel a quantum military advantage over the Arab states that was at least the equivalent of cannon over bow-and-arrow. Why then did Israel not respond? The answer to this riddle may have been supplied unwittingly by U.S. Secretary of State Kissinger after the 1973 war while he was working out the terms of the disengagement. Referring to the new Israeli Prime Minister, Kissinger was quoted as saying "I ask [Yitzhak] Rabin to make concessions and he says he can't because Israel is weak. So I give him more arms and he says he doesn't *need* to make concessions because Israel is strong."[9]

As we now know, neither Egypt's Anwar Sadat nor Syria's Hafez Al-Assad had ever expected their October 1973 surprise attack to accomplish anything more than limited objectives. Nor did they have illusions about 'driving the Jews into the sea.' Angry rhetoric aside, Sadat and Assad were well aware of Israel's nuclear arsenal and, as a consequence, knew that a decisive Arab victory was simply not possible, since total war might compel Israel's leaders to play their nuclear trump card. Instead, they gambled from the outset on a limited war by which they hoped to win a political victory, namely, to create a situation which would compel the superpowers to intervene, bringing irresistible pressure to bear on Israel to withdraw from the Sinai and to negotiate a comprehensive political settlement.[10]

An abundance of persuasive evidence supports this view of a limited though ferocious war. Most important, Egypt's deployment of forces following its hugely successful surprise crossing of the Suez Canal was organized *in situ* under an umbrella of Soviet ground-to-air (SAM) missile batteries. The Egyptian plan was to offset Israeli aerial superiority along the length of the canal, enabling Egypt to fight what the London *Times* Insight Team called a 'meat-grinder' war. It was anything *but* an offensive alignment. In fact, while consolidating their new positions along the canal's eastern shore, Egyptian forces hesitated for four crucial days, a 'mobilizational pause' which may have cost Egypt the war by allowing Israel the opportunity to regroup and regain the initiative. When the Egyptian tank attack finally did come, the Israelis were ready. The Egyptians were cut to pieces within miles of the canal.

Indeed, far from being part of a grand design to destroy Israel, even the ill-fated Egyptian tank attack had a limited objective, namely, to relieve the Syrians, who by this time were being routed on the northern front.[11] In his memoirs Kissinger reported that the Israelis learned after the war, from captured Egyptian soldiers, that Sadat had no expectation of seizing the Sinai passes some thirty miles from the canal, let alone attacking Israel. "Egyptian forces had drilled for years to perfect the technique of crossing the Suez Canal; beyond it they had no operational plan except to hang on."[12]

The 'limited war' scenario is supported by the testimony of other eyewitnesses as well, one of whom was interviewed by Alan Hart, a former BBC Journalist. The observer was a PLO senior military advisor who experienced the war first-hand from near the Egyptian front line. According to this witness, whom Hart does not name, the moment the truth about Sadat's intentions came as early as the second day of the conflict:

> *By the beginning of the second day of the war the Egyptian crossing of the Suez Canal had been completed. Egyptian forces had, in fact, established a firm line five miles inside what was previously Israeli-occupied territory. At the beginning of this second day I said to myself, "This is really it! In two or three days we're going to be in Tel Aviv! Sadat is actually going to achieve what Nasser said was impossible!" Really, for a short time that's what I was telling myself. Then I began to see that nothing was happening. The Egyptian army was at a standstill. Very slowly I walked around the War Room, and one by one I looked into the faces of the Egyptians who were directing the war. I knew them all as former colleagues. Finally I asked the questions which they knew had been passing through my mind. "What is happening?" I said. "Why have you stopped? Why are you not continuing the advance when the gate to Tel Aviv is open?" They looked at the ground. They looked at the ceiling. Everywhere but at me. So I said again, "Why?" Then I got the answer. "No orders. We are not advancing because we have no orders. There is no plan and there will be no advance." In that moment I knew what had happened. We all knew. As far as Sadat was concerned, the war was over....For the first time in my life I was ashamed to be an Arab. I left the War Room and I cried my heart out.[13]*

Reckless as Sadat's and Assad's plan surely was – it brought the world to the brink of nuclear war[14] – their strategy of fighting a limited war in the shadow of nuclear weapons had historical precedents in Korea and Vietnam. What is more, the plan nearly succeeded.

Aftermath

A few weeks after the war, a poll taken in Israel revealed how wide the disparity between perception and fact can be. The poll showed that more than 80% of Israelis believed the goal of the war had been the destruction of Israel.[15] Indeed, one of the effects of the war was resignation to the necessity of a nuclear arsenal. The debate then shifted to the questions: How *far* should the country's nuclear potential be allowed to develop? And, should Israel publicly announce its nuclear policies?[16]

The other important aspect of the security debate joined during this period centered on the severe economic dislocations caused by the October 1973 War and by the continuing high levels of military spending – in fact, the highest rate in the world. At this time Israel was facing astronomical inflation and, for the first time, an actual drop in the standard of living.[17] Because of these problems, some military experts such as Moshe Dayan doubted whether the country could afford the continuing levels of spending required to maintain conventional superiority, and argued forcefully for a declared national commitment to the nuclear path.[18]

As usual, the government was divided, with Defense Minister Shimon Peres endorsing Dayan's nuclear agenda, and the more moderate Prime Minister Yitzhak Rabin, together with his Foreign Minister Yigal Allon, favoring reliance on conventional weaponry.[19] With the advantage of 20-20 hindsight, we now know that Rabin and the other so-called moderates in the cabinet succumbed in the end to the combined pressures of expedience and compromise. In effect, the government pursued *both* paths simultaneously, covering the fact by encouraging ambiguity on the matter – even espousing ambiguity as a form of deterrence.[20]

Rabin and the Nixon Doctrine

Rabin had previously served as Ambassador to the United States, and understood the crucial importance of continued American support. He also knew that a visible Israeli nuclear buildup might endanger that support. During the mid-1970s his government therefore attempted to project an image of moderation and reasonableness to allay American fears about Israeli nuclear capabilities. An image of restraint was regarded as essential to forging the special relationship between the two countries, which was Rabin's main objective. Rabin's strategy was to use Israel's existing nuclear arsenal as a means of levering political and diplomatic support from the U.S. as well as conventional military assistance.[21] The precedents for such a policy had been established by Prime Minister Eshkol in 1966 and again – much more dramatically – during the recent 1973 war when Golda Meir threatened nuclear escalation if the United States did not open up an emergency arms pipeline.[22]

Rabin's initiative was fortuitous in that it coincided with a new U.S. strategy, the Nixon Doctrine, which aimed at strengthening selected allies militarily in order to create American watchdogs to police the world.[23] In the Middle East the two states designated for such aid were Iran, under the Shah, and Israel. The outcome of these concerted moves made Rabin look like a winner; soon the stream of U.S. aid became a flood. By 1976 Israel was not spending a penny of its own money for conventional arms imports from the U.S. In fact, during 1976-1980 the average American contribution to the cost of Israel's military imports was 129% – in other words, 29% *more* than the actual cost.[24]

Meanwhile nuclear weapons development was proceeding apace – secretly. According to Amos Perlmutter, a former member of the IAEC, nuclear development went forward during this period in several different areas, widening the program in both quality and quantity. Nuclear cooperation agreements were also initiated with both Taiwan and South Africa.[25] Under this triple alliance various projects were kindled, including a common effort to develop a neutron bomb, as well as a cruise missile with sufficient range (2400 km) to target the southern Soviet Union from Israel. Perlmutter also reported that two Israeli physicists, Yeshayahu Nebenzahl and Menahem Levin, achieved a breakthrough in 1972 by developing a new inexpensive method of enriching uranium using laser technology.[26] Though the research had been carried out secretly, the two scientists were issued a West German patent for the breakthrough in 1973. The research project was inexplicable except as part of a weapons program, and should have alerted disarmament activists. The new techniques were reportedly shared with South Africa.[27]

A Nuclear Alliance

In this context the Israel-South Africa connection deserves special note. Forged during a visit to Israel in 1976 by South African Prime

Minister – and former Nazi collaborator – John Vorster,* the alliance served mutual needs. Commenting on Vorster's visit, on April 17, 1976, the Johannesburg *Star* wrote: "Clearly the pact goes well beyond the usual trade and co-operation agreements that normally round off a state visit between friendly countries....At the root of the pact is a mutual exchange of materials and military know-how which both countries desperately need. For both, it is a question of survival. Very likely, that is the strongest imperative of all." The word 'nuclear' was never mentioned.

For their part, the South Africans had much to offer Israel, including investment capital, a steady supply of inexpensive uranium and other strategic raw materials, plus vast open spaces for testing. On the other hand, Israel had the scientific and technical expertise South Africa lacked, besides offering a trade outlet enabling the apartheid regime to evade the economic sanctions which threatened to strangle the country's economy. Following Vorster's visit, a trade boom began between the two states with the main items, arms and diamonds, going unreported.[28]

The September 22, 1979 Flash

In August 1977 the Soviet Union notified the United States that one of its Cosmos spy satellites had detected preparations for an underground nuclear test in South Africa's Kalahari desert. After confirming the Soviet report with photo-intelligence from a high-flying U.S. SR-71 spy satellite, the U.S. and its allies were able to exert sufficient pressure on South Africa to block the test.[29] The crucial leverage was provided by France, which because of its civilian nuclear contracts with Pretoria was able to apply the necessary muscle. According to *Newsweek* "some U.S. intelligence analysts concluded that the bomb the South Africans had planned to set off actually had been made in Israel."[30]

On October 25, 1979 John Scali of ABC News reported that a U.S. Vela satellite had detected a telltale double-flash of light off the South African coast on September 22, 1979, indicating a nuclear explosion.[31]

---

* Vorster had been jailed for 20 months during World War II by the British for pro-Nazi Activities. *Time,* April 16, 1976. For a more exhaustive review of the Israeli-South Africa relationship dating back to 1953, see Chapter Five of Beit-Hallahmi's hook, *The Israeli Connection.*

Later the same day, in response to the Scali report, the State Department issued its own statement:

> *The United States government has an indication suggesting the possibility that a low-yield nuclear explosion occurred on September 22 in an area of the Indian Ocean and South Atlantic including portions of the Antarctic Continent, and the southern part of Africa. No corroborating evidence has been received to date. We are continuing to assess whether such an event took place.[32]*

The next day Secretary of State Cyrus Vance announced that air sampling for radioactive debris over a 4500 square mile area was underway, though nothing yet had been detected.[33]

In January 1980 the CIA informed a Congressional committee that a task force of South African warships was conducting night maneuvers at the time of the event in the vicinity of Prince Edward and Marion Islands – the flash zone, 1500 miles off the coast of South Africa.[34] The CIA also indicated possible Israeli involvement.

No further reports occurred until February 21, when CBS News quoted two Israeli journalists who confirmed – from sources in Israel – that the suspicious flash had been an Israeli nuclear test "conducted with the help and cooperation of the South African government."[35] The next day the *Washington Post* carried a follow-up story based on the same sources, claiming that Israel had received requests from South Africa to test nuclear weapons as early as 1966 but had not accepted the offer until shortly before the 1979 test.[36]

Much later, these reports received some degree of confirmation when on December 21, 1980, Israeli state television aired, without denials or comment, a British-made documentary which described the September 1979 flash as the test of a newly developed naval nuclear shell, part of a combined Israeli-South African nuclear development program.[37]

The Blue-Ribbon Panel Report

Initial evidence that a nuclear test had occurred was strong. Prior to the September 22, 1979 signal, the U.S. Vela spy satellites had established a perfect record of monitoring nuclear explosions. The satellites had correctly identified tests forty-one out of forty-one times.[37] According to the Los Alamos scientists who designed the satellite, the signature of a nuclear fireball is unmistakable, impossible to confuse with other natural phenomena. "This is what the Vela saw the night of September 22," one said. In fact, a document released by the Los Alamos Lab in November 1979 explained in detail why Vela was so hard to fool. The paper described the two-peaked signature of a nuclear explosion, explaining how it was unique:

> *The two-peaked character of the light pulse, together with the very large energy radiated during the second maximum, makes it unmistakable that this light signature originated in a nuclear explosion....Pulsed light sources do occur in nature, or can be built, that match either [the] power level [of a nuclear explosion] or the pulse duration. However, no other source is known that matches both.*[40]

Unfortunately, follow-up efforts by the Air Force to detect radioactive debris failed to produce samples which would have conclusively verified the test. The failure was probably explained by the extreme remoteness of the flash zone – the fact that Air Force high-altitude reconnaissance aircraft were not able to begin the search until nearly three weeks after the event[41] – and to the vast 4500 square mile area of ocean involved. Because of the delay, radiation could have been dispersed by wind and storm long before the search began. In fact, some scientists were not surprised by the failure of a high altitude search. One Los Alamos expert told the *Washington Post* that, unlike high-yield tests which spew debris high into the atmosphere, a 1-5 kiloton explosion would not have sufficient energy to carry radiation to high altitudes.[42] Rapid dispersion would therefore be more likely. Other experts speculated the lack of fallout suggested a neutron bomb.[43]

In mid-November 1979 one initial reading of fallout was reported downwind of the suspected test zone, by scientists at the Nuclear Institute of Science at Gracefield, New Zealand.[44] The trace radiation was detected in rainwater samples. However, the report was later withdrawn when reanalysis failed to confirm the initial readings.[45] Inability to produce fallout did not rule out a test, but it did cast doubt on the U.S. government's capacity to verify nuclear arms testing at a time when President Carter was seeking Congressional ratification of his Strategic Arms (SALT) agreement with the Soviet Union.[46]

The White House response was to convene a panel of distinguished scientists, including several Nobel laureates, whose task was to:

1. Review all available data from both classified and unclassified sources that could help corroborate that the Vela signal originated from a nuclear explosion;

2. Evaluate the possibility that the signal in question was a 'false alarm' resulting from technical malfunction; and

3. Investigate the possibility that the signal recorded by Vela was of natural origin.

Over the next several months the blue-ribbon panel heard testimony from a number of government agencies and private labs, including the U.S. Naval Research Laboratory, the U.S. Air Force, the Los Alamos National Laboratory, the Sandia Lab, The Arms Control and Disarmament Agency, the Livermore Lab, the Department of Energy, and the State Department, as well as civilian scientists from the giant radio observatory at Arecibo, Puerto Rico.

After eight months' deliberation, the panel announced on July 15, 1980 that in all likelihood the flash had been due to a meteorite:

> *Although we cannot rule out the possibility that this [Vela] signal was of nuclear origin, the panel considers it more likely that the signal was one of the zoo events [receptions of signals of unknown origin under anomalous circumstances], possible consequence of the impact of a small meteorite on the satellite.*[49]

Response to the finding ranged, in the words of one informed observer, from "caution to incredulity."[50] Indeed, the day before, on July 14, the Pentagon had released its own report, which reached the *opposite* conclusion.[51] And on June 30, two weeks before release of the White House report, the Naval Research Laboratory (NRL), which had been commissioned by the White House Office of Science Technology Policy (OSTP) to gather geophysical data worldwide on the flash, released *its* report, which also determined that a nuclear test probably had occurred.[52] As if this were not enough, just days before, the CIA had followed up its earlier testimony to Congress by delivering *its own* secret report to the National Security Council.[53] The report informed the NSC – and the President – of the strong possibility that Vela *had* detected a 2-3 kiloton nuclear burst on September 22, detonated at an altitude of 26,000 feet. The CIA report reiterated the earlier assessment that the test may have been carried out jointly by Israel and South Africa. In other words, the White House panel report was the only one of four released by various agencies of the government to conclude there had been no test.

Enter: the 'zoo animal'

Because of the important ramifications of the White House panel's conclusion – its findings were designated as the official position of the White House – a general review of the panel's reasoning in rejecting all the presented evidence of a nuclear test is in order.

The possibility of instrument failure or malfunction was ruled out immediately. It was revealed to the panel that the satellite's two optical-sensing devices, called bhangmeters – both of which detected the September 22 flash – had been recalibrated just one week prior to the event.[54] Furthermore, follow-up tests demonstrated that the sensors, despite nine years of service, remained in good working order.[55]

The panel admitted in its report that the light signals of the September 22 flash closely matched previous signals of confirmed nuclear tests. (See charts in Appendix B) The panel's basis for rejecting the Vela signal as conclusive lay elsewhere, in a curious anomaly discussed on page ten of the panel's report.[51] The panel discovered that the relative intensity of the two bhangmeters' signals, with respect to one another – i.e., their ratio – was at variance with all previous signals of confirmed tests recorded by Vela satellites. The panel argued, therefore, that whatever caused the flash could *not* have occurred at a great distance from the satellite, and could only be explained if the flash had been produced in the vicinity – within 30 meters – of the satellite itself, as it circled the earth at an altitude of 60-70,000 miles.[57] The panel's explanation seemed to rule out a nuclear test.

What, then, caused the double flash of light? After an extensive review, the panel eliminated nearly all natural phenomena, such as cosmic rays, solar flares, sun glint, meteor flashes, and superlightning bolts. In the end they turned to a category of events known as 'zoo animals,' described as "strange signals for which no satisfactory explanation has been forthcoming."[58] The panel speculated that a meteoroid may have struck the satellite, ejecting particles which, in turn, reflected a double-glint of sunlight into the register, mimicking the distinctive signal of a nuclear explosion. Unexplainable signals had occurred previously, on at least sixty other occasions, but none had so closely matched the characteristic two-peaked signature of a nuclear explosion.[59]

The panel's judgment was greeted with considerable skepticism. According to *Science* magazine, one expert at the Sandia Lab claimed that a plausible explanation existed for the discrepant readings, *short* of discounting them, but could not discuss it for fear of violating security regulations. Another criticized the panel's theory, suggesting the anomaly could have been caused by a difference in the alignment of the Vela's bhangmeters, relative to the earth's axis. When asked about the likelihood of a small meteoroid bouncing off the satellite, producing the near-perfect image of a nuclear bomb flash, the scientist answered: "It strains credibility." The same scientist, who helped design the satellite, acknowledged that the September 22 signal was unusual, but was annoyed that the panel resorted to the 'zoo event' category so quickly. Suddenly, when an explanation was needed, he said, "the zoo animals came marching out of the woodwork."[60]

Other potentially corroborating evidence, including acoustic wave data gathered by technicians of the U.S. Air Force Technical Applications Center (AFTAC), evidence of a traveling ionospheric disturbance (TID) recorded by the giant radio telescope at Arecibo, Puerto Rico, and radar data picked up by the Air Force's early-warning radar net were all, in turn, discounted by the White House panel[61] as unrelated to the September 22 event.

The panel also reviewed hydroacoustic data compiled in an extensive investigation conducted by the Naval Research Laboratory (NRL). According to *Science,* the NRL search, carried out by a team of 75 naval scientists and technicians, demonstrated that two monitoring sites had detected a hydroacoustic signal, received at the right time and from the right direction to be linked with the Vela flash. In fact, two pulses were reported. The initial weaker pulse was a direct signal transmitted through the South Atlantic. It was theorized by Navy scientists that the original strength of this first pulse had been considerably dampened because, due to the pulse's angle of propagation, the traveling wave had encountered considerable interference with the African mainland. The second signal, on the other hand, was much stronger because, rebounding off the Antarctic continent, it had moved more nearly due north through the corridor of the Atlantic relatively unimpeded by the continents of Africa and South America. The Director of the Naval Lab, Dr. Alan Berman, described the signal as the strongest hydroacoustic pulse he had ever seen, comparable in its signature only to those recorded following previous announced nuclear tests in the Pacific.[62]

However, the White House panel was not convinced, and dismissed the naval hydroacoustic analysis in two brief paragraphs of its unclassified report as "preliminary" and "incomplete."[63] According to *Aviation Week and Space Technology* magazine, the panel judged that "the NRL analysis was not complete enough to determine whether distinctive signals were generated *only* at the time of the September 22 event."[64] In its report, the panel even went so far as to claim that "had a search been made for corroborating data relevant to a nonexistent event chosen to occur at a random time, such a search would have provided 'corroborative data' of similar quantity and quality to that which has been found during analysis of the September 22 signal."[65] In other words, the panel took the position that the evidence was no more significant than data which might have been gathered randomly.

Later Dr. Berman publicly disputed the panel's conclusion that the NRL report was 'incomplete.' Berman stated that NRL scientists had searched the log for thirty days before and after the September 22 event in an effort to find comparable signals caused by natural phenomena. That they found none demonstrated, in his view, the relative uniqueness of the hydroacoustic signal's strength and timing.[66] Dr. Berman further pointed out that the White House panel reached its final decision on the hydroacoustic evidence at its last meeting on April 2, weeks *before* the finished naval study was released.[67] As already noted, the completed 300-page NRL report was not submitted until June 30. When asked to comment, panel-member Richard Muller, a distinguished physicist from UC Berkeley, told the author that the Navy's completed report was not significantly different from the preliminary draft reviewed by the panel in April. Muller described the NRL report as "flawed."[68]

The Van Middlesworth Sheep Thyroids

Fresh evidence pointing to a nuclear test continued to turn up long after the Blue Ribbon panel's final report was released. On September 25, 1980, Dr. L. Van Middlesworth of the Department of Physiology and Biophysics of the Tennessee College of Medicine reported to Dr. Berman that he had detected radiation six times above normal in thyroid tissue taken from Australian sheep on November 12-13, 1979.[69] He explained that for 25 years he had routinely examined Australian cattle and sheep thyroids without ever previously discovering radioactive iodine levels above background. The discovery was made nine months after the fact when he received additional funding making possible a re-examination of a broader sample of thyroid tissue. A follow-up by NRL confirmed Dr. Van Middlesworth's finding at a level of five times above normal.[70] Because the samples were taken from sheep grazing in rural areas, the NRL determined the probable source had been grass contaminated by rainwater.[71]

NRL scientists had already concluded from meteorological data that storms moving through Prince Edward and Marion Islands, the zone of the flash, would track eastward across the southern Indian ocean toward Australia. In fact, one such storm had deposited substantial amounts of rain on Victoria, Australia on September 26-27.[72] Naval analysis showed that the 'footprint' of a 'fallout trajectory' could have taken potential radiation debris from the suspected test site to southern Australia, carried by the storm.[73] The Navy found that the storm could also have reached New Zealand, possibly accounting for fallout detected at Graceland.[74] Though re-analysis of the Graceland rainwater samples had failed to duplicate the earlier finding, no satisfactory explanation was ever offered to account for the initial 'false' report.[75]

Subsequent statistical analysis of the sheep thyroid radiation by the Department of Energy (DOE) resolved the significance of the radiation level at 3.1 standard deviations, a figure described as "in a middle ground where it cannot be dismissed as a frequent occurrence nor can it be claimed with certainty to be different from background.",[76] In other words, rigorous statistical analysis weakened *but did not* refute Van Middlesworth's sheep thyroid data, which was attached as an annex to the June 30 NRL report. When asked to comment on this supplementary evidence, Dr. Muller acknowledged the sheep thyroid data but discounted it, claiming that – even at five times above normal – it fell within the range expected from random sampling.[77] In other words, Dr. Van Middlesworth's 25-year history of routine thyroid examinations without a single previous unusual reading was regarded, statistically, as an insufficient basis from which to argue that the November 12-13, 1979 findings constituted significant evidence.

If the hard evidence was not conclusive, taken together, it certainly was indicative. Sufficiently indicative, in fact, that – despite the White House panel's conclusion – civilian specialists, technical experts in the U.S. Department of Energy, U.S. Navy scientists, and the Director of the Los Alamos Laboratory all remained convinced that a small, tactical-size, nuclear test had occurred.

Some also believed that the panel's inconclusive judgment had been the result of political interference.[78] One such observer, Stephen Green, concluded on the basis of personal interviews with well-placed sources in Washington that the White House panel did not have full access to "to all available data" – in particular, to military and CIA intelligence.[79] In his recent book, Green cites remarks by former CIA Director Stansfield Turner, who told him categorically that no request for supplementary intelligence information regarding the September 22 event was ever made to the CIA by anyone associated with the White House panel.[80] When Turner was asked to comment on the blue-ribbon panel's report, he referred to the panel's conclusions as "absurd."[81] Green concluded that the panel's review had been an academic exercise, a sterile debate of "how many angels could fit on the head of a nuclear detection pin," as he phrased it.[82]

When I recently discussed the matter of technical evidence versus evidence from intelligence sources with former panel member Richard Muller, he insisted that the panel had been fully briefed by intelligence experts.[83] However, I was surprised to hear Dr. Muller explain that the CIA had *supported* the panel's conclusions – an opinion directly contradicted by Stansfield Turner's statements. Furthermore, Dr. Muller seemed unaware of the secret CIA report delivered to the National Security Council in June 1980. The obvious question arises: Were efforts made by White House staff close to the investigation to screen the channels of intelligence made available to the distinguished panel?

A Staged Test?

On the basis of their own separate investigations, Howard University Professor Ron Walters and author Stephen Green independently speculated that the test had been staged by South Africa and Israel so as to maximize – by design, should it be detected – ambiguous readings by those monitoring stations known to be listening. The fact that the test had been extremely low-yield, on the order of 1-5 kilotons, almost insured from the outset that fallout and other acoustical evidence would be gathered at the margins of detection capability, making absolute verification difficult.

According to Dr. Berman, U.S. hydroacoustic detection equipment had been designed – "thresholded," as he put it – to verify nuclear tests in the 10-20 kiloton range, or larger, rather than low-yield tests.[85] For this reason, Dr. Berman believed that the panel's negative conclusion was misleading. In a conversation with the author, Berman explained that re-analysis of signal data from older confirmed low- yield nuclear tests (conducted by China) showed a similar pattern at the margin when compared with the September 1979 flash. In other words, the record of the September 1979 'event' was compatible with a nuclear test.[86]

In an earlier article, reporters Robert Manning and Stephen Talbot argued that because of the long history of intelligence-sharing among Israel, South Africa and the United States, Israel and South Africa undoubtedly "knew a great deal about U.S. detection capabilities," and thus how best to evade them. According to Manning and Talbot, sources close to the White House investigation stated that whoever set off the blast must have known the Vela satellite's course and schedule and hence its 'blind spots.'[87], In fact, within days of the flash U.S. intelligence learned that the South African military attaché in Washington had recently made his country's first-ever request to the U.S. National Technical Information Service for a computer search of the Vela satellite's detection history.[88]

That the flash was detected at all – at 5 A.M., minutes before dawn, in one of the most remote areas of the planet – may have been due mostly to luck.[89] According to one report, the Vela satellite had been slowly losing altitude and was out of its usual position on the night of the incident. "We were lucky the Vela picked up the fireball because if it had not been out of position it would have missed it," the Pentagon source said, adding that "there is a chance the same Vela missed other explosions before September 22 when it was in the position it was supposed to be in."[90]

The Political Fallout

Though debate continued in the scientific community, press coverage of the incident abruptly ceased in the wake of the White House panel's report, the administration's official position, probably owing to the prestige of the Oval Office. President Carter certainly had good reason to hope that the blue-ribbon panel would succeed in discrediting evidence presented by the government's own scientists. An inconclusive finding insured that Carter's administration would escape wide-ranging political fallout over the embarrassing implications of a South African nuclear test.

For one thing, positive confirmation would lead to media scrutiny of the true extent of U.S. involvement with Pretoria's nuclear program. In 1976 the Chairman of the South African Atomic Energy Board (SAAEB), Dr. A.J.A. Roux, acknowledged the key U.S. role, telling a group of visiting Americans, "We ascribe our degree of advancement today, in large measure, to the training and assistance so willingly provided by the U.S.A. during the early years of our nuclear program."[91]

The assistance referred to by Dr. Roux was outlined by the *Middle East Journal* in June 1980: Beginning as early as 1953, U.S. involvement included help with the development of a South African uranium mining and processing industry; training of nuclear scientists; assistance in the construction of South Africa's first research reactor, Safari I, which included supplies of enriched uranium and access to classified nuclear information; U.S. participation in a series of 'weapons effect tests' off the South African coast in 1958, as well as the supply of advanced computers.[92] Admittedly, much of this involvement occurred in the days of blissful ignorance *before* the nuclear link between 'atoms for peace' and weapons development was widely understood. Even so, there was still ample reason for the President to shudder at the implications of a confirmed nuclear test.[93]

In particular, the specter of Israeli participation would not only be embarrassing, it threatened to be a political nightmare. As one State Department official put it, coming clean on the test "would be a major turning point in our relations with South Africa and Israel....It makes me terribly nervous just to think about it."[94] Indeed, official acknowledgement of a South African bomb – *especially* one involving Israel – would trigger a veritable earthquake in U.S. foreign policy. Not only would it demonstrate in a most dramatic way the failure – indeed, the hypocrisy – of U.S. nonproliferation efforts, it would also doom U.S. South African policy and the 'special relationship' with Israel to the ashbin, all in one fell swoop.[95]

In 1977 the United Nations had voted to slap a mandatory arms embargo on South Africa, banning all sales of conventional arms and directing all states to "...refrain from any cooperation with South

Africa in the manufacture and development of nuclear weapons."[96] Moreover, under the terms of Carter's own 1978 Nuclear Non-proliferation Act, the United States would be forced to convene a series of meetings with allies to initiate some form of economic sanction against South Africa, and possibly Israel.[97] In addition, by this time several U.S. laws mandated a cut in aid to countries engaged in secret nuclear proliferation. Laws applicable in the cases of Israel and South Africa were the 1976-77 Symington-Glenn Amendments.[98]

All this must have seemed unthinkable to President Carter, who by early 1980 was engaged in a tough re-election campaign.

In fact, Carter committed the U.S. to covering possible Israeli involvement in a South African test months before the panel's report was even released. On December 11, 1979 the UN General Assembly adopted a resolution calling on Israel to open all its nuclear facilities to IAEA inspections. The bill also instructed nations to take steps to prevent the transfer of nuclear weapons technology and fissionable material to Israel, a non-signatory of the NPT.[99] In short, there was nothing radical about the resolution; it was consistent with official U.S. policy – frequently stated on many occasions – opposing clandestine development of nuclear weapons. Nevertheless, even though the CIA had long suspected Israel of secret nuclear weapons proliferation – having warned the White House of a secret Israeli bomb program as early as 1968[100] – the U.S. voted against the 1979 U.N. resolution. Had the President wished to maintain a posture of strict impartiality, because of the blue-ribbon panel's pending review, he could easily have instructed the U.S. delegation to abstain from the General Assembly vote. He did not. The U.S. decision to oppose the resolution was an unmistakable signal to the world of United States complicity with Israel's secret nuclear weapons agenda. There is no other explanation.

The same month of the UN vote, as U.S. government agencies continued to study the flash, both Israel and South Africa – without fanfare – established research stations on Antarctica, i.e., near the flash zone.[101]

The Doctrine of Reliable Supply

The Carter policy on nonproliferation had been hamstrung from the beginning because of contradictions inherited from previous administrations. The Carter position, stated in October 1977 and reiterated again in March 1978, was that a complete severance of nuclear relations would only "encourage separate development of South Africa's own nuclear potential."[102] This approach, which President Reagan later adopted in the context of 'constructive engagement,'[103] was a holdover from the old 'atoms for peace' program of the 1950s.*

The approach, which has been called the 'doctrine of reliable supply,' in essence holds that nuclear supplier states such as the U.S. can retain important influence over the internal nuclear policies of states like South Africa by continuing to serve as a reliable supplier of nuclear materials. Without an incentive to develop their own fuelcycles the theory goes, these states tend to remain dependent on supplier nations such as the U.S., who in turn gain the diplomatic leverage to introduce the necessary safeguards/oversight.[104]

Notwithstanding the inability of five previous U.S. presidents to perceive the failure of this approach in halting nuclear proliferation – as demonstrated repeatedly over at least a quarter-century – [105] it should not surprise anyone that the Carter White House did not awaken to the fact immediately.** By 1978-79 however, when Carter's efforts to bring South Africa into compliance with the Nuclear Nonproliferation Act of 1978 ground to a halt, the contradictions had become inescapable.[106] Unfortunately, by this time Carter's decision to halt additional shipments of South Africa-bound uranium came too late to make a difference.

On May 21, 1985, while announcing the publication of Ronald Walters' critical study of the September 22, 1979 flash, the Congressional Black Caucus publicly challenged the National Academy of Sciences and the National Academy of Engineers to reopen the investigation of the 'mystery flash.' The Caucus also called for Congressional hearings in order to "release to the public all pertinent information."[107] As of February 1988, however, the matter remained officially 'dead' in Washington, buried for want of a politician brave enough to revive it.[108]

---

* The Atoms for Peace Program was inaugurated by President Eisenhower in a speech to the United Nations General Assembly delivered in December 1953.

** Some of President Carter's moves were clearly in the right direction; namely, his 1977 cancellation of the Clinch River Breeder Reactor, the shutdown of the Barnwell, S.C. reprocessing plant, the tightening of nuclear exports, and a more aggressive approach in establishing and implementing safeguards. For these steps he deserves credit.

The 155 mm Nuclear Howitzer

As already noted, on December 21, 1980, Israeli television aired – without denial or comment – a British-made program which claimed that the September 22, 1979 flash had involved the test of a naval nuclear shell developed jointly by Israel and South Africa.[109]

Nearly two years after the report, Amos Perlmutter and two associates elaborated additional details in their book *Two Minutes over Baghdad*. Referring to CIA sources and other un-named "intelligence services in the West," the authors confirmed the British report, adding that the nuclear shell had been launched from an advanced 155 mm howitzer cannon surreptitiously acquired by South Africa in 1977 from the Space Research Corporation (SRC), a U.S. defense contractor.[110]

Originally, the cannon had been developed by American-Canadian inventor Gerald Bull to launch satellites, which suggests a hint of its power. A smaller military prototype was also developed, the G-4, which soon became SRC's main focus of research and marketing. The SRC howitzer has been called "the finest artillery piece in the world" for range, accuracy and destructive power.[111]

The covert operation by which South Africa acquired this advanced technology – in direct violation of U.S. law and the UN arms embargo – was recounted by London *Sunday Times* defense correspondent James Adams in a chapter of his 1984 book *The Unnatural Alliance*.[112] It is a tale which reads like an Ian Fleming novel – once again proving the real world to be at least as improbable as mere fiction. In the end, with the willing collusion of Israel, the U.S. State Department and the CIA, and with the cooperation of the U.S. Army, South Africa not only acquired the gun and thousands of custom-made shells, but also the blueprints, machine tools, expertise, patents and in fact everything needed to produce the weapon. So bold was the operation that various components of the technology continued to be smuggled out of the United States even after a U.S. Customs Investigation into the scam was in progress.[113]

Later a Senate subcommittee conducted an investigation into the sorry failure of various U.S. agencies to monitor arms trade from the United States consistent with U.S. export laws. In March 1982 the subcommittee found that:

> *The causes of the [U.S.] government's failure to adequately implement the arms embargo were structural rather than accidental in nature...failures reflected the*

governments lack of capacity to adequately enforce arms licensing regulations. Office of Munitions Control [OMC] officials acknowledged their lack of sufficient technical expertise to make reliable judgments on applications of their own regulations.... The Army's slip-ups were due to loose and ill-defined procedures.. At the CIA a preoccupation with the immediate...need to move arms efficiently into Angola through South Africa appeared to supersede the larger U.S. policy of enforcing the arms embargo against South Africa. Finally, SRC's successful implementation of its plans revealed that there is a 'non-system' of enforcing the arms embargo in the U.S. government. U.S. foreign policy agencies did not interrupt this scam because collecting information on the embargo's operation was not high on the list of any agencies' priorities. . . [114]

The subcommittee also recommended steps to strengthen enforcement of the UN arms embargo, steps which at the time of writing in 1988 have yet to be fully implemented.[115]

Eventually Gerald Bull served four-and-a-half months in a minimum security prison for his part in the $30 million arms scam. His company, SRC, was fined $45,000 – a slap on the wrist. Meanwhile South Africa gained another powerful means to devastate and/or intimidate its African neighbors.[116] It also gained another potential arms export industry. At a champagne breakfast on September 26, 1982, barely two years after the flash, Pieter Marais, bead of ARMSCOR, an important South African arms producer, announced plans to manufacture an improved G-5 version of the howitzer capable of firing a nuclear shell. Marais also announced plans to market a smaller G-6 prototype billed as a "new mobile artillery system."[117]

It is worth pointing out that Israel already possessed the earlier G-4 model of the SRC artillery, and according to Adams, made good use of its superior accuracy and 30-50 km range to stem the Syrian assault on the Golan Heights during the 1973 war.[118] A recent study by authors Terry Asher and Eric Hammel confirmed that Israel had deployed seven batteries of the 155-mm howitzer on the Heights during the war.[119]

In a later chapter of this study we will return to discuss the SRC howitzer's possible role in a future Middle East war.

The Dimona reactor.   © The *Sunday Times*, London

Photo taken by Mordechai Vanunu of what experts believe to be a scale
model of an advanced Israeli nuclear weapon design.

© The *Sunday Times*, London

Photo taken by Mordechai Vanunu of what experts believe to be the control room of Israel's underground plutonium separation plant, housed in the Machon II Lab.   © The *Sunday Times*, London

This key photo, taken by Mordechai Vanunu in Machon II, reveals what experts believe to be a "cooling tower" apparatus involved in the separation of the rare isotope Lithium-6. Lithium-6 is used in the production of thermonuclear weapons.   © The *Sunday Times*, London

Mordechai Vanunu as a young boy (circa 1956) with his brother Albert (on the left), brother Meir (on stool) and mother Maazel in their home in Morocco.

Mordechai with his girlfriend, Judy Zimmet at archeological ruins south of Bersheba in winter of 1985 just before leaving Israel.

Mordechai at friend's home in Israel, winter of 1985.

The Reagan Legacy

Ronald Reagan's attitude toward South Africa, expressed in an interview with Walter Cronkite shortly after his inauguration, was positive, almost friendly. Reagan's views on nuclear proliferation were no more inspired. In response to Cronkite's question regarding a possible leadership role for the U.S. in opposing nuclear weapons development by other nations, Reagan was quoted saying: "I just don't think it's any of our business."[120] Though he later backed off from that position somewhat, Reagan's early remark set the tone for the new administration, one of 'business as usual.' Within months the White House was finding ways to sell $30 million worth of enriched uranium to South Africa for its new 1844-megawatt Koeberg nuclear station, even though the sale was a clear violation of Carter's 1978 Nuclear Nonproliferation Act (NNPA). In the end the administration succeeded – evading the law – by arranging the sale via third-party brokers.[121]

In 1982 Reagan outdid even himself by reversing a prior Carter ruling and approving the sale to South Africa of the advanced 170/750 Cyber computer, built by Control Data Corporation. The computer had important military uses, namely, the capacity to model nuclear weapons. According to *Newsweek*, the deal went through "simply because no one in the administration made a compelling enough case against it."[122] Apparently, handing over to the South African military the means to run computer tests of nuclear weapon designs, thereby eliminating the need for live tests, was not considered reason enough for concern.[123] Or, more likely, given that the White House – as a result of the classified Pentagon and CIA reports in June 1980 – was informed that South Africa *already* had the bomb, the President and his men may have decided, since the bird had already flown the coop anyway, they might as well salvage a lucrative business arrangement. As Ronald Walters put it: "Both parties' success in managing ambiguity makes possible continued nuclear commerce and other relations, resolving the contradictions by avoiding challenges."[124]

Walters' speculations are not without foundation, and even more applicable in the case of Israel, which has managed over the years to walk a tightrope, repeatedly evading closer U.S. scrutiny and possible sanctions by stressing non-nuclear uses of new dual-purpose weapons systems. The Jericho 11 missile, which can carry both conventional and nuclear warheads, is an obvious case in point.[125] While such waltzes have 'fooled' the U.S. Congress, they certainly have not fooled the Soviets. Israel's recent tests of its latest Jericho, with a range estimated at up to 900 miles, have prompted Soviet warnings on at least three occasions since 1986. This disturbing pattern and its implications will be explored in greater detail in a following chapter.

The European Role

In addition to U.S. and Israeli aid, South Africa bas received major nuclear assistance from France and West Germany. The French company Framatome provided the know-how for the giant 1844-megawatt Koeberg Reactor, capable of producing 400-600 kilograms of plutonium per year, sufficient in theory for the production of up to 50 bombs a year.[127] And while at present it is not known whether South Africa possesses a plutonium weapon, several sources have reported a small plutonium reprocessing plant.[128] Recent testimony before U.S. Congressional hearings have also indicated that spent plutonium fuel from the large reactor could have been stockpiled inside South Africa or even clandestinely reprocessed by other nations, while escaping detection by the IAEA.[129] At the very least, the hearings demonstrated the enormous difficulties of effectively monitoring and safeguarding radioactive materials in an international marketplace, difficulties which clearly favor proliferators.[130] Materials with nuclear weapon fuel potential, as the Plumbatt Affair (the 1968 Israeli hijacking of 200 tons of West German uranium ore; see Chapter Four) showed, are so desirable as commodities that nations determined to acquire them will invariably seek out and exploit weak links in the oversight/security network.

While the existence of a South African plutonium bomb remains uncertain, the issue may be moot, considering South African development of a uranium enrichment capability in the early 1970s. By 1973 a pilot-scale plant was completed with West German assistance and later expanded, removing the final obstacle to weapons production via the uranium path.[131] The agreement was only made public when documents revealing the top-secret uranium-for-technology exchange fell into the hands of the African National Congress (ANC) in 1975.

Later the French government used the existence of this enrichment facility to excuse its own participation in the Koeberg project. In February 1977 the *Washington Post* quoted French Prime Minister Raymond Barre's defense of the lucrative French sale: "South Africa already has nuclear military capability."[132] The French were sufficiently self-interested to argue that their involvement would not alter the strategic balance. The French view had been summed up as early as 1973 when Dr. Bertrand Goldschmidt, the father of French plutonium extraction, told a meeting of the IAEA that while no nation could build a sizeable nuclear arsenal in secret, almost any nation could build a few bombs without anyone knowing. "That", he insisted, "was practically unstoppable."[133]

West German involvement began as early as 1968, when the South African Ministry of Defense contracted a West German firm to construct a missile test-range at St. Lucia, 100 miles north of Durban and 40 miles from the Mozambique border. The project also included development of Advocaat, a $25 million radar communications system headquartered at Silvermine, near Capetown. Over the years the system has continued to expand, with additional technology supplied by Italy, France and the United States. At present, it is rated as one of the world's most advanced communications centers. According to a study prepared by the Stockholm International Peace Research Institute (SIPRI), the system has been used by South African security agencies to monitor the country's Black population, as well as air and naval traffic off the South African coast.[134]

Even Sweden, whose voters rejected nuclear power development in a 1981 referendum, has contributed to South African nuclear weapons development, though perhaps unwittingly. In May 1986 the magazine *Ny Teknik* reported that in late 1985 South Africa had obtained two 600-kilovolt flash X-ray machines from Sweden through a clandestine purchasing scheme. The devices, which fall into the category of dual-use technology, can be used in testing triggers for nuclear weapons.[135]

The Neutron Bomb – Nuclear Grail?

While this discussion of the various Western nations' nuclear involvements with South Africa is far from exhaustive, it nevertheless establishes the needed backdrop for the Israeli connection. A critical analysis such as this would be derelict in the extreme to single out Israel – or any state – for condemnation when at least several are implicated. The United States, France and West Germany are in varying degrees all guilty of complicity with South Africa in nuclear weapons development, and they all deserve condemnation.

Yet the Israeli connection stands apart from the rest for several important reasons. In the first place, the extent of Israeli military involvement with South Africa, both conventional and nuclear, is simply on another scale, a full quantum leap beyond other nations.*

Of at least equal importance, several of the sources already cited in this study either stated categorically or noted the strong possibility that the Israeli-South African nuclear alliance included development of a neutron bomb. If true, the fact holds serious implications for Africa's Black masses, not to mention Israel's Arab neighbors.

---

* James Adams' 1984 reference to the two states' "joint arms industry" bas been substantiated recently by none other than the U.S. government. See Adams, *The Unnatural Alliance*, p. 125. On April 2, 1987, the State Department released a report to Congress documenting massive Israeli violations of the 1977 UN arms embargo. The report bad been mandated by the Mathias Amendment (Section 508) of the 1986 Anti-Apartheid Bill. While the bulk of the report remains classified, a summary was made public, stating in part:

Prior to the Israeli government's decision on March 18 [1987] not to sign new military contracts [with South Africa] and to let existing contracts expire, Israel appears to have sold military systems and sub-systems and provided technical assistance on a regular basis. (for the text of the summary see Appendix C)

The total Israeli involvement was estimated to be at least $400-800 million per year. "Congress Gets Report on Israeli Military Aid to South Africa," *New York Times*, April 2, 1987.

Though the report summary did not provide specifics, they were already available from other sources, including Professor Beit-Hallahmi: missile boats, Kfir jets, Gabriel missiles, howitzers, communications equipment, radar systems and intelligence technology, airplane parts, and ammunition. See Beit-Hallahmi, *The Israeli Connection*, p. 118. Though far from being an exhaustive list, the point is made.

The Israeli promises mentioned in the report – paraded as "limited sanctions" before Congress – constituted an eleventh-hour effort by Israel's leaders to head off the unfavorable consequences of being identified as a violator nation. The Mathias Amendment explicitly stated that once violators were known, U.S. military assistance to those countries would be terminated. Judging from the lack of any response in Washington – other than silence – to the State Department Report, Israel's attempts to stave off Congressional action have succeeded thus far. In 1987 new anti-apartheid legislation (HR 1580/5556) introduced jointly by Rep. Ron Dellums (D-CA) and Sen. Alan Cranston (D-Ca) called for a total trade embargo and complete withdrawal of U.S. corporations from South Africa. Yet, despite the State Department Report, neither bill included penalties affecting Israel. Not surprisingly, over the years Senator Cranston bas been one of Israel's strongest supporters in Congress, and bas received massive financial support during bis campaigns from AIPAC, the Israel lobby. Rita McWilliams, "Sanctions law squeezes some friends of Israel," *Washington Times*, April 2,1987.

Neutron bombs are tactical thermonuclear weapons based on the principle of nuclear fusion. In essence, the neutron device can be described in terms of a 'reversal of energy partition,' meaning that its radiation and blast effects are nearly opposite those of simpler fission weapons.[136] Fission bombs create enormous blast, relatively small amounts of intense short-lived radiation, and significant long-term fallout. Low-yield fusion devices are characterized by much reduced blast and much increased short-term radiation, with little fallout. For these reasons the neutron (Fusion) design bas been called the 'clean' bomb. When detonated thousands of feet above the ground, its destructive punch to material structures such as homes and factories can be reduced as much as 90% or more, with even greater reductions

---

According to Beit-Hallahmi, Israel's conciliatory move to blunt criticism, called a "gesture" by Prime Minister Shamir, was perfectly consistent with the Israeli government's previous duplicitous record. For years Israeli foreign policy has consisted of two components: one part official policy for public consumption, and a second – the real policy – remaining covert. *The Israeli Connection,* p. 68. That Israel's limited sanctions against Pretoria were worthless – mere public relations – was even admitted by one Israeli official, who called the "gesture" meaningless. Y. Melman, "Israel Will Continue All Contracts with South Africa," *Davar,* January 18, 1987 (Hebrew).

The logic behind covert defiance had been clearly stated as early as 1977 in the *Economist:* "The Israelis, for their part, believe that should the UN Security Council impose a mandatory arms embargo against South Africa, Israel itself could be next in line; that if the West can be pushed into endorsing one against South Africa, it can equally be pushed into one against Israel. Israel, therefore, would not adhere to an arms embargo against South Africa." "The Israeli Connection," *The Economist,* November 5, 1977. Apparently this view is not exclusive to Likud and the right. Recently a left-wing MAPAM party intellectual, Eric Lee, was quoted saying "the movement for sanctions against South Africa may be a prelude to similar campaigns against other 'racist' and unpopular regimes, such as 'the colonial Zionist entity in Palestine.'" Lee urged continued resistance to the UN embargo. Nor was Ice's cynicism an aberration. The same article noted a recent-opinion survey showing that 68% of Israelis favor continued military/economic relations with South Africa. Raphael Medoff and Mordechai Haller, "South Africa in the Mind of Israel," *National Review,* April 15, 1988, p. 38.

Meanwhile, reports of Israeli arms shipments to South Africa continue. In May 1988 the Danish Seamen's Union disclosed that three ships staffed by its members have been delivering weapons to South Africa The ships were chartered by an Israeli company name Mano Seaways. The most recent shipment, made earlier this year, came to light when a fire aboard the ship damaged part of the cargo – supposedly canned sardines – which turned out instead to be weapons. *Har'retz,* April 22, 1988; also see "More Arms Shipments to South Africa," *Israeli Foreign Affairs,* June, 1988.

in long-term contaminating radiation.[137] At the same time, the bomb's killing power is effected by a brief but intense shower of gamma radiation and highly energized neutrons. For these reasons the neutron bomb has been euphemistically described as the bomb which kills people instead of destroying property.*

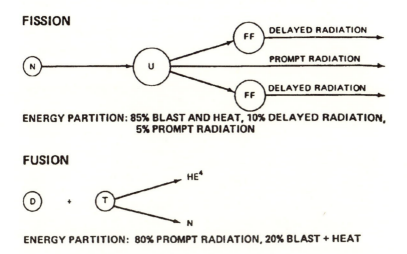

FISSION

DELAYED RADIATION

PROMPT RADIATION

DELAYED RADIATION

ENERGY PARTITION: 85% BLAST AND HEAT, 10% DELAYED RADIATION, 5% PROMPT RADIATION

FUSION

HE⁴

N

ENERGY PARTITION: 80% PROMPT RADIATION, 20% BLAST + HEAT

---

* In principle there are two types of neutron designs. The first, the fission-fusion design – a technology which already exists in the American arsenal – incorporates a fission trigger and represents a modified 'mini' version of the boosted fission bomb. The second design, the pure-fusion type, is still theoretical, as far as we know. Of this weapon Cohen wrote: "The second design represents a much more formidable challenge. We've never done anything like this before. Were we to be successful in such a development, this would represent a great breakthrough in nuclear weapons... Such a warhead would not produce any significant levels of radioactivity. From a psychological standpoint, this would greatly enhance political acceptability... Such a capability would represent the ultimate in discriminate nuclear weapons as we now understand them." Sam Cohen, *The Truth About the Neutron Bomb*, pp. 126-157, particularly p. 130 and 134.

Neutron bomb destroys only life, not property. (News item)

© With Permission of the Chicago-Sun Times Inc. 1988

Beit-Hallahmi's Warning

Originally neutron weapons were designed for NATO defense of Western Europe against a theoretical Soviet tank attack. However, in recent years their usefulness in the European theater has been seriously questioned.[138] Nonetheless, their effectiveness in other applications, as for example in the very different geopolitical context of South Africa or in the Middle East, has, to my knowledge, never been assessed.

One Israeli scholar, Benjamin Beit-Hallahmi, did raise the issue in 1987 in his book *The Israeli Connection*. Though the author's comments were directed primarily at the Israeli program, they also apply in the case of South Africa:

Most reporting and speculation about Israel's nuclear weapons have suffered from being locked into the pattern of generalizing from well-known nuclear development programs, while ignoring Israel's specific situation. Israel's needs are different from those of the United States, France, or China. Israel's nuclear weapons are designed... to fit local conditions.... Israel like South Africa, needs low-yield 'clean' bombs. This idea has shaped the Israeli nuclear effort since the 1960s.

> *The solution for this need has been original and stunning, going beyond conventional breakthroughs. The world has been watching Israel, and sometimes South Africa, using the old conventional notions about nuclear weaponry, as developed by all nuclear nations. What some brilliant minds in Israel have developed is an original...solution. South Africa has been the planner and the beneficiary...The real achievements of the joint Israeli-South African nuclear program are possibly beyond anybody's dreams, or nightmares.[139]*

Yet Professor Beit-Hallahmi remains the exception. In general, the nuclear threat posed by possible new applications has not been widely recognized. Indeed, the question of neutron weapons has been all but ignored by the peace and nonproliferation movements. Mr. Leonard Spector is a highly regarded authority on nonproliferation issues and a good case in point. Soon after his third book on the subject, *Going Nuclear,* appeared in 1987 it was called "the most comprehensive and sophisticated analysis of nonproliferation issues we have today" by journalist/author Seymour Hersh. Yet the 350 page Carnegie-endowed study not only did *not* discuss neutron weapons, it never even mentioned them.[140]

Mr. Spector did point out that because of advances in nuclear weapons technology, bomb development need no longer be tied to actual weapons testing.[141] Had the author followed his own logic just a bit further, he would have approached Beit-Hallahmi's disturbing conclusions. As already noted, South Africa acquired advanced computer technology in 1982, and with it a powerful means with which to advance nuclear weapons development. It should not take a great leap of imagination therefore – particularly in the context of a joint arms-industry with Israel – to speculate that Pretoria has joined the search for an optimal weapon configuration.

True, neutron bombs are not the only atomic weapons which could be used on the African continent. Far from being the only threat, they may not even be the primary threat. An arsenal of tactical atomic (fission) bombs of almost any design would make South Africa's thinly inhabited borders impregnable to a conventional assault. And almost any deliverable atomic design would give the apartheid regime the capability to execute nuclear threats and/or reprisals against the front-line states, none of which possess nuclear technology.[142]

Nevertheless, Third World leaders have generally assumed that nuclear weapons would be ineffective in countering guerrilla warfare and hence not a decisive factor in shaping the outcome of a grassroots liberation movement. The views of Dr. Ali A. Mazrui, a prominent African intellectual from Kenya, are probably typical of many:

> *In the final racial conflict, nuclear weapons could not be used internally without endangering the whites themselves. When the war does end, blacks will inherit the most advanced [nuclear] infrastructure on the continent. Out of the ashes of apartheid will emerge a black-ruled republic with convincing nuclear credentials.* [143]

Unfortunately, such views reflect wishful thinking more than a thorough assessment of the risks. Bishop Desmond Tutu probably came closer to identifying the nuclear threat in a 1986 address:

> *I myself actually fear that in the end, because they [South Africa's whites] are so irrational they seem to have a Samson complex...they are going to pull down the pillars and everybody must go with them.... If, as most of us believe, they do have a nuclear capability, I don't put it past them to have their own version of a scorched earth policy.*[144]

Yet even Bishop Tutu may be overlooking the special dangers posed by 'clean' weapons. Because of their unique radiation signature, best characterized as intense but short-lived and very local, deployment of neutron weapons need not imply a final suicidal immolation, as suggested by Tutu.[145] Far from it. In a political landscape defined by apartheid, the unthinkable becomes possible. In the hands of frightened white leaders who, to borrow a phrase from ANC activist Denis Goldberg, "will stop at nothing,"[146] it is not inconceivable that such weapons could become one more tool of repression. At the very least, the possibility cannot be excluded that in a crisis, the South African regime – desperate to suppress a mounting insurgency by any means necessary – would be tempted to unleash its nuclear arsenal internally. The government might judge it had the means – neutron weapons – to annihilate a perceived enemy at close quarters without endangering white South Africa at the same time. Or the government might gamble that a ruthless demonstration of power – perhaps one or two strikes – would be sufficient to crush Black resistance by instilling fear. The will to struggle against great odds is one thing. Certain nuclear liquidation is quite another.

Nightmarish scenarios are all too possible because of the segregated nature of South African society. A significant percentage of the country's Black population is known to live in 'homelands' geographically separate from white South Africa. Since the mid 1960s at least 3.5 million South African Blacks have been forcibly relocated to these enclaves.[147] With the heating up of guerrilla warfare, the homelands are almost certain to become staging areas for rebel attacks against government bases. For this reason they could easily become targets. Given the incredible killing power of the smallest tactical nuclear weapons, even one 'surgical nuclear strike' could result in many thousands of Black casualties. And since the struggle for the liberation of the subcontinent (Azania) has only just begun, it is reasonable to suppose that the risks to the peoples of the region will increase as the conflict intensifies.[148]

Is the Talking Over?

Unfortunately, substantive evidence already exists suggesting that the South African government has contingency plans for deploying tactical nuclear weapons. In 1979 Dr. Frene Ginwala of the ANC produced a document during a UN seminar in London revealing alleged plans for exploding nuclear weapons along South Africa's borders.[149] The ANC claimed that the plans had been drawn up by the SAAEB as early as 1972. The document reportedly called for the deployment of 10-kiloton weapons along the country's borders.[150]

Nor have statements by South African government officials been reassuring. In 1977 South African Information Minister Connie Mulder was quoted as saying: "If we are attacked, no rules apply at all if it comes to a question of our existence. We will use all means at our disposal, whatever they may be."[151] More recently Prime Minister Botha told a cheering crowd in Cape Town: "If there are people who are thinking of doing something, I suggest they think twice about it. They might find we have military weapons they do not know about."[152]

Skeptics who, despite the evidence, would still discount the possibility of a South African holocaust, should ponder the name given the location of the South African military establishment's nuclear research complex near Pretoria which has remained off-limits to international inspectors. It is called *Pelindaba,* a Zulu expression which means "the talking is over."[153]

The Unraveling of Apartheid

Whatever the risks, they have not deterred the ANC. After delivering an address in Berkeley, California recently, an ANC official was asked to comment on the role of South Africa's nuclear arsenal in the struggle to abolish apartheid. The speaker, Pallo Jordan, a member of the ANC executive committee, emphasized the ANC's first commitment to freedom, and flatly denied that Black leaders had been deterred from active struggle by the South African government's military prowess, even if it did include nuclear weapons.[154]

Reports that ANC guerrilla activities are indeed expanding support Mr. Jordan's statement. According to Donald Woods, former South African news editor and author of *Biko,* guerrilla units continue to operate within South Africa, and the frequency of attacks has increased. Despite extensive counterinsurgency efforts by the government, at least 144 raids were mounted by the resistance in the period since the current news blackout went into effect.[156] Though the raids represent a military escalation of the conflict, they have gone almost unreported in the Western media.

Apparently the ANC strategy is to minimize the nuclear threat through a prolonged campaign of attrition. By dispersing forces widely, presenting no fixed targets (such as permanent rural bases), adopting hit-and-run tactics, and staging carefully selected acts of sabotage, a war of incremental steps can perhaps evade the dangers of tempting the South African Defense Force (SADF) to unleash its nuclear arsenal. Assuming such a strategy works, the defeat of apartheid will come about *not* as the result of one great final battle, but through internal exhaustion coupled with international pressure – what Mr. Woods called the "unravelling of apartheid."[157]

Corroboration by Vanunu

Besides testifying that South African nuclear scientists had worked at Dimona – confirming previous reports of Israeli-South African nuclear ties[158] – former Israeli nuclear technician Vanunu also revealed that Israel had launched a thermonuclear weapons program. Vanunu told the London *Sunday Times* that some time in 1980 the Defense Ministry began installing new labs in the *Machon* II bunker alongside the plutonium extraction plant in order to produce the special materials required for thermonuclear weapons. Unit 93 produces tritium as a by-product of irradiated lithium and aluminum. Unit 95 separates lithium-6 from commercially available lithium. Unit 98 is a deuterium production plant. These are materials used in the manufacture of 'boosted' weapons, and in hydrogen bombs – weapons *many* times more powerful than the relatively simple fission bombs used on Hiroshima and Nagasaki.[159] The same materials are also used in the production of neutron weapons. Vanunu thus confirmed the basis for reports of an Israeli-South African neutron bomb.

A Step Toward Peace?

Even as the new fusion research/production lab was being installed at Dimona, Israeli delegates at the United Nations were, to all appearances, taking an important step toward peace. In December 1980, Israel voted in favor of a UN resolution calling for the creation of a Nuclear Weapons Free Zone (NWFZ) in the Middle East.[160] Though Israeli diplomats had publicly supported the idea as early as 1975, they bad continued to vote against the UN bill – jointly sponsored each year by Egypt and Iran. As might be expected, the apparent shift in the Israeli position was much welcomed as a hopeful sign.

The world was unaware that the step toward peace was being more than offset by other Israelis who, with a different agenda, i.e., the production of thermonuclear weapons, were dragging their country and the world two steps nearer the abyss.*

* In fact, it is quite likely that Israel's 1980 decision to support the NWFZ Resolution was an example of Zionist public relations in action. The Arab states had based their support for the free zone idea on the precondition that all states must sign the 1974 Nonproliferation Treaty (NPT), a reasonable position of substance. Israel was not a signatory to the NPT, and did not intend to become one. (Israel's rationale in rejecting the NPT was discussed in an official statement released in June 1981 after its pre-emptive attack destroyed Iraq's Osirak nuclear plant. For the text see Spokesman, *Israel's Bomb: the First Victim,* p. 15; also see Green, *Living by the Sword,* p. 135.) Therefore, Israeli support for the 1980 UN resolution was certain to generate positive images of Israel in the American media while leading precisely nowhere. Israel could achieve a publicity 'coup' at no cost. See Sadat's interview on ABC Television, February 27, 1977.

Notes to Chapter Five

1. Guest Lecture, School of Law, Tel Aviv University, December 24, 1987, reprinted in *Yediot Aharonot*, December 25, 1987.

2. Cape Province paper of the National Party.

3. Steve Biko, 1986. *I Write What I Like*, San Francisco, Harper and Row, p. 79.

4. Chomsky, op cit, pp. 64-65; also see Sadat's interview in *Newsweek*, April 9, 1973, pp. 44-45.

5. Edward Witten, "Cold Silence," *Ha'aretz*, January 6, 1973; Chomsky, op cit, pp. 64-65.

6. By 1972, Sadat admittedly was preparing for war against Israel, and his expulsion of the Soviets was designed to increase pressure on Moscow to supply the offensive weapons needed. However, at the same time Sadat's policy was two-fisted. Even as he armed for war Sadat continued to hold out the option of a negotiated settlement. The Soviet expulsion was therefore a highly ambiguous move. Had the U.S. or Israel shown any interest, it could even have led to peace talks. In fact, what is astonishing about the Yom Kippur War is that the debacle might have been averted up until almost the last moment, had Washington recognized the opening and pressed Israel into talks. By this time however, Nixon was up to his neck in Watergate and U.S. intelligence experts who knew a Middle East disaster was brewing simply did not have access to the President. Moreover, Jordanian warnings to Kissinger went unheeded. For a brilliant analysis of these events, and the war itself, see the study by the London *Sunday Times* Insight Team, op cit, pp. 43-45 for the Israeli rejection; also see Seymour M. Hersh, 1983. *The Price of Power: Kissinger in the Nixon White House*, New York, Summit Books. pp. 402-414; the Sadat interview in *Newsweek*, December 13, 1971 and again in March, 1972; Mohammed Heikal, 1975. *The Road to Ramadan*, Quadrangle, pp. 114-155; William Quandt, 1977. *Decade of Decision*, University of California, pp. 128-164.

7. Golda Meir was quoted at the time as saying that "Israel will continue to pursue her enlightened policy in Judea and Samaria." Meir's political adviser, Israel Galili, in charge of settlement in the occupied territories, amplified the Prime Minister's remark by adding that, henceforth, the Jordan River should be "Israel's agreed border – a frontier, not just a security border." In Chomsky's view, the latter term previously had implied the possibility of some form of self-government for Palestinians. Cited by Chomsky, op cit, p. 65.

8. Sadat had offered Israel a full peace treaty on the pre-June 1967 borders, with security guarantees and recognized borders. According to Noam Chomsky (citing writer Amos Elon), the offer caused a panic in Israel and was promptly rejected "with the statement that Israel would not return to the internationally recognized pre-1967 borders." Interestingly, Sadat's 1971 offer was more favorable to Israel than proposals made later during the Egyptian President's historic 1977 trip to Jerusalem, since in 1971 he made no reference to Palestinian rights. This was in keeping with the international consensus of that time, which in 1971 still regarded the Palestinians as a refugee problem. This changed after 1974. Sadat's 1971 peace offer was recognized by Israel's Labor party but rejected on the grounds that more territorial gains would be possible if Israel held out. In fact, as reported by Chomsky, Israel's only overt response, apart from the rejection, was an immediate announcement of new West Bank settlements near Jerusalem. Amos Elon, *Ha'aretz*, November 13, 1981; also see Jon Kimche, *There Could Have Been Peace*, pp. 286f. Both sources cited in Chomsky, op cit, pp. 64-65.

In April 1973 – as he prepared for war – Sadat referred to his 1971 ace offer in an interview with Newsweek: "When I made my [peace] initiative in February 1971, I was genuine and I told the U.S. it was a test of peace. Secretary Rogers told me it was now up to Israel. But Israel told the U.S. it was just the beginning of Egyptian concessions. I told Nixon I wanted a successful effort with the U.S. for an overall settlement. But there was no response from the U.S. or Israel – except to supply Israel with more Phantoms.. Every door I have opened has been slammed in my face by Israel – with American blessings." "The Battle is Now Inevitable," *Newsweek*, April 9, 1973, p. 45.

9. In earlier years, Golda Meir had shown similar inflexibility. According to Seymour Hersh, Yitzhak Rabin recalled meetings where Kissinger had raged at Meir: "There is serious fear that what you really want is to evade any settlement that requires concessions on your part so that you can remain along the lines you hold at present." Hersh, op cit, p. 406.

Kissinger suggests as much in his own memoirs: "Golda had two objectives: to gain time, for the longer there was no change in the status quo, the more Israel would be confirmed in the possession of the occupied territories; and to achieve Nixon's approval of a new package of military aid for Israel." Henry Kissinger, 1982. *Years of Upheaval*, Boston, Little, Brown and Co., p. 221; also see Richard R.F. Sheehan, 1976. *The Arabs, Israelis and Kissinger*, New York, Readers Digest

Press, p. 199.

Stephen Green offers documentation in his new book confirming Kissinger and Hersh's assessment, quoting (then) Deputy Minister Gideon Raphael: "Mrs. Meir had come to Washington (a) to discuss additional arms purchases, and (b) to avoid discussion of peace plans." Green also identifies the main item on the 'wish list' referred to by Kissinger: additional Phantom F-4E fighter jets, the most advanced aircraft in the Middle East at that time. According to Green, Israel did receive the new Phantoms in December 1969 and within weeks launched a series of deep-penetration bombing raids on Egypt's heartland. According to Green, the raids were never even reported in the U.S. media. Green, *Sword,* op cit, pp. 47-48.

10. This was also Yitzhak Rabin's view: "The Yom Kippur War was not fought by Egypt and Syria to threaten the existence of Israel. It was an all-out use of their military force to achieve a limited political goal. What Sadat wanted by crossing the canal was to change the political reality and, thereby, to start a political process from a point more favorable to him than the one that existed. In this respect, he succeeded." Milton Viorst, 1987. *Sands of Sorrow,* New York, Harper and Row, p. 170.

11. Plenty of corroboration on this point can be drawn from the following literature. The London *Sunday Times* Insight Team, op cit, pp. 46-420; also see Edgar O'Ballance, 1978. *No Victor No Vanquished: the Yom Kippur War,* San Raphael, Ca., Presidio Press, pp. 147-149; Perlmutter, *Two Minutes,* op cit, pp. 45-48; Dana Adams Schmidt, 1974. *Armageddon in the Middle East: The New York Times Survey Series,* New York, The John Day Company, p. 205.

The battle for the Golan Heights is more difficult to interpret. A recent book suggests the near-breakthrough by Syria probably has been overstated. According to the authors of the new study, Terry Asher and Eric Hammel, the Syrians were so decisively beaten they never even achieved their initial objectives. For this reason it is difficult to assess Syria's overall strategy. Asher and Hammel concluded on the basis of the evidence that, although heavily outnumbered, the tenacious Israeli defenders achieved one of the greatest tank victories of all time. Terry Asher and Eric Hammel, 1987. *Duel for the Golan: the 100 Hour Battle That Saved Israel,* New York, William Morrow and Co., Inc.

12. Kissinger, op cit, p. 459.

13. Hart, op cit, pp. 372-373.

14. The details of this near-miss will be examined in a subsequent chapter.

15. London *Sunday Times* Insight Team, op cit, p. 461-462.

16. Perlmutter, *Military and Politics in Israel* (1969), op cit, p. 48.

17. Joel Beinin, "Challenge from Israel's Military," *Merip Reports,* November-December, 1980, pp. 6-7.

18. Inbar, op cit, p. 63; also see *Ha'aretz* March 15, 1973; Uri Bar-Joseph, "The Hidden Debate: the Formation of Nuclear Doctrines in the Middle East," *The Journal of Strategic Studies,* June, 1982, pp. 216-217.

19. Inbar, op cit, p. 63; also see Perlmutter, *Two Minutes,* op cit, pp. 48-50; Bar-Joseph, "The Hidden Debate," op cit, 218-223.

20. Gerald M. Steinberg, "Deliberate Ambiguity: Evolution and Evaluation," in Berès, ed., op cit, pp. 29-43; also see Inbar, op cit, p. 63.

21. Perlmutter, *Two Minutes,* op cit, pp. 47 and 49; also see Inbar, op cit, pp. 62 and 66-67; Bar-Joseph, "'The Hidden Debate," op cit., pp. 218-219; Robert W. Tucker, "Israel and the US: From Dependence to Nuclear Weapons?" *Commentary,* November, 1975, p. 41.

22. Perlmutter, *Two Minutes,* op cit, p. 47; also Safran, p. 489; *Time,* April 12, 1976, p. 39; the London *Sunday Times* Insight Team, op cit, pp. 282-284.

23. Nixon News Conference, November 12, 1971; also see Kissinger, op cit, pp. 339 and 668-669; also see Hersh, op cit, p. 121.

24. Beinin, op cit, p. 7; also see the profile on Senator Clifford Case (R-NJ), former ranking Republican on the Senate Foreign Relations Committee, prepared by his staff in 1978: "Senator Clifford Case: a Profile On His Record On Israel and Related Matters." Note: For an exhaustive review of U.S. military and economic assistance to Israel, see the uncensored text of the June 24, 1983 report prepared by the General Accounting Office (GAO) in *El-Khawas,* op cit, pp. 117-191.

25. Perlmutter, *Two Minutes,* op cit, pp. 50-52.

26. *Ibid,* pp. 50-52; also see "Three Nations Begin Cruise Missile Project," Washington Post, December 8, 1980.

27. J.K. Cooley, "Ten More Nations May Have Nuclear Arms on the Drawing Board – If Not in Hand," *Christian Science Monitor,* June 6, 1985. A recent report indicates South African involvement in the new Israeli Jericho II project: see *Yediot Aharonot,* November 27, 1987, cited in *Israeli Foreign Affairs,* March, 1988, p. 4.

28. In fact, trade between Israel and South Africa had been on the rise since 1971. Between 1971-1975 total trade between the two countries almost tripled, from R13 million to R37 million. For a

detailed analysis of Israeli-South African economic/military coopera-tion see Birgit Sommer, 1976. "Military-economic collusion," in *Israel-South Africa: Cooperation of Imperialist Outposts,* Bonn, PDW; also see Robert Manning and Stephen Talbot, "American Cover-Up on Israeli Bomb," *The Middle East,* June, 1980. pp. 8-12; Martha Wenger, "Recipe for an Israeli Nuclear Arsenal," *The Middle East Report ,* November-December, 1986. p. 12; "Need Unites," *The Economist,* December 20, 1980.

29. "Halting Pretoria's A-Test," *Newsweek,* September 5, 1977; also see TASS, August 8, 1977. The TASS statement was later quoted in *Pravda:* "The possession of nuclear weapons by the racist regime of Pretoria would constitute a most direct threat to the security of the African states; it would lead to a sharp escalation of instability and tension in southern Africa and would increase the nuclear threat to all mankind....The leaders of the Soviet Union feel that the most urgent and effective efforts on the part of all states, the United States and international public opinion are needed in order to prevent.. the proliferation of such weapons."

30. Jane Hunter, 1987. *Israeli Foreign Policy: South Africa and Central America,* Boston, South End Press, p. 36; *Newsweek,* September 12, 1977.

31. Ronald W. Walters, 1987. *South Africa and the Bomb,* Lex-ington, Massachusetts, Lexington Books. p. 42.

32. *New York Times,* October 26, 1979, p. 1.

33. *Washington Post,* October 26, 1979, p. A-1d.

34. Thomas O'Toole "New Light Cast on Sky-Flash Mystery," *Washington Post,* January 30, I980,p. A-1; see also Thomas O'Toole, "South African Ships in Zone of Suspected N-Blast," *Guardian,* January 31, 1980. Other evidence existed as well: a Navy official had revealed that U.S. spy planes flying over the region where the flash was detected had been waved off by the South African Navy and forced to land in Australia. Ronald W. Walters, and Kenneth S. Zinn, "South Africa's Bomb," *Africa Asia* (Paris), September 1986, p. 12.

35. The two Israelis who leaked the story were the same jour-nalists noted in chapter four, Eli Teicher and Ami Dor-On, who authored the book on the Israeli A-bomb program censored by the Israeli government in 1980. Subsequently, the CBS reporter who reported the leak, Dan Raviv, had his press credentials canceled by the Israeli government censor. "CBS Evening News With Walter Cronkite," CBS NEWS, 6, no. 52, February 21, 1980, pp. 4-5; also see Shipler, "Israel Bans...," op cit.

Author James Adams later claimed that he had read significant parts of Teicher and Don-On's manuscript. Adams was convinced that the writers had "extremely good connections within the political establishment." James Adams, 1984. *The Unnatural Alliance*, London, Quartet, p.210.

36. *Washington Post*, February 22, 1980, p. A-6.

37. Beit-Hallahmi, op cit, p. 134.

38. *Washington Post*, January 17, 1980, p. A-11.

39. *Ibid*

40. Guy E. Barasch, November, 1979. *Light Flash Produced by an Atmospheric Nuclear Explosion*, Los Alamos, Los Alamos Scientific Laboratory, LASL Mini Review 79-84.

41. Green, *Sword*, op cit, pp. 117-118.

42. Thomas O'Toole, "Officials Hotly Debate Whether African Event Was Atom Blast," *Washington Post*, January 17, 1980, p. A-11.

43. Thomas O'Toole, "Neutron Bomb Suspected in Africa Blast," *Washington Post*, March 9, 1980.

44. Thomas O'Toole, "Fallout Studied to Confirm Blast Near S. Africa," *Washington Post*, November 14, 1979, p. A-1.

45. Eliot Marshall, "Flash Not Missed by Vela Still Veiled in Mist," *Science* November 30, 1979.

46. On October 26 the *New York Times* carried two front-page stories, side-by-side: one on SALT, and one on the suspected South African test. *New York Times,* October 26, 1979, p. A-1.

47. The panel was appointed by White House Science Advisor Dr. Frank Press. A transcript of the White House report is included in Appendix B, including a list of the panel members. *Ad Hoc Panel Report on the September 22 Event*, Executive Office of the President, Office of Science and Technology, July 15, 1980.

48. *Ibid*

49. *Ibid*

50. Walters, *South Africa,* op cit, p. 52.

51. "DIA Concludes Mystery Flash Probable A-Test," *Washington Post*, July 15, 1980.

52. Eliot Marshall, "Navy Lab Concludes the Vela Saw a Bomb," *Science,* August 29, 1980.

53. Jack Anderson, "The Mystery Flash: Bomb or Phenomenon?" *Washington Post*, September 16, 1980; also see Green *Sword*, op cit, p. 125; Adams, op cit, p. 194. Note: details of the CIA report are presented in a documentary produced by Granada Television. "South Africa's Bombshell," *The World in Action,* transcript P568/536, issued

October 21, 1980.

54. Marshall, "Flash Not Missed by Vela," op cit, p. 1051.

55. *Ibid*

56. Appendix B.

57. Telephone conversation with panel member Dr. Richard Muller, May 13, 1988. Also see Appendix B, p 10.

58. Eliot Marshall, "Scientists Fail to Solve Vela Mystery," *Science*, February 1, 1980, p. 504-5.

59. *Ibid*, also see See Appendix B.

60. Marshall, "Navy Lab Concludes," op cit.

61. Appendix B; also see Green, *Sword*, op cit, pp. 118-119.

62. Marshall, "Naval Lab Concludes," op cit, p. 996.

63. Appendix B.

64. (emphasis added); Philip J. Klass, "Clandestine Nuclear Test Doubted," *Aviation Week and Space Technology*, August 11, 1980.

65. Appendix B.

66. Marshall, "Naval Lab Concludes," op cit.

67. *Ibid*

68. Conversation with Dr. Richard Muller, June 1, 1988.

69. References cited regarding Dr. Van Middlesworth's sheep thyroid data were gleaned from Dr. Ronald Walters' review of the NRL study, which he acquired via the Freedom of Information Act. To this date the NRL study, and the three other reports remain classified. Walters, *South Africa*, op cit, pp. 48-51.

70. *Ibid*

71. *Ibid*

72. *Ibid*, p. 50.

73. *Ibid*

74. *Ibid*

75. The report submitted by New Zealand to the United Nations stated that "We are still not certain what this radioactivity is." Nor did the report explain how it occurred. "Policies of Apartheid of the Government of South Africa," *UN General Assembly*, A/34/674/Add. 1, November 26, 1979, Annex, p. 12; cited in Walters, *South Africa*, op cit, p. 50.

76. Walters, *South Africa*, op cit, p. 51.

77. Conversation with Dr. Richard Muller, June 1, 1988.

78. Green, *Sword*, op cit, pp. 130-132; also see Walters, *South Africa*, op cit, p. 54.

79. Green, *Sword*, op cit, pp. 126-130.

80. *Ibid*, p. 130.

81. *Ibid*, p. 130.

82. *Ibid*, pp. 130-132.

83. Conversation with Dr. Richard Muller, June 1, 1988.

84. Walters, *South Africa*, op cit, pp. 17, 54 and 58; also see Green, *Sword*, op cit, p. 128.

85. Conversation with Dr. Alan Berman, June 6, 1988.

86. *Ibid*

87. Manning and Talbot, op cit, p. 9.

88. Stephen Talbot, "The Case of the Mysterious Flash," *Inquiry*, April 21, 1980, p. 16; also see Green, *Sword*, op cit, p. 128.

89. Green, *Sword*, op cit, p. 111.

90. Manning and Talbot, op cit, p. 9; also see O'Toole, "Neutron Bomb Suspected," op cit.

91. *Washington Post*, February 16, 1978, p. A12.

92. Manning and Talbot, op cit, pp. 10-11.

93. Documents declassified in 1982 and obtained by Mark Evanoff of the Friends of the Earth through the Freedom of Information Act revealed that as early as 1952 the AEC understood the connection between 'atoms for peace' and war. At that time the AEC commissioned feasibility studies and invited industry proposals for 'dual purpose' reactors which would integrate commercial generation of electricity with production of plutonium weapons. Soon thereafter a joint study by Pacific Gas and Electric and the Betchel Corporation concluded that such dual-purpose reactors were technically feasible. However, the program never got off the ground, despite generous subsidies offered by the AEC in the form of a 'plutonium credit,' because the utilities were not prepared to take the risk on expensive and untried technology which had not been shown to be financially competitive – even with the subsidy. Amory Lovins, 1980. *Energy/War: Breaking the Nuclear Link*, San Francisco, Friends of the Earth; also see "Pacific Gas and Electric Company – Betchel Corporation Industrial Reactor Study," *Reactor Science and Technology*, October 1952, pp. 81-103.

One of the chief players in this drama, IAEC Chairman Ernst Bergmann, was certainly under no illusions as to the link. In 1969 he was quoted as saying: "By developing atomic energy for peaceful purposes you reach the nuclear option. There are no two atomic energies." Quoted in Leonard Beaton, "Israel's Nuclear Policy Under Scrutiny ," *The London Times*, January 16, 1969.

94. Talbot, "Mysterious Flash," op cit.

95. Walters, *South Africa*, op cit, pp. 42-59.

96. UN Resolution 418, Mandatory Arms Embargo, passed

November 4, 1977.

97. The Nuclear Nonproliferation Act, Public Law 95-242, S. 1432 and H.R. 4409, established the adoption of International Atomic Energy Agency (IAEA) safeguards – and, hence signing of the NPT – as the criteria for future nuclear exports and cooperation with trading partners. Article III, section 128(a), no. 1 states: "No such export shall be made unless IAEA safeguards are maintained with respect to all peaceful nuclear activities in, under the jurisdiction of, or carried out under the control of such a state at the time of the export." In addition, Article IV, section 403(a), no. 5 stated: "No nation or group of nations will assist, encourage, or induce any non-nuclear weapons state to manufacture or otherwise acquire any [nuclear] explosive device." *Congressional Record,* February 9, 1978, p. H. 914.

98. The Symington-Glenn Amendments, Public Laws 94-329, and 95-92, were intended to toughen the 1961 Foreign Assistance Act, with respect to proliferation. The Glenn Amendment explicitly mandated that no U.S. military/economic aid would he appropriated to any country that "is not a nuclear-weapon state as defined in article IX (3) of the Treaty on Nonproliferation of Nuclear Weapons [the NPT] and which detonates a nuclear explosive device – or to a country that "delivers nuclear reprocessing equipment, materials or technology to any other country or receives such equipment." Section 669-670, International Security Assistance Act of 1977.

99. UN General Assembly Resolution 34/89. 97th plenary meeting, December 11, 1979. The important sections of the Resolution stated: "The General Assembly...

1. Appeals to all states to put an end to any cooperation with Israel which may assist it in acquiring and developing nuclear weapons and also to dissuade corporations, institutions and individuals within their jurisdiction from any cooperation that may result in providing Israel with nuclear weapons;

2. Calls upon all states to take necessary measures to prevent the transfer to Israel of fissionable material and nuclear technology which could be used for nuclear arms;

3. Calls upon Israel to submit all its nuclear facilities to inspection by the International Atomic Energy Agency;

4. Strongly condemns any attempt by Israel to manufacture, acquire, store, or test nuclear weapons or introduce them into the Middle East."

100. Hedrick Smith, "U.S. Assumes the Israelis Have A-Bomb or its Parts," *New York Times,* July 18, 1970, p. 1; also see "Israel reported

behind A-Blast off S. Africa," *Washington Post,* February 22, 1980; O'Toole, "New Light Cast on Sky-Flash Mystery," op cit; William Beecher, "Israel Believed Producing Missile Capable of Atom Capability," *New York Times,* October 5, 1971.

101. Memo, "Project Status Report," Goodman to Berman, March 21, 1980. NRL. Cited in Walters, *South Africa,* op cit, p. 61.

102. *Washington Post,* November 1, 1977, p. A18; also see a restatement of the Andrew Young position by Zbigniew Brzezinski, *The Johannesburg Star,* March 10, 1978.

103. See President Reagan's speech on nuclear power and proliferation, July 16, 1981.

104. Ford Foundation and Mitre Corporation, 1977. *Nuclear Power: Issues and Choices,* Cambridge, Mass., Ballinger, p. 372; also see *The Washington Post,* August 8, 1982, p. Al.

105. For a discussion of how such leverage actually works in reverse see Amory B. and L. Hunter Lovins and Patrick O 'Heffeman, 1983. *The First Nuclear World War,* New York, William Morrow and Company, Inc., pp. 206-208.

106. "Top South African Aide Denies Knowledge of Nuclear Explosion," *New York Times,* October 26, 1979, p. 22; also see Walters, *South Africa,* op cit, pp. 94-99 and 150.

107. Dr. Walters' study was based, in large part, on his review of the classified NRL study, obtained via the Freedom of Information Act. Dr. Ronald Walters, 1985. *The September 22 Mystery Flash: Did South Africa Detonate a Nuclear Bomb?,* Washington Office on Africa Educational Fund in cooperation with Congressman John Conyers, the Congressional Black Caucus Foundation and the World Campaign Against Military and Nuclear Cooperation with South Africa, p. 17.

108. Conversation with Professor Ronald Walters, February 10, 1988; also confirmed by sources close to Congressman Ron Dellums, February 10, 1988. To date, all four reports on the mystery-flash remain classified.

109. Beit-Hallahmi, op cit, p. 134.

110. Perlmutter, *Two Minutes,* op cit, pp. 50-51; also see Walters, *South Africa,* op cit, p. 34.

111. The quote was by Pieter Marais, head of ARMSCOR. Adams, op cit, pp. 38-71.

112. *Ibid,* pp. 38-71. The CIA's part in subverting U.S. law was 'justified' by the same rationale used later in the Iran-Contra Affair. The artillery was to be used by UNITA/South African troops fighting Cubans in Angola. As it turned out, the realities of Southern Africa

showed the CIA's cold-war logic to be absurd. In this case the Cuban (enemy) troops ended up protecting U.S.-owned oil facilities and drilling platforms from certain destruction or capture by South African (friendly) forces.

113. *Ibid*

114. *Ibid*, p. 68.

115. For a transcript of the Senate subcommittee's recommendations see *Ibid*, pp. 68-71.

The U.S. arms pipeline to South Africa is known to have continued long after the facts concerning the SRC howitzer fiasco were made public. Pursuing its own cold war agenda, in 1985 the U.S. Congress voted military aid for Jonas Savimbi's UNITA rebels, which had been struggling for years to overthrow the Socialist government of Angola. The aid was 'justified' by Washington due to the presence of Cuban troops in Angola, troops which in the 1970s prevented the South African Defense Force (SADF) from occupying the country. Unfortunately, Washington failed to perceive the reality: that UNITA, along with its RENAMO counterpart in Mozambique, amounted to little more than an extension of the South African Defense Force, comprising an important part of South Africa's campaign to intimidate, destabilize, and dominate its neighbors. In Angola, South Africa also had another direct interest: capture of the Cabinda oilfields, to supply Pretoria's energy needs in the event of a tightening UN oil embargo.

Given all this, U.S. military aid for UNITA – the South African equivalent of the Reagan Administration's Contras – can only have had the effect of supporting apartheid. Indeed, such a conclusion had been drawn by the reputable British daily *The Independent* as early as 1980. On December 9 of that year the paper reported a large-scale covert operation involving transport of arms from the U.S. and Europe to UNITA via South Africa. The report cited evidence detailing secret shipment to Johannesburg of forty tons of machine guns and twenty tons of rocket launchers. The shipments constituted a flagrant violation of the UN embargo. Incredibly, the State Department denied all knowledge, claiming U.S. military aid ended in 1962.

For their part, Africans are well aware of the U.S. role in support of South African terrorism, à la UNITA. Denis Goldberg, an African National Congress activist released after 22 years in a South African prison for opposing apartheid, claimed in an address in Berkeley, California on February 1, 1988 that 6000 or more Angolans – mostly civilians – had been killed or crippled over the past few years by U.S. made/supplied claymore mines. Goldberg called on Americans to demand real enforcement of the UN arms embargo.

In fact, the figure cited by Goldberg is probably conservative. In early 1987 the Angolan government estimated that some 23,000 of its people, mostly peasant farmers, had been crippled in the war with South African/UNITA forces. Many of those crippled were amputees. Andrew Meldrum, "At War With South Africa," *Africa Report* , January-February, 1987; also see James Brooke, "War Turns Angolan Breadbasket Into Land of Hunger," *New York Times,* December 28, 1985.

116. According to recent reports, the advanced 155 mm artillery was used by South Africa in a devastating attack on Angola in late February, 1988. In launching the attack the South African Defense Force (SADF) used tactics previously employed by Israel in its 1982 pre-emptive assault on Syria. Israeli technicians reportedly assisted in the operation. *Africa Analysis,* March 4, 1988; also see "Israelis Help South African Air Force," *Israeli Foreign Affairs,* April, 1988.

117. Adams, op cit, p. 70.

118. *Ibid*

119. Apparently the Israelis were sufficiently impressed by its performance during the Yom Kippur War that they tried to acquire SRC themselves – without success. Later, they were more successful in assisting South Africa. Adams, op cit, p. 42; also see Asher and Hammel, op cit, pp. 125-127.

120. CBS Evening News with Walter Cronkite, March 5, 1981; for a printed version see *The New York Times,* February 1, 1980, p. A12.

121. Two U.S. corporations served as brokers: Edlow International and Swuco. Walters, *South Africa,* op cit, pp. 101-113 and 29.

122. *Newsweek,* April 12, 1,982, p. 17.

123. *Washington Post,* August 8, 1982. p.A1 and A11.

124. Walters, *South Africa,* op cit, p. 17; also see Leonard Spector, "Proliferation: The Silent Spread," *Foreign Policy,* Spring 1985, p. 56.

125. As we now know, the development of Jericho II and Cruise missiles after 1980 conspicuously coincided with the secret development of strategic (fusion) weapons at Dimona. A 1981 report in *Aerospace Daily* described the Jericho II as a solid- fuel rocket with an inertial guidance system and a range of 400 miles – constituting a quantum leap beyond the earlier Jericho I. "Israel said to Deploy Jericho Missile," *Aerospace Daily,* May 1981. Also see "Three Nations Begin Cruise Missile Project," op cit. A more recent report indicated

South African participation in the latest Jericho II test program. Apparently South Africa is providing secluded desert sites for testing of the new prototype, which has a potential range of 900 miles. *Yediot Aharonot,* November 27, 1987.

126. "Soviets Warn Israel on Missiles," *San Francisco Chronicle,* July 30, 1987; also see "USSR Warns Israel on Missile," *Israeli Foreign Affairs,* September, 1987, p. 2.

127. Walters, *South Africa,* op cit, pp. 28-29.

128. Cervenka and Rogers, op cit, p. 198; also see Ted Greenwood, Harold Feiveson, and Theodore Taylor, 1977. *Nuclear Proliferation,* New York, McGraw-Hill, p. 18; "Resource Development in South Africa and U.S. Policy," in Hearings, Subcommittee on International Resources, Food and Energy, Committee on International Relations, U.S. House of Representatives, May 25, June 8 and 9, 1976, appendix 6, p. 293

129. "U.S. Policy Toward Africa," *Hearings, Subcommittee on Africa, Subcommittee on Arms Control, International Organizations and Security Agreements, Committee on Foreign Nations,* 1976. U.S. Senate, May 27, 1976, U.S. Government Printing Office, 1976, p. 290.

130. A report filed by the Nuclear Regulatory Commission's (NRC's) own staff in 1980 revealed that the agency's statistical checks on fuel shipments and stockpiles had become so muddled as to be meaningless. For material on this, plus a detailed account of the many reasons why the IAEA has failed to safeguard nuclear materials, see Lovins and O'Heffeman, op cit, p. 94 and pp. 225- 247; also see Kohn, "widening gaps," op cit.

131. Expansion of the plant to a commercial capacity of 5000 tons of enriched uranium annually was completed by late 1984. Walters, *South Africa,* op cit, pp. 26-27 and 132. For a more complete record see A.J.A. Roux, and W.L. Grant, "Uranium Enrichment in South Africa: Nuclear Energy Maturity," Proceedings of the European Nuclear Conference, Paris, April 21- 24, 1974; also see A.J.A. Roux, W.L. Grant, R.A. Barbour, R.S. Loubser, and J.J. Wannenburg, "Development and Progress of the South African Enrichment Project," a paper presented at the International Conference on Nuclear Power and its Fuel Cycle, IAEA, Salzburg, Austria, May 2-13, 1977; D.K. Palit, and P.K. Namboodiri, op cit, p. 127. For a report of the involvement of West Germany see Cervenka and Rogers, op cit; also see Virginia Foote, "South Africa: Another Loophole in Non-Proliferation Policy," *Country Notes,* March 1, 1982, p. 4 ff; *Nuclear Engineering International,* April, 1974, p. 255.

132. *Washington Post,* February 18, 1977, p. A28.

133. Weissman and Krosney, op cit, p. 73.

134. Stockholm International Peace Research Institute (SIPRI), 1976. *Southern Africa; Escalation of a Conflict,* New York, Praeger, pp. 131 and 134.

135. Christer Larsen and Jan Melin, "Third World Countries Buy Swedish Nuclear Weapons Technology," in *Ny Teknik,* May 2, 1986, p. 12, translated in JPRS/TND, July 30, 1986, p. 1.

136. "The First Neutron Bomb Briefing," Sam Cohen, 1983. *The Truth About the Neutron Bomb: the Inventor of the Bomb Speaks Out,* New York, William Morrow and Co., Inc. p. 131; also see MIT Faculty, 1984. *The Nuclear Almanac: Confronting the Atom in War and Peace,* Reading Mass., Addison-Wesley Publishing, pp. 185, 199, 202 and 212.

137. *Ibid,* p. 127-139; also see Harold M. Agnew, "A primer on Enhanced Radiation Weapons," *Bulletin of the Atomic Scientists,* December, 1977, p. 6.

138. As, for example, by the bomb's inventor. See Cohen, op cit, pp. 221-226; also see Frank Barnaby, "World Arsenals in 1977," SIPRI Report, *Bulletin of the Atomic Scientists,* May, 1978, p. 11; George Kistiakowsky, "The Folly of the Neutron Bomb," *Bulletin,* September, 1978; Jorma K. Miettinen, "Time for Europeans to debate the presence of tactical nukes," Bulletin, May 1976.

The debate has not been limited to neutron weapons, however. In debunking tactical defensive weapons in general, one analyst, Alain Enthoven, testified that "twenty years of efforts to find an acceptable doctrine for the use of [tactical] nuclear weapons for the defense of Western Europe have failed because one does not exist. The planned first use of nuclear weapons for the defense of Western Europe simply doesn't make sense. It amounts to saying 'We'll have to destroy this continent in order to save it.'" Cited in Robert Shreffler, "The New Nuclear Force," *Proceedings of the Tenth Anniversary of SIPRI,* November, 1977, p. 5.

139. Beit-Hallahmi, op cit, pp. 135-136.

140. Mr. Spector has made important contributions to the growing body of literature on nuclear proliferation. See Leonard S. Spector, 1987. *Going Nuclear,* Cambridge, Ballinger Publishing Company, pp. 217-235.

141. A recent article in *Newsweek* explained in greater detail why extensive testing is no longer a necessity: "Sophisticated laboratory equipment, pre-tested bomb plans...and the technique of zero-yield

tests [tests too small by design to be picked-up by detection equipment] have allowed the new nuclear-club members to build atomic bombs without the political fallout of an explosion." Rod Norland, "The Bombs in the Basement," *Newsweek,* July 11, 1988, p. 42; also see Spector, *Going Nuclear,* op cit, p. 137.

142. South Africa's present capacity to deliver conventional and/or nuclear weaponry is well-documented. In 1986 South Africa acquired 707 Boeing jets outfitted with Israeli assistance as in-flight refueling platforms and flying electronic warfare stations – effectively extending the range of South African Cheetah fighter jets to much, if not all, of Africa. As a result, in 1988 South Africa commands the skies of the continent. One immediate practical consequence is that South Africa can now target a vital railroad line – formerly out of range – spanning the continent from Angola to Tanzania. South Africa's destabilization policy has included the destruction of key links in its neighbors' rail transport systems, to force dependence on South Africa rail/port facilities. Thus South Africa raises tax revenues from its own victims – much as Israel taxes Palestinians. South African involvement in Israel's Jericho II missile program will be discussed in a later chapter. Beit-Hallahmi, op cit, p. 124; also see Martin Streetly, "Israeli Airborne SIGINT Systems," *Jane's Defense Weekly,* December 27, 1986, cited in Hunter, op cit, p. 42; "A Farewell to Arms," a documentary produce by Diverse Production, available via *Israeli Foreign Affairs.*

143. Mary Battiata, "Author Defends 'Africans'", in *Washington Post,* September 6, 1986; also see David K. Willis, "South African Blacks to Have the Bomb by the Year 2000?" *Christian Science Monitor,* July 1, 1985.

144. In an address given January 9, 1986. Cited in Spector, *Going Nuclear,* op cit, p. 217

145. Cohen, op cit, p. 129.

146. In an address by Denis Goldberg delivered at the South Berkeley Senior Center, Berkeley, California, February 1, 1988.

147. Walters, *South Africa,* op cit, p. 70.

148. Mr. Spector, already mentioned, has estimated South Africa's stockpile of nuclear weapons to be as high as 40 or more. See Leonard S. Spector, 1984. *Nuclear Proliferation Today,* New York, Vintage/Random House, p. 305. Note: Mr. Spector's most recent book inexplicably downgrades this estimate to around 20 war-heads. See Spector, *Going Nuclear,* op cit, pp. 217-239.

149. Adams, op cit, p. 178.

150. Adams, op cit, p. 178.

151. *Washington Post,* February 16, 1977.

152. Cited in Adams, op cit, p. 186.

153. Manning and Talbot, op cit, p. 10; also see Adams, op cit, pp. 177 and 186.

154. Lecture by Pallo Jordan, Director of Research, ANC, at UC Berkeley, California, May 6, 1988.

155. In an address by Donald Woods to an Oakland audience, February 20, 1988.

156. *Ibid*

157. *Ibid*

158. Jane Hunter compiled these reports in her book. Op cit, p. 32-39.

159. London *Sunday Times,* op cit, p. 5; also see Frank Barnaby "The Nuclear Arsenal in the Middle East," in *Technology Review,* May-June, 1987: pp. 27-34.

160. UN Resolution 35/147, passed at the 94th plenary meeting, December 12, 1980. For a discussion of the Israeli position see the London *Observer,* October 26, 1980; also see Inbar, op cit, p. 74.

Chapter Six

Israeli Nuclear Strategy: "Polite Blackmail"

The Israeli nuclear option has every possible quality; its non-exercise can be sold for the thing that really matters, sophisticated conventional armaments, and remain to serve another day; in the meantime the stockpile grows steadily; the transmission of assurance tends to discourage countermoves in Arab countries; and should the conventional balance shift at some future date, the option remains to be exercised at a time when it would make the maximum emotional impact.
— *Leonard Beaton*[1]

In the early days, Israeli strategists probably regarded a nuclear capability as purely supplementary to conventional military strength. After all, because Israel's defensive strategies – summarized by Yigal Allon in his treatise *A Curtain of Sand* – emphasized interceptive war and pre-emptive attack, the integration of nuclear with conventional weapons must have seemed unlikely, to say the least, given the weapons' vast destructive power. It follows they would be regarded as weapons of last resort, without qualification.

As the nuclear program advanced, however, and as the Israeli-Arab stalemate became more entrenched, opinion began to change. The first hint of a shift in strategy was offered by Shimon Peres in a 1962 interview with the Labor daily, *Davar.* At the time Peres was Permanent Secretary of the Israeli Defense Ministry. Peres spoke of the IDF concept of nonconventional 'compellence.'[2] The concept was subsequently explained by another Israeli nuclear expert, Yair Evron:

Acquiring a superior weapons system would mean the possibility of using it for compellent purposes – that is, forcing the other side to accept Israeli political demands, which would presumably include a demand that the territorial status quo be accepted and a peace treaty signed.[3]

Fuad Jabber, one of the early writers on Israeli nuclear strategy, described the new reality: "Nuclear weapons could thus be conceived as an effective instrument for the attainment of the primary objectives of her [Israel's] foreign policy. Insomuch as they would fulfill the same deterrent functions as the conventional forces, they would fit the requirements of Israeli strategic doctrine."[4]

The "territorial status quo" Evron was referring to coincided with Israel's frontiers after the June 1967 war, when the IDF occupied the Sinai, the Gaza Strip, the West Bank, and the Golan Heights in six remarkable days of blitz warfare. It was a war most Israelis continue to regard in defensive terms, a viewpoint which is true only if one accepts the Israeli definition of 'defense.' If one agrees with former Chief-of-Staff General Chaim Bar-Lev that "the best defense is to attack", then assuredly the Six-Day War was defensive.[5] If, on the other hand, one believes that attack constitutes offensive action (as Webster defined the word and at last glance its meaning still), then a far different conclusion becomes inescapable.[6]

In fact, the inclination of Israelis to regard the IDF's pre-emptive launching of the 1967 war as 'defensive' is consistent with the deeper problem of Zionism. That problem is *not* the historical link between the Jewish people and the land of Palestine (Israel) – a relationship that has never been denied, even by Israel's enemies – but rather, the commitment to *Eretz Israel,* a concept of 'greater' Israel implying Jewish control of lands extending to the Jordan River and beyond, to the exclusion of the indigenous Palestinian Arabs. Its legitimization was supposedly based on the authority of the ancient kingdoms of David and Solomon, as recorded in Hebrew Scripture. Yet because the territories of the ancient kingdoms shifted constantly, scriptural definitions of *Eretz Israel's* borders remain ambiguous to this day and open to wide interpretation among Jews.

Ben Gurion's reluctance to declare Israel's borders, therefore, becomes understandable. Though Israel had formally accepted the 1947 UN Partition, in practice things were very different. Zionists like Ben Gurion had their own pragmatic reasons for encouraging a maximalist concept of Israel rather than a compromise solution. First and foremost, Zionists were state-builders, concerned with practical solutions to immediate problems. Aside from security considerations, the greatest perceived need was for 'elbow room' – new lands in which to settle the anticipated waves of Jewish immigration, called *aliyahs,* which were to follow the creation of the new state. The writings of David Ben Gurion after the 1948-49 war are filled with passages reflecting his dissatisfaction with Israel's then current boundaries:

> *Every state consists of land and a people. Israel is no exception, but it is a State identical neither with its land nor with its people....It must now be said that it has been established in only a portion of the Land of Israel. Even those who are dubious as to the restoration of the historical frontiers, as...given form from the beginning of time, will hardly deny the anomaly of the boundaries of the new state.[7]*

Some of his writings were even more to the point. Years earlier Ben Gurion wrote to his son that:

> *A partial Jewish State is not the end, but only the beginning...I am certain that we will not be prevented from settling in the other parts of the country, either by mutual agreement with our Arab neighbors or by some other means...[If the Arabs refuse] we shall have to speak to them in a different language.[8]*

The hopes and plans of Zionists for a vast ingathering of world Jewry to Palestine explains the assumption – already discussed in Chapter Three – that a compromise solution would never be satisfactory. Given Israel's need for new lands, and the smallness of the country, it was assumed that no Jewish concessions could be made which would satisfy the Arab states. This line of thinking was summarized in 1965 – almost in anticipation of the coming war – by Yehoshafat Harkabi, one of Israel's leading strategists:

> *Israel because of its smallness enjoys very limited latitude in making concessions. Israel may suspect that any territorial concession is of importance to the Arabs if it is calculated to weaken Israel as a step towards a final onslaught....Israel, by the nature of her position, will prefer living dangerously rather than offering a concession incurring the danger of non-existence. Any concession which may weaken Israel is too big for her; for the Arabs, it is too small if it leaves the existence of Israel intact.[9]*

Notably, Harkabi's thinking was shared by the three men responsible for Israel's nuclear agenda – Ben Gurion, Peres, and Dayan. The rub is that Ben Gurion and his allies never imagined that Palestinian leaders would one day agree to accept a homeland in a small fraction – less than 30% – of the original Palestine Mandate. Yet such a shift *did* occur in the largest faction of the PLO, Fatah, in the mid-1970s, and led to the two-state compromise formula currently supported by the PLO[10] and virtually the entire world community – with the lone exceptions of Israel and the United States.

Optimal Defensive Borders?

In the euphoric days following the 1967 war, probably most Israeli generals believed that the nation had achieved optimal defensive boundaries, and that the country should content itself with consolidating its gains. This was Dayan's view: "Speaking purely theoretically, I doubt whether we could find more ideal borders than the present lines."[11] His view was shared by Chief-of-Staff Rabin: "From a military point of view, at least, our borders are now ideal."[12]

But it was Defense Minister Dayan, by virtue of his perceived leading role in the smashing victory, whose reputation was most enhanced by the 1967 war and who emerged as the dominant figure in the Eshkol government.[13] During this period Dayan's control expanded beyond the Defense Ministry. He soon became the principal architect of Israeli policy toward the Arab states. The rise in his fortunes as a result of the war also helps to explain his success in scuttling the nuclear nonproliferation policy of Levi Eshkol's government, and launching the country's nuclear build-up. Later, in Prime Minister Golda Meir's 'kitchen' cabinet, Dayan's influence became even greater. Before long Dayan was shaping government policy in other key areas. It was during this period that Dayan, as Chief Administrator of the newly occupied territories, assumed the leading role in formulating the policy of occupation. This included, but was not limited to, confiscation of Arab lands.[14] By 1969 Dayan was actively encouraging construction of the first Jewish settlements on the occupied West Bank, even though the cabinet supposedly frowned on the policy.[15] Years later, after Camp David, Dayan unabashedly explained the need – from a military standpoint – for introducing settlers into the territories:

> *I myself viewed an Israeli military presence in the West Bank and Gaza as inextricably bound up with settlement. I did not believe it was politically possible to maintain Israeli troops in these territories unless there were also an Israeli civilian population. I thought that several groups of Jewish*

villages should be established, with army units stationed in
or near them. If the population of the territories were
exclusively Arab, the role of the Israeli units would appear to
be that of an occupation force stationed among a resentful
population, and Israel would be under constant pressure to
remove it.[16]

In other words, settlers 'legitimized' IDF occupation all the way to the Jordan River, the favorable new defensive perimeter established by the 1967 war.

During this period Israel's nuclear program was being dramatically expanded and transformed, creating new political conditions at the same time. In addition to the bomb itself, Israel had gained a potent psychological weapon. All this was obvious to author Fuad Jabber as early as 1971, and noted in his classic study, *Israel and Nuclear Weapons*. By virtue of the nature of the threat embodied by nuclear weapons, they had become particularly useful for the perpetuation of a status quo which, "as a result of the Six-Day War," quoting Jabber, was now "markedly favorable to Israel territorially, economically, and strategically."[17] To be successful, however, perpetuation of the status quo required a policy of consolidation entailing the suppression of Palestinian resistance and culture. By the end of the Meir cabinet Jewish settlement of the West Bank had become official government policy.[18]

The same pattern continued and, if anything, was intensified following the Yom Kippur War during the Rabin government. This time, however, the torch was carried by Defense Minister Shimon Peres, who helped open the door for the fanatic Gush Emunim (Bloc of the Faithful) settlers. In his memoirs Rabin claimed that:

On a number of occasions...the Defense Minister [Peres]
behaved as if he was out to challenge the cabinet's authority
by taking his differences to the public. When we clashed over
the defense budget...Peres chose to make the issue a subject
of public debate. When the cabinet adopted a policy that
excluded the establishment of new settlements in the heavily
populated area of Samaria on the West Bank (in the belief
that Jewish settlement there was not justified by security
considerations and would only serve as a provocation to the
Arab population), Peres raised the banner of "settlement
everywhere."[19]

As for Rabin's own roots: during the War of Independence he commanded the second batallion of the *Palmach,* an elite commando unit dominated by MAPAM party members. Later, when Ben Gurion disbanded the force in a purge of left-wing officers from the army, Rabin was recruited to serve Ben Gurion's government. (Eventually MAPAM joined with Ben Gurion's party, MAPAI, to forge the Labor coalition.) It was the beginning of a long political career which at one time or another included nearly every important post in the cabinet.

As one of Israel's most 'moderate' leaders during the 1970s, Rabin had long been on record opposing the nuclear program and its agenda – though, as I have already stated, he made no overt attempt to block it.* In his memoirs, in a number of passages, Rabin as much as called Shimon Peres a liar. And he accused him outright of undermining the Labor party and contributing to its defeat by the right-wing Likud bloc in the elections of 1977. Surely Rabin understood the implications of linkage. Given the country's widening nuclear program, the pattern of consolidation advocated by Peres (echoing Dayan) could mean only one thing: a commitment to eliminate Palestinian nationalism as a factor in a future 'peace settlement' by creating new irreversible facts backed up by unprecedented military power. However, Rabin's memoirs revealed no hint: "...it is difficult to fathom why a cabinet minister would be interested in encouraging defiance of his own government's policy."[20]

This is not to suggest that Rabin's 'moderation' extended to Palestinian self-determination. Rabin the 'moderate' *never* supported the principle of Palestinian self-determination and freely admitted that "...there is really no ideal solution to the Palestinian problem."[21] As Noam Chomsky pointed out, Israel's two major political parties, Labor and Likud, have never disagreed on the essential point that Jordan would become the Palestinian homeland in a future peace agreement to be imposed on the Arab states. Rabin's opposition to Jewish settlement in certain areas of the West Bank and Gaza reflected the view held by some in the Labor party that heavily populated, predominantly Arab areas should be returned to Jordan to overcome the 'demographic' problem. By such an arrangement, Palestinians in selected areas would gain some administrative control (limited self-rule) over their

---

* Yoram Peri suggests Rabin may have attempted to frustrate Peres' nuclear agenda by forcing spending cuts on the Defense Ministry, even as he sought increased U.S. aid. Assuming such efforts were made, they failed. *Between Battles and Ballots*, pp. 170-171.

communities – enough to ensure that 'democratic' Israel would retain its Jewish character.[22] However, Labor fully agreed with Likud on the need to maintain military control, which explains why the 'moderate' Labor party could not endorse a Palestinian state. Most believed that Israel's security demanded the West Bank be so criss-crossed by IDF outposts, lines of communication and transport, that a truly independent Palestinian entity was simply not viable.

Likud had its own 'solution' for the 'demographic' problem, designed to preserve the best features of annexation (control) while avoiding its worst (i.e., the lamentable necessity of granting Arabs the political rights that come with Israeli citizenship.) The 'solution' amounted to political limbo for Palestinians. Menachem Begin coined a name for the fraud; he called it 'sovereignty.'[23] More recently, Begin's successor, Prime Minister Yitzhak Shamir, openly called for formal annexation of the West Bank, an alternative which, should it ever occur, would almost certainly lead to the forced expulsion of Palestinians to Jordan or elsewhere. Such a 'final solution' has long been advocated by elements within Likud as well as by those on the extreme right, such as the racist Meir Kahane.

As regards the West Bank and Gaza, Dayan's position was somewhere in between Labor and Likud. Initially Dayan supported the Labor formula of land for peace, the so-called Allon plan: partial Israeli withdrawal and limited Palestinian autonomy in association with Jordan. Following the Yom Kippur War, however, Dayan's views changed. Henceforth he rejected in principle the return of territories to Jordan.[24] In other words, Dayan's views moved nearer to Likud. Apparently the shift was an aftershock of the 1973 war, which to Dayan's way of thinking vividly demonstrated the strategic importance of the West Bank. His drift away from Labor no doubt explains why he was invited by Menachem Begin to cross the aisle and participate in the Camp David peace talks. Dayan continued – at least in his own mind – to distinguish between his own views and Likud. He always claimed that he opposed formal annexation and Begin's version of 'sovereignty' as much as he opposed autonomy.[25]

Dayan's 1976 Proposal

Dayan was an intellectual who dabbled in archaeology and even cultivated an appreciation for Arab history and culture. He continued to speak of the importance of reaching a mutual understanding – an 'arrangement' – with the Palestinians, a 'normalization' of relations based on a carrot-and-stick approach. But there was never any doubt about where he stood on the matter of Palestinian self-determination. In this regard, Dayan's readiness to extend strategic doctrine to the Jordan River perimeter is illuminating. In a lecture to the Israeli-American Chamber of Commerce in March 1976, Dayan proposed that Israel move to an openly-declared nuclear strategy. As explained by Avraham Schweitzer, a reporter from the daily *Ha'aretz,* the proposed new doctrine called for a solution to the Arab-Israeli conflict by making territorial concessions to Egypt and Syria, presumably involving land exchanges in the Sinai and the Golan Heights in return for peace.[26] Just as important, the newly-declared nuclear policy would 'give practical authorization' to such a peace settlement.

While it is true that Dayan was out of favor at the time due to the near-defeat suffered by Israel in the Yom Kippur War, it would be a serious mistake to discount his proposed new doctrine for this reason. Dayan was a perfect example of the old warrior who never dies. His role continued to be important, despite the ups and downs of his career. Even as an older man, Dayan was never far from the major developments shaping policy within Israel's military establishment. When it came to strategy, his views often prevailed. Dayan's pivotal role in the evolution of Israel's warfighting doctrine of retaliation, the nuclear agenda, and the West Bank settlement policy have already been described. The proposal he unveiled in 1976 therefore deserves careful attention, in retrospect.

While a nation's nuclear strategy defines the outer limits of its military doctrines, it is important to understand that nuclear strategy also incorporates essential political relationships. Dayan's proposed new doctrine was particularly interesting in that it never mentioned the Palestinians. Far from being a coincidence, the omission was Dayan's way of declaring the matter of Palestinian self-determination a dead letter. 'Practical authorization' implied that henceforth there would be linkage between nuclear strategy and the new realities on the West Bank. Years of creeping consolidation would be backed up by the ultimate coercive means. The proposal was a public announcement of facts recognized by Fuad Jabber and Yair Evron years before.

Nor were the implications of the proposed strategy lost on perceptive Arab observers. The Egyptian journalist Muhammad H. Heikal, for example, clearly understood that a separate peace with Egypt and Syria would mean increased pressure – backed up by constant intimidation and ultimately by nuclear threats – on the Arab states to keep the Palestinians in line. The new doctrine amounted to a new pecking order, with the Palestinians at the bottom:

> *With the bomb it [Israel] can deter Egypt and Syria....*
> *But what good is the bomb against the Palestinians? They*
> *have no cities, or factories, water reservoirs or anything at*
> *all. [ie., no targets.] The answer is that if Israel can deter*
> *Egypt and Syria with the bomb or threaten them without*
> *actually using it, we could imagine a new situation in which*
> *Egypt and Syria would be afraid of Israel's [nuclear]*
> *deterrent....The Palestinians would be afraid of the*
> *Egyptian-Syrian force of [conventional] arms. This would*
> *mean that Syria and Egypt would find themselves compelled*
> *to maintain Israel's security against the Palestinians. Thus*
> *they would be transformed into a police force for Israel.*[27]

It is noteworthy that Heikal's statement appeared several months *before* Dayan's new doctrine was announced. Clearly, the strategy was 'in the air,' obvious to anyone at the time who cared to know the facts. Dayan's proposal articulated developments already in the process of unfolding.

Dayan's 1976 proposal was probably also an effort to institute policy where none officially existed. It is shocking to suggest, but quite possible, that in a larger sense Israeli nuclear strategy had never been systematically thought out. As Major General Israel Tal once said, "Instead of operational thinking being tailored out of...military strategy, there has been confusion and the process has sometimes taken the opposite direction."[28] Dayan no doubt realized that nuclear weapons development was rapidly creating new realities which badly needed to be addressed. Creating a policy for facts already on the ground was essential. Nuclear strategy was simply too important to be allowed to ferment in an ad hoc way. An operationally defined nuclear strategy made foreign policy look like an afterthought, as indeed it was: the proverbial cart before the horse.

The 1976 doctrine was also consistent with other changes in conventional strategy which occurred in the aftermath of the Yom Kippur War.[29] The failure of static 'defense in depth' (the Bar-Lev Line) in that war – along with the Maginot Line mentality it represented – was generating a return to the former battle-proven doctrine of interdiction and pre-emptive attack.[30] The October 1973 war had demonstrated that the Sinai was as much a military liability as an asset. Specifically, holding the Sinai was not essential for Israel's security, provided the state of 'no war-no peace' in the south could be stabilized by a modest peace arrangement with Egypt.[31] Dayan's proposal was the perfect complement to such a deal: Israel would back up a treaty with nuclear power.

Camp David

The doctrine proposed by Moshe Dayan in 1976 anticipated the Camp David 'peace process' to a considerable degree. As we know, Dayan went on to play an important role in those talks which forged a separate peace between Israel and Egypt. The hallmark of that agreement was the return of the Sinai by Israel in exchange for diplomatic recognition, cultural and economic ties, and – of central importance – the capitulation of Egyptian President Anwar Sadat on the Palestinian issue. For this, Egypt was rewarded by the United States with a payoff amounting to billions in U.S. assistance – with which Sadat hoped to bail his country out of a deepening economic crisis.[32] In public, Sadat continued to speak of Palestinian rights during the negotiations. But according to writer David Hirst, the transparency of the arrangement became obvious the day of the signing ceremony on the White House lawn, as demonstrated by a conspicuous omission in Sadat's prepared statement. At the last minute the Egyptian President deleted the following paragraphs from his speech:

> *No one is more entitled to your support and backing than the Palestinian people. A grave injustice was inflicted on them in the past. They need a reassurance that they will be able to take the first step on the road to self-determination and statehood.*
>
> *A dialogue between the United States and the representatives of the Palestinian people will be a very helpful development. On the other hand, we must be certain that the provisions of the Camp David framework on the establishments of a self-governing authority with full autonomy are carried out. There must be a genuine transfer of authority to the Palestinians in their land. Without that, the problem will remain unsolved.[33]*

After the speech Mohammed Hakki, spokesman for the Egyptian Embassy, claimed that "the President inadvertently turned two pages, instead of one" while reading his address. Author David Hirst had a different interpretation: "It was an appropriate omission. The betrayal of the Palestinians lay at the heart of this separate peace which he [Sadat] swore he would never sign."[34]

Though the Camp David Accords provided for autonomy talks on the Palestinian question, in addition to a separate peace with Egypt, in reality it was all mirrors and smoke. In the interests of facilitating an agreement, Jimmy Carter decided that the issues should not be conditional on one another, thus abandoning the goal of a comprehensive settlement. Viewed with hindsight, Carter's two-track approach was obviously predicated on the assumption that *any* agreement was preferable to none. Adoption of a two-track approach took Menachem Begin off the hook, providing the slack he needed to achieve his own objectives without making concessions on the central Palestinian issue. Nor did the U.S. press the matter.[35]

In the weeks before the signing, the Israeli negotiators managed to tiptoe around the question so as not to undermine the treaty by embarrassing Sadat in public. In one interview in Paris, Dayan refused to enter into a debate on Palestinian autonomy since, as he put it, "...if the Egyptians understand Israel's real intentions on this matter they will not sign the peace treaty."[36] On that occasion Dayan did not elaborate what those "real intentions" might be. There was no need to do so in any case. The real linkage was obvious: it had been created by years of creeping annexation and military expansion. In fact, Dayan had laid out the formula – an Israeli-imposed military solution – in his 1976 press conference.

The fact that the entire world regarded the continuing occupation as illegal was unpleasant and inconvenient, but it mattered less than the speedy creation of even more settlements to thicken the Jewish presence and cement the irreversibility of Israeli control. Within days of the signing, Prime Minister Begin told the Knesset and the world that "Israel will never return to the borders of 4 June 1967."[37]

The Perennial Tension:
Economic Dependence/Military Independence

Moshe Dayan's 1976 proposal to 'go public' with the bomb did not become official government policy. Far from being a high-level repudiation of his views on strategy, however, the decision probably reflected the perennial tension between military independence on the one hand and Israel's need for positive foreign relations on the other.

The trade-off between the two factors is more than sufficient to explain the persistence of nuclear ambiguity, even following Vanunu's revelation,[38] despite Dayan's urging toward a public policy.

As already mentioned in an earlier chapter, in 1977 and 1978 the U.S. Congress passed legislation making continuing American aid conditional on nuclear nonproliferation.[39] And in 1977 the UN passed an arms embargo aimed at South Africa. In such an unfavorable climate Israel could not 'go public' without damaging its all important image – especially in America – and running the very real risk of an economic embargo.[40]

On the other hand, Israeli cold warriors like Moshe Dayan and Ariel Sharon instinctively gravitated to the other side of the equation: military independence. Their prime consideration was always freedom of action. This was the rationale offered by Dayan in the mid-1950s in rejecting an Israeli security pact with the United States:

> ...such a pact will only constitute an obstacle for us....The security pact [with the U.S.] will only handcuff us and deny us the freedom of action which we need in the coming years. Reprisal actions which we couldn't carry out if we were tied to a security pact are our vital lymph...they make it possible for us to maintain a high level of tension among our population and in the army. Without these actions we would have ceased to be a combative people and without the discipline of a combative people we are lost. We have to cry out that the Negev is in danger, so that young men will go there.[41]

It should be recognized that Dayan was not slavish in the pursuit of military independence. On occasion he could show a keen appreciation for political realities. For example, in the hours immediately preceeding the 1973 Yom Kippur War, when an Arab attack appeared imminent, Dayan advised Prime Minister Golda Meir to overrule the request of Chief-of-Staff General Elazar to launch a pre-emptive air strike against Syrian missile (SAM) batteries and airfields. On that occasion Dayan believed the political disadvantages of striking first outweighed the military gains.[42]

Still, Dayan's basic philosophy never changed. His proposal in 1976 to make limited territorial concessions on Israel's southern and northern frontiers was a rejection of static defense-in-depth and a return to the former reliance on freedom of movement. Nor did Camp

David moderate his basic views. During an interview in 1980, a year before he died, Dayan reiterated almost verbatim the ideas he had expressed in 1976, adding: "I don't want to enter into any details here. The concept of quality is enough for me; and it really is a diversified concept ranging from nuclear weapons to electronic weapons and conventional arms."* At the time that Dayan was speaking, the diversification to which he referred was proceeding full steam ahead. Thanks to Mordechai Vanunu's testimony, we know that by 1980 Israel was developing fusion weapons; in other words, strategic thermonuclear weapons, and possibly neutron bombs.[43] Soon after, in 1981, Israel conducted the first tests of the new Jericho II missile, a solid-fuel rocket far more accurate than its predecessor, the Jericho I, and with twice the range. According to expert Leonard Spector, documents abandoned at the Israeli trade mission in Tehran after the fall of the Shah in 1979 pointed to Dayan's involvement in the joint Israeli-Iranian project, "Operation Flower," which developed the missile: "One of the documents...contains the minutes of a 1977 conversation in Tel Aviv between the then Israeli Foreign Minister Moshe Dayan and Iranian General Hassan Toufanian in which the missile was discussed." Later Toufanian acknowledged the authenticity of the documents. They prove that Dayan was privy to the latest advances on the frontier of Israeli research and development.[44] All this, together with his remarkable candor – frequently mentioned in various accounts – make Dayan's public statements extremely valuable in assessing Israeli strategies.

Officially, Israel would continue to have no bomb, and therefore, no nuclear strategy. Meanwhile, the pressing need for such a policy was no less real. For these reasons, as we shall see in a subsequent chapter, a national security debate on the issue eventually became inevitable.

---

* Jimmy Carter recently claimed that during the Camp David talks Dayan stated "That one of his greatest desires was to stop the occupation, because it was not only damaging to the Palestinians who lived under it, but it was also destroying the moral structure of life among Israeli Jews as well." It should be obvious that this statement is irreconcilable with the position re-stated by Dayan in 1980. How is this seeming contradiction to be explained? In the author's view, it *cannot* be explained – which is the whole point. The irresolvable contradiction nakedly epitomizes the tragedy of Zionism. "Interview: Jimmy Carter," *American-Arab Affairs,* Winter, 1987-88, p. 32; *Ha'aretz*, August 27, 1980.

Nuclear Leverage

Before discussing Israel's use of threats, an important qualification must be attached to this study. In no way does this section seek to single out Israel for special condemnation – to the exclusion of others equally culpable. It is a matter of public record that successive U.S. presidents employed nuclear threats to implement foreign policy on at least a dozen occasions since 1946.[45] Citing Israel without also condemning the initial source of such threats – i.e., the White House – would be unpardonable hypocrisy.

It is my conviction that all nuclear threats – past, present and future – undermine the legitimate authority of governments in general by institutionalizing the exercise of terror as an instrument of state policy. Indeed, this is also the fundamental moral argument against nuclear weapons. As Phillip and Daniel Berrigan and others have unceasingly tried to point out, the mere existence of nuclear weapons is blasphemous in a spiritual sense, because by their very existence fear is granted a sanction and official status it does not deserve – binding men everywhere in a covenant of death. It follows that all attempts to justify such weapons are fraudulent, amounting to complicity with moral blackmail and political extortion. Is it any wonder in 1988 that grassroots liberation movements the world over scoff at the nuclear-armed club? Apparently it is the poor and the dispossessed who – with little or nothing to lose – perceive more clearly the deeper spiritual reality.

Unfortunately, political leaders time and again have proven themselves 'immune' to moral arguments; so perhaps it is too much to hope that 'mere' moral persuasion can effect the necessary changes before it is too late. Hence the urgent need to go straight to the people with the pertinent documentation. (Obvious precedents: Mordechai Vanunu, Daniel Ellsberg.) As the U.S. proxy, Israel provides the clearest possible lens through which to see how U.S. foreign policy has gone wrong. At very least, this study ought to demonstrate the bankruptcy of previous arguments – such as Blechman's 'prestigious' Brookings study – purportedly showing the value of 'force without war'.[46] Clearly, the Israelis have well learned their trade (in threats) from us. Sooner or later, one is led round-about to the inevitable conclusion that *any* nuclear threat directed at any state ultimately becomes a threat to all.

In 1988 one can justifiably wonder whether these lessons will be learned in time. The rebounding of threats has had a crippling effect in Washington. The American people have yet to be heard on the issue.

Threats – or the hint of threats – have been a part of U.S.-Israeli relations since at least the period of the 1973 Yom Kippur War. The fact was recognized by Johns Hopkins scholar Robert Tucker in an influential 1975 article in *Commentary* magazine. In the article Tucker called an Israeli nuclear arsenal "..a form of insurance against Israel's desertion by America and, more concretely, a bargaining chip in Israel's requests for conventional arms – in effect, a polite form of blackmail."[47]

While the use of nuclear weapons as leverage had its roots in the Israeli A-bomb program of the late 1950s and early 1960s, exactly when the strategy's full potential was consciously recognized remains open to question. Certainly Levi Eshkol's 1966 deal with Lyndon Johnson freezing Israel's nuclear program in return for conventional arms was an early example of leverage. Recent statements by one highly credible source suggests that a strategy of 'polite blackmail' was intended from the beginning. The week following the October, 1986 Vanunu revelation in the London *Sunday Times*, the paper carried an interview with Francis Perrin, the former French High Commissioner for Atomic Energy. In addition to confirming Vanunu's basic story, which disclosed the existence of an Israeli nuclear arsenal of 100-200 warheads, Perrin went on to summarize his view of Israeli nuclear strategy:

> We thought the Israeli bomb was aimed against the Americans, not to launch it against America but to say "If you don't want to help us in a critical situation we will require you to help us; otherwise we will use our nuclear bombs."[48]

As France's top nuclear scientist during the 1950s, Perrin led the French team which helped Israel construct the Dimona reactor. Because of his intimate association with the Israeli program, of all non-Israelis, Perrin was uniquely placed to know the facts.

Perrin's statement offers an invaluable insight – though it is worth pointing out that initially it was the United States which used, or attempted to use, pressure. On different occasions Presidents Kennedy and Johnson each employed a carrot-and-stick approach with Israel, promising conventional arms in return for promises to abstain from developing a nuclear weapons option. The failure of their efforts is now history.* On the other hand, *after* Israel crossed the nuclear threshold the tables were suddenly reversed; from then on it was Israel who applied leverage – with great success. So while Perrin is probably correct in claiming that Israel had always intended to use its nuclear weapons to blackmail the U.S., in actual fact the mechanism necessary to implement the threat was only achieved by the production of nuclear weapons.

As late as 1970 Golda Meir suggested in an interview in the German magazine *Der Speigel* that the United States should force the Soviets out of the Middle East, even if it brought about another 'Cuban missile crisis.'[49] Meir's statement, apart from being shocking, suggests that in 1970 Israeli thinking had not strayed far beyond the American nuclear shield. On the other hand, it also implies that Meir was perfectly willing to risk World War III to shore up Israel's position.

The Yom Kippur War

A case could probably be made that the strategy of leverage did not assume real prominence until the circumstances of the 1973 Yom Kippur War demonstrated its efficacy in a crisis situation. It was during the critical first phase of that war, when the tide appeared to have swung against Israel, that Moshe Dayan reportedly told Golda Meir, "I am not sure we can hold out much longer. This is the end of the Third Temple." By the same account, Meir then approved the arming of Israel's doomsday weapons for the first time.[50] Hours later, the battle on the Golan Heights turned in Israel's favor; but to counterattack on the southern front Israel still needed resupply. It was at this stage of the

* Meyer Feldman, a former assistant to John F. Kennedy, confirmed that Kennedy offered Hawk surface-to-air missiles in return for an Israeli commitment not to develop nuclear weapons. Similar pressure was continued under President Johnson. This time, however, the carrot was the F-4 Phantom jet. *New York Times,* June 16, 1968. In the end, however, Israel got the Phantoms – without making *any* concessions on nuclear regulations/controls – even though President Johnson had been informed of the secret diversion of enriched uranium from NUMEC. In his study, Leonard Spector argued that the sale of the Phantoms to Israel marked a weakening of U.S. resolve and a turning point in U.S. nonproliferation policy: from a posture of actively opposing secret Israeli weapons development to outright complicity. Spector, *Nuclear Proliferation Today,* p. 126.

war, as recounted by Nadav Safran, that Israel delivered its first thinly veiled nuclear threat to Washington:

> *On October 13, 1973 [Israeli Ambassador] Simha Dinitz reiterated his country's case and needs, complained bitterly about the runaround given to its arms request and concluded with an ominous warning. "If a massive airlift to Israel does not start immediately, then I will know that the United States is reneging on its promises and...we will have to draw very serious conclusions from all this...." Kissinger, along with a few people in the top government echelons, had long known that Israel possessed a...nuclear option...but he had not dwelt on this issue because of the remoteness of the contingency that would make it relevant. Suddenly...the scenario of...Israel...on the verge of destruction resorting to nuclear weapons, hitherto so hypothetical, assumed grim reality. The Secretary of State, whose policy had been inspired by the desire to preserve detente and by fear of a total Israeli victory, did not need much pondering to imagine the catastrophic consequences....Very late that night [Kissinger] met the President and reviewed the situation with him. The next morning the President summoned his principal advisors to an emergency conference at the White House and ordered them...immediately to provide Israel with all the arms it needed....All the previous insuperable problems vanished like a morning mist and by dawn the next day the first flights of a massive airlift were on their way to Israel.[51]*

Partly as a result of the United States arms pipeline, the momentum of battle swung back against Egypt. Soon Kissinger's efforts to stave off a superpower confrontation were stretched to the limit. It was at this stage of the war that U.S. intelligence reported a Soviet transport, probably loaded with nuclear weapons, passing from the Black Sea through the Bosphorus, headed for Alexandria, Egypt.[52] Apparently the Soviets, having detected Israeli preparations for nuclear escalation through their own intelligence-gathering spy satellites, had dispatched the shipload of nuclear warheads from their naval base of Nikolayev near Odessa. The warheads were designed to fit Egyptian SCUD missiles. At the same time Soviet leader Brezhnev announced that the Soviet Union was contemplating "unilateral action."[53]

The specter of Soviet intervention brought an immediate U.S. display of counter-force. President Nixon ordered a worldwide nuclear alert. According to a *Washington Post* report, "another U.S. signal at the time," never before made public, was "a private message to the Soviets that said...the United States 'might not be able to restrain someone else [Israel] from "taking out" Soviet nuclear warheads.'" In other words, the U.S. consciously played to Soviet fears of an Israeli 'wild card' to force the Soviets to back down – which they did. Fortunately, the Soviet transport turned around and headed for home.[54]

At the same time the U.S. brought tremendous pressure to bear on Israel. In the course of those critical hours – made all the more urgent by the bold Israeli counterthrust behind the Egyptian lines and General Adan's threatened encirclement of the Egyptian Third Army – world order seemed to be slipping from Kissinger's grasp.* In this context, his less-than-tactful cease-fire ultimatum to Golda Meir becomes understandable. As we now know – since we live to talk about it – on that occasion U.S. pressure succeeded. Golda Meir flew to the southern front in a helicopter to personally deliver the order to cease the battle.[55] Yet because American pressure deprived the IDF of victory, it was deeply resented in Israel – notwithstanding the narrow escape from World War III – and had the effect of overturning Israeli confidence in Israel's position vis-à-vis the United States. Whether the Israeli interpretation was warranted or not,[56] the crisis certainly did reveal the full spectrum of psychological effects of nuclear threats, from power to impotence. It was a hair-raising illustration of how weapons of mass destruction could be used without even touching the trigger.

Arguably, Israel's decision to develop strategic thermonuclear weapons, in addition to cruise and Jericho II missiles – with range sufficient to target the southern Soviet Union – was the progeny of those events, which had revealed an apparent gap between Israeli and American vital interests.[57] In her memoirs, published after the war, Golda Meir warned "the world in general and Israel's enemies in particular" that the circumstances of the Yom Kippur War would never be allowed to recur.[58] Her meaning: Israel would take steps to guard against being pressured in a similar fashion in a future crisis.

---

* This is a figure of speech. I do not mean to imply that world order was ever really in Kissinger's hands – though the former Secretary of State may have convinced himself and others of this delusion. It is my conviction that world order has always rested in hands far greater than Kissingers'.

None of this was obvious in 1975. Robert Tucker's article in *Commentary,* which probably reflected the views of many American conservatives and liberals at the time, had cautiously endorsed an Israeli nuclear deterrent – then thought to consist of a 'scant' 20-25 atomic weapons of last resort. To be sure, the endorsement was not without qualification. To his credit, Tucker accurately foresaw the inherent dangers of a strategy which included threats, however 'polite.' Knowing what we know today, the close of Tucker's 1975 essay rings almost like prophecy:

> *It is ironic that perhaps the most serious danger attending an Israeli nuclear strategy...is so seldom mentioned. A nuclear deterrent would, I have argued here , largely deliver Israel from the dangers it presently faces. But what would prevent Israel, once delivered...from pursuing a hawkish policy and employing a nuclear deterrent to freeze the status quo?[59]*

Tucker's 1975 warning needs to be repeated in 1988. After all, it is in the nature of wild cards to be wild. The same card aimed at the Soviets in 1973 could, under different circumstances, be played elsewhere.

"Diplomacy by other means"

That such a fearful possibility had real substance was later borne out by events. Specifically, at the time of King Fahd's Saudi Arabian peace proposal in August 1981, Israel's response – in addition to categorical rejection of the plan – was to mount provocative military overflights of Saudi airspace. Apparently a form of "diplomacy by other means," the flights conveyed the threat of an irrational reaction should Washington apply pressure on Israel to negotiate. What that "irrational behavior" might consist of was discussed by writer Daniel Bloch in the Labor party daily, *Davar:*

> *Last week both Begin and [Foreign Minister] Shamir gave strong hints that the adoption of the Fahd plan by the world might cause Israel to reconsider various policies, among them the planned evacuation of the rest of Sinai [part of the Camp David Accords]. This [and the flights over Saudi Arabia] must have caused many foreign intelligence*

*agencies to reach for old files containing statements by
Israeli generals about Israel's capacity to bomb the Saudi
oilfields. After the bombing of the Iraqi reactor, Israel is
thought capable of such acts.*[60]

The Saudi plan called for a two-state settlement with recognized
borders and security guarantees for Israel. In other words, it was
consistent with previous UN resolutions calling for Israeli withdrawal
from the occupied territories and was anything but a repudiation of
Israel's existence. Nevertheless it was denounced by Foreign Minister
Yitzhak Shamir, who claimed the plan was "dangerous to Israel, was
rejected in the past and is rejected now." It was also criticized by Labor
leaders, including Yitzhak Rabin and Shimon Peres.[61] Some Israeli
moderates were horrified by the irrationality of their government's
response. One such writer, Amos Elon, described it as "shocking,
frightening, if not downright despair-producing."[62]

"..it will make Beirut look like peanuts."

Another instance occurred the following year, during the IDF's
invasion of Lebanon, at the time of the siege of West Beirut. After
weeks of Israeli saturation bombing of the city, White House patience
began to wear thin when commander Ariel Sharon abrogated cease-
fires arranged by U.S. Ambassador Phillip Habib, and intensified the
bombardment in an attempt to kill the PLO leadership.[63] At that point
even President Reagan was no longer able to ignore mounting public
outrage at the indiscriminate destruction – its scale was horrifying –
and mildly criticized the Israeli assault, calling it "a disproportionate"
move. In a letter to Prime Minister Begin, the President stated that
Israel's actions raised questions about whether American weapons and
ammunition were being used by Israel for "legitimate self defense" – a
historic bit of understatement, according to former Under-Secretary of
State George Ball.[64] In the letter Reagan urged Begin to return to the
cease-fire lines of the previous day and end the "unnecessary
bloodshed." Begin's angry response to the mildly worded criticism
was: "Nobody should preach to us. Nobody, nobody is going to bring
Israel to her knees. You must have forgotten that the Jews kneel but to
God." The Israeli cabinet brusquely rejected Reagan's appeal for
restraint. Soon after, a "senior Israeli official" warned that any U.S.
pressure on Israel would provoke "an unpredictable" reaction;

according to the official, such an action "will have a contrary effect and America will lose all of its leverage. Then what Israel will do is unpredictable, but it will make Beirut look like peanuts."[65] The threat was unmistakable, but instead of meeting it with strength, the U.S. response was, as George Ball put it, to turn the other cheek.[66]

"Don't get Jerusalem too nervous...."

A different kind of threat occurred in early 1983. It was delivered by Tom Dine, the executive director of the Israeli lobbying organization, AIPAC (American Israel Public Affairs Committee). Dine had just returned from Jerusalem, where he had met with Israeli government officials. In a blistering speech delivered in Atlanta shortly after his return, Dine warned that "U.S.-Israeli relations are seriously strained," with the two nations on "a collision course" because of Reagan Administration policies. Dine cited numerous complaints. He criticized Caspar Weinberger for "his readiness, indeed eagerness, to assume the worst about Israel." He accused the Administration of "removing all pro-Israeli voices from the inner circles of decision-making," of pursuing a policy of "systematically excluding Israel from U.S. defense planning while fawningly courting certain Arab regimes whose conduct contradicts and conflicts with U.S. foreign policy." And Dine contended that the White House had "invoked more sanctions over a longer period than any preceding administration."

In actual fact, the circumstances Dine cited were nothing more nor less than the direct fallout from Israel's unprovoked invasion of Lebanon the previous year.[67] Dine's so-called sanctions were delays in U.S. arms shipments to Israel imposed as a *direct consequence* of the Lebanon invasion.

This explains Israel's recourse to open threats; in the aftermath of a brutal invasion, polite leverage was, from the standpoint of tonality, out of key. "All of this" Dine claimed, "is having a disastrous effect on the Israeli side....An important minority of Israelis are coming to believe that the U.S. is not a reliable ally, that sooner or later it will sell out Israel to appease the Arabs." For these reasons, he continued, "an increasing number of Israelis believe...they must end their dependence on U.S. support." Accordingly, Dine warned, if U.S. sanctions continue they might tempt Israel to "consider sweeping measures to eliminate the [Arab] threat while the IDF is still comparatively strong." *Jerusalem Post* correspondent Wolf Blitzer described the content of the new threat: "A possible pre-emptive strike by Israel against its Arab adversaries designed to cripple their military capabilities for a long time to come. Don't get Jerusalem too nervous, Dine implied."[68]

During this period the Soviets were in process of rearming Syria, replacing the military hardware Israel had destroyed the previous year. In fact, a week earlier, on February 24, Israel's new Defense Minister, Moshe Arens, had publicly warned Moscow that Israel "might make a pre-emptive strike against Syria if the build-up of long-range Soviet missiles there continued."[69] In reality, the new missiles were tactical weapons, with a range of under 100 miles. However, given the compressed geography of the region, from Israel's standpoint they were regarded as strategic weapons. Nor did the cycle of threats end there. On March 17 the Soviets countered with a threat of their own, explicitly warning Israel against a surprise attack on the new Syrian missile batteries.[70]

Dine's warning to Washington had been carefully timed; it came while the administration's request for aid to Israel was before Congress. In fact, after his Atlanta speech Dine carried the Israeli warning directly to Capitol Hill, in testimony before the Senate Foreign Relations Committee – testimony which pandered to President Reagan's fantasies of the Soviet 'evil empire':

> *Israel must now take into account even the Soviet Union itself as a potential threat....Russia has seven airborne divisions whose troops and equipment could be introduced rapidly into a Middle East conflict. It also has several thousand military personnel already on the ground in Syria.[71]*

Dine urged Congress to improve on President Reagan's aid request, emphasizing "Israel's strategic value to the U.S. Thanks largely to Israel" he said, "the Mediterranean basin is now largely an American lake," a fact "which has not escaped the attention of Moscow."[72]

Washington's response to Dine's onslaught was full retreat. As Blitzer put it, "If [the] intention was to scare senior White House officials, then [it] succeeded." Congress voted to expand the next economic and military aid package, even though this could only be interpreted as a U.S. endorsement of Israel's Lebanon invasion. Nor did President Reagan insist on attaching conditions, despite the undeniable fact that the aid package would be used in support of Israel's West

Bank settlement policy – which Reagan had explicitly opposed just months before. *

Nor was there a public response from the 'peace' movement to what should have been equally obvious: that by pushing the day of reckoning on the central matter of the Palestinians into the future, Ronald Reagan and the U.S. Congress virtually guaranteed that the final shocks, when they came, would be magnified many times over.

'Polite blackmail' has continued in recent years. In a January 1987 interview in the *Christian Science Monitor,* Amos Rubin, an economic minister to Prime Minister Yitzhak Shamir, unveiled a plan to reverse the present net emigration of Jews from Israel to America by raising the Israeli standard of living. Rubin called on the United States "to help restructure the Israeli economy by at least sustaining, if not increasing, its current level of grants, which this year [1987] will total $3 billion in civilian and military aid" (about $8 million per day). The basis for aid, as stated by Rubin, goes beyond a shared belief in democracy and the common Judaeo-Christian heritage – beyond even a mutual determination to defend the West from any Soviet threat. The overriding reason why America should continue easing Israel's financial burden of fielding massive conventional forces was pragmatism:

> *If left to its own, [Israel] will have no choice but to fall back on a riskier defense which will endanger itself and the world at large....To enable Israel to abstain from dependence on nuclear arms calls for $2-3 billion [per year] in US aid.*

In this case no attempt was made to conceal the underlying nuclear threat. Rubin even called for increases in what he called "direct payments."

Rubin did not point out other pertinent details, namely, that Israel built up its nuclear arsenal during the very period when the spigot of American aid had opened, and largely *because* of that aid – not in its

* As a part of the Reagan Peace Plan, proposed on September 1, 1982, President Reagan had called for a freeze on construction of new Israeli settlements on the occupied West Bank. Menachem Begin's response two days later: defiant announcement of plans for 57 new settlements over four years, in addition to a stern letter to Reagan, amounting to a lecture on the historic connection of the Jewish people to Judea and Samaria. *New York Times,* September 2, 3, 4, 5, 6, 9, 1982.

absence – since Israel did not possess the financial resources to pursue both paths simultaneously without assistance. Moreover, Rubin's unstated assumption that U.S. conventional arms would enable Israel to maintain Israeli hegemony in the region in the future consistent with its role as a U.S. ally – without resorting to nuclear weapons – is itself open to serious question, as we shall see.

Notes to Chapter Six

1. Leonard Beaton, "The International Political Context," in Mason Willrich, Editor, 1971. *Civil Nuclear Power and International Security,* New York, Praeger, p. 78.

2. Cited in Green, *Taking Sides,* op cit, p. 151.

3. Yair Evron, "Israel and the Atom: the Uses and Abuses of Ambiguity 1957-1967," *Orbis,* Volume 17, Winter, 1974, p. 162.

4. Jabber, op cit, p.147.

5. Quoted in the Jewish Observer and Middle East Review, January 5, 1968, p. 8.

6. Zionists called Israel's blitz attack a defensive move to preempt an imminent Egyptian assault, a view that is not supported by the facts. Nasser's closure of the Straits of Tiran was as much a pretext as it was a provocation. U.S. intelligence, as well as UN reports, discounted the likelihood of an Egyptian attack on Israel. U.S. high altitude reconnaissance demonstrated Nasser's forces were in a defensive posture. Nasser himself denied he wanted war. Nor was there any threat to Israel's existence in any case. Secretary of Defense MacNamara told Israeli Ambassador Abba Eban that – based on U.S. intelligence – in a fight Israel would win regardless of who struck first; he therefore urged restraint. The Israeli General Staff also was informed of Israel's overwhelming military superiority, despite official government pronouncements to the contrary. Neff, *Warriors for Jerusalem.* op cit, pp. 120-121 and 136, 140, 163 and 315.

As cited by Chomsky, the Israeli Air Force Commander Ezer Weizmann later stated there had been "no threat of destruction." *Ha'aretz* March 29, 1972. Similar statements were made by other Israeli military leaders, such as Chief-of-Staff Chaim Bar-Lev and General Mattityahu Peled. John Cooley, 1973. *Green March, Black September.* London, Frank Cass, pp. 161-162; also see Chomsky, op cit, p. 100.

Even arch-hawk Menachem Begin admitted in a 1982 speech that there was no threat to Israel's existence: "In June 1967 we had a choice. The Egyptian army concentrations in the Sinai approaches do not prove that Nasser was really about to attack us. We must he honest with ourselves. We decided to attack him." Begin knew what he was talking about. In the days preceding the 1967 war he had been invited into the war cabinet by Prime Minister Levi Eshkol. Speech given at the National Defense College August 8, reprinted in the *New York*

Times August 21, 1982; also see Bar- Joseph, "The Hidden Debate," op cit, p. 215; S. Aronson, 1978. *Conflict and Bargaining in the Middle East,* Baltimore, Johns Hopkins, pp. 95-96; Beit-Hallahmi, op cit, p.117.

According to former French President Charles de Gaulle, as early as 1959 David Ben Gurion "revealed to me his intention of extending [Israel's] frontiers at the earliest opportunity." de Gaulle, op cit, pp. 256-266.

Nasser's closing of the straits was provocative, but it had some legal basis. Egypt had continued to insist that the straits lay within Egyptian territorial waters. As David Hirst put it: "The Israelis' claim to right of passage. . . .was indeed an exceedingly dubious one; it was based on possession of a thin sliver of coastline, and this itself had been secured, on the Israelis' own admission, by one of those 'calculated violations [of the cease-fire] which we had to carefully weigh against the political risks.' That was in 1949, during the final stages of the war of independence, when in defiance of a UN sponsored cease-fire, an Israeli patrol thrust southward to the Arab hamlet... of Um Rashrash, expelling its inhabitants and founding the port of Eilat in its place." Incidentally, the 1949 thrust to the Gulf of Aqaba signaled the abandonment of Ben Gurion's collusion with King Abdallah. In other words, besides being an act of pure expedience, arguably it was also a betrayal. The thrust southward placed Abdallah in an utterly compromised situation, vis-à-vis his own people. The Israeli advance occurred under the very guns of Abdallah's troops, who were in perfect position along the Jordanian border to intervene. Abdallah, remaining true to the collusion, ordered his guns to remain silent – conspicuously so – damning the King in the eyes of own own people. Not long afterward, Abdallah was assassinated. Hirst, *Olive Branch,* op cit, p. 208; also see pp. 213-215 for a study of the Israeli provocations on the Syrian border which led to Nasser's fatal decision to close Tiran.

Though it did not threaten Israel's existence, Nasser's closing of the straits did represent a challenge of a different sort. As noted by the perceptive Egyptian journalist/editor M.H. Heikal, it was the first time an Arab state had imposed a *fait accompli* of any kind on Israel. This explains why Israel's military men favored a preventive war. Israeli military doctrine insisted that no challenge could go unanswered: to do so would be interpreted as weakness. As Heikal put it: "It is not a matter of the Gulf of Aqaba but of something bigger. It is the whole philosophy of Israeli security. Hence I say that Israel must attack."

Thus Heikal predicted the Israeli response days before it came. What he could not predict was the overwhelming nature of that attack. Nasser's closing of Tiran provided Israel's leaders with a convenient pretext to continue Ben Gurion's plans for expansion of Israel's borders based on the commitment to *Eretz* Israel. Muhammad H. Heikel, *Al-Ahram* (Cairo), May 26, 1967; also see Jabber op cit, pp. 113-115.

A few months after the war, Shimon Peres admitted in an interview by the Histadrut newspaper *Davar* that Israel had attacked to stave off a possible diplomatic defeat. The reasoning was as follows: by choosing not to re-open Tiran by force, Israel laid itself open to international pressure. The issue of Tiran was certain to face arbitration, as for example in the World Court, taking a favorable settlement of the issue out of Israeli hands. It was this 'threat' which prompted a preventive war. *Davar,* November 25, 1967.

Former President Carter's inability to recognize these important facts, as indicated in his own 1985 account, helps explain why he was handily out-foxed at Camp David by Menachem Begin. Jimmy Carter, 1985. *The Blood of Abraham,* Boston, Houghton Mifflin Company, p. 37-38.

7.   David Ben Gurion, "Israel Among the Nations," *Israel Government Year Book:* 1952, p. 15.

8.   Cited along with other examples in Chomsky, op cit, p. 162.

9.   Yehoshafat Harkabi, "The Arab-Israeli Confrontation: An Israeli View," (paper presented at the 7th annual conference of the Institute for Strategic Studies, London, October 3, 1965), pp. 4-5.

10. For extensive documentation on this important point see Noam Chomsky's essay and footnotes to "The Continuing Threat of Peace" in *The Fateful Triangle,* op cit, pp. 75-80.

11. Hodes, op cit, p. 142.

12. Quoted in the *Jewish Observer and Middle East Review,* January 5, 1968, p. 7.

13. Perlmutter, *Politics and the Military in Israel,* (1978), pp. 64-65; also see Bar-Joseph, "The Hidden Debate," op cit, p. 221; Avram Schweitzer, 1986. *Israel: The Changing National Agenda,* London, Croom Helm, pp. 40-49.

14. Peri, *Between Battles,* op cit, p. 96.

15. Perlmutter, *Politics and Military in Israel* (1978), op cit, pp. 64-65 and 75; also see Chomsky, op cit, p. 104.

16. Moshe Dayan, 1981: *Breakthrough: a Personal Account of the Egypt-Israel Peace Negotiations,* New York, Alfred A. Knopf, p. 185.

17. Jabber, op cit, p. 147¡18. The endorsement became known as

the Galili Document, or the Galili Protocols. Perlmutter, *Politics and the Military in Israel* (1978), p. 65.

19. Rabin, op cit, p. 307.

20. Rabin was not alone in his criticism of Peres' demagoguery. Dayan later reported that his old ally Peres played a similar divisive role during the Camp David negotiations. See Dayan, *Breakthrough*, op cit, pp. 73 and 193; Rabin, op cit, p. 308.

21. Rabin, op cit, p. 332.

22. Chomsky, op cit, pp. 453 and 457.

23. *Ibid*, pp. 48-49.

24. In an address to the UN General Assembly on October 6, 1977 Dayan stated: "For ten years, between 1967 and 1977, the government of Israel was committed to territorial concessions in return for genuine peace, and this implied the redivision of the area, but to no avail. Now our view is that redivision is not the answer. Nowhere is it possible to draw a dividing line which will satisfy not only the security, but also the historical, economical, and social needs of all sides. Bethlehem, a satellite town of Jerusalem, dependent on Jerusalem for its tourist trade and indeed its very existence, cannot be cut off from the Holy City. Mount Scopus, the site of Hebrew University, and the Hadassah Hospital, cannot be separated from Israel. The Arabs in Gaza cannot once again be bottled up in an intolerably narrow strip of land, unable to get out without passing an international frontier. The model for the future must be united Jerusalem – where since 1967 Jews and Arabs have proved they can live together harmoniously to their mutual benefit, where all residents enjoy freedom of movement in all parts of the Holy City, and where freedom of access to the holy places is assured for all. There is no need, no room, for barbed wire any more." Chaim Herzog, 1978. *Who Stands Accused? Israel Answers its Critics*, New York, Random House, p. 82; also see Amos Perlmutter, "Unilateral Withdrawal: Israel's Security Option, *Foreign Affairs* Fall 1985, p. 141.

During the Camp David camp talks Dayan, by his own account, told President Carter: "...in my view, if the West Bank were annexed to Jordan, it would lead to destruction of the State of Israel." *Breakthrough*, pp. 61 and 304.

25. Dayan: "I too was firmly opposed to the rise of a Palestinian State, but I thought the only way to maintain a dialogue with the Palestinian Arabs was to tell them this, and to add at the same time that neither would annex the territories without their agreement." *Breakthrough*, op cit, p. 305.

26. Amos Perlmutter reported Dayan's support for similar ideas as early as the post-1967 period. Perlmutter, *Two Minutes Over Baghdad*. op cit, p. 44; Avraham Schweitzer, "The Importance of the Nuclear Option," *Ha'aretz*, March 15, 1976; also see Schweitzer's 1986 book, op cit, pp. 40-49.

27. Muhammad H. Heikal, "Frankly Speaking: The Israeli Atomic Bombs... Why was Israel Obliged to Make the Bomb?," *Al-Ra'y Al-Am* (Jordan), January 20, 22, 24, 26, 1976.

28. *Al Hamishmar*, December 31, 1976.

29. It is important to understand that Dayan's 1976 proposal was compatible with de facto U.S. policy, which had diverged from the international consensus by 1971 – thanks to Henry Kissinger, who backed Israeli occupation of the territories. Henry Kissinger, 1976. *The White House Years*, Boston, Little, Brown and Co., pp. 1279, 1291; also see Hersh, op cit, pp. 232 and 402-414; Chomsky, op cit, pp. 64-66; Sheehan, op cit.

30. This was the view offered by retired General Mattityahu Peled, as well as by Ariel Sharon. M. Peled, "First Lessons," *Ma'ariv*, October 17, 1973, p. 9; also see Amos Perlmutter, "The Covenant of War," *Harper's*, February, 1973, pp. 51-63; Perlmutter, *Politics and Military in Israel* (1978), op cit, pp. 82-86.

31. This view is supported by a secret 1978 U.S. State Department study, recently obtained by the *Washington Post*. Among other things, the study documented that Israel privately offered to return the Sinai as early as June 19, 1967, within days of the June 1967 war. David Ignatius "The 20-Year U.S. - Israeli Battle Over Land for Peace," *Washington Post*, April 10, 1988, B-1.

This interpretation implies that the Israeli withdrawal from the Sinai negotiated at Camp David did not amount to a precedent – though the claim is often made – for eventual Israeli withdrawal from the West Bank and Gaza. It is worth noting that economic realities also support this view. Noam Chomsky has pointed out that, aside from its half-depleted oil fields, the Sinai had little economic importance to Israel – in sharp contrast to the occupied territories, which provide cheap manpower for the Israeli economy, – a ready made market for Israeli goods, tourist income, and at least a third of Israel's water supply. The loss to the Israeli economy by withdrawal (in 1983 figures) from the West Bank would be on the order of one billion dollars a year. Chomsky, op cit, pp. 46-47; also see Thomas R. Stauffer, *Christian Science Monitor*, January 13, 1982 Amos Perlmutter, "Unilateral Withdrawal: Israel's Security Option," *Foreign Affairs*, Fall 1985, p. 144.

Israeli plans to further exploit the West Bank's water resources have moved forward in recent years, generating new protests from Palestinians. See Alan George, "Palestinians Seek Support Over Israeli 'Water Theft,'" *Earth Island Journal,* Spring, 1988. p. 21.

32. Egypt's economy continued to deteriorate after Camp David in spite of U.S. aid. In fact, things had become so bad by 1987 that *Insight* magazine referred to the Egyptian economy as "the new sphinx." One foreign banker interviewed by *Insight* deciphered the 'handwriting on the wall' as follows: "If Egypt was a horse," as he put it, "you'd have to shoot it." *Insight (The Washington Times).* January, 1987, p. 8; also see Paul Jabber, "Egypt's Crisis, America's Dilemma," *Foreign Affairs,* Summer, 1986, p. 961.

33. Sadat Text (Speech at Signing of Camp David), March 26, 1979, Carter Archives, Folder: Mid-East, Israeli-Egyptian Peace Treaty, Collection: Press Office, Granum.

34. David Hirst and Irene Beeson, 1981. *Sadat,* London, Faber and Faber, p. 321.

35. Carter's decision to de-emphasize the Palestinian issue may have been spurred, in part, by the Iranian Revolution of February 1978, and its aftermath. The interesting way William Quandt's book on Camp David buried the crucial significance of Carter's adoption of a two-track approach also deserves to be noted. William B. Quandt, 1986. *Camp David: Peacemaking and Politics,* Washington, D.C. The Brookings Institution, pp. 178, 211-212, 261, 270, 280, 321, and 320-323.

36. Amnon Kapeliouk, *Le Monde Diplomatique,* Paris, January 1979.

37. Hirst and Beeson, op cit, p. 325; also see Dayan, *Breakthrough,* op cit, p. 305.

38. "Peres Attacks Report on Israeli A-Arms," *New York Times,* October 7, 1986.

39. As already noted, the pertinent legislation were the Glenn and Symington Amendments of the Foreign Assistance Act of 1961, and the Nuclear Nonproliferation Act of 1978.

40. Zionists always cultivated special relations with carefully chosen benefactor nations. According to the historian Lenni Brenner, before World War I leading Zionist figures – Vladimir (Ze'ev) Jabotinsky and even Theodor Herzl – attempted without success to curry favor with the Ottoman Turks, who ruled Palestine at the time. With the imminent collapse of the Ottoman Empire, the Zionist diplomatic front shifted to Great Britain. Years later, when the passing

of the British Mandate paved the way for Israeli independence in 1948, Zionist leaders sought assistance elsewhere, first with France, and then with the United States. More recently, Israel developed strong ties with South Africa – though the latter case seems more an alliance of near equals. Due to the tiny size of Israel's economy, in addition to the country's relative lack of natural resources, favorable alliances were crucial to its continued development, as well as to its security. Lenni Brenner, 1984. *The Iron Wall,* London, Zed Books, pp. 42-52.

41. Dayan's statement was reported to Moshe Sharett by Ya'acob Herzog and Gideon Raphael, and duly recorded by Sharett in his diary. Sharrett went on to add his own thoughts. "The conclusions from Dayan's words are clear: This state has no international obligations, no economic problems, the question of peace is non-existent... It must calculate its steps narrow-mindedly and live on its own sword. It must see the sword as the main, if not the only, instrument with which to keep its morale high and to retain its moral tension. Toward this end it may, no – it *must* – invent dangers, and to do this it must adopt the method of provocation and revenge... Above all – let us hope for a new war with the Arab countries, so that we may finally get rid of our troubles and acquire our space. (Such a slip of the tongue: Ben Gurion himself said that it would be worth while to pay an Arab a million pounds to start to a war.) Sharrett, *Personal Diary,* May 26, 1955, p. 1021. Cited in Rokach, op cit, p. 41.

For a summary of Dayan's views during the mid-1950's see Moshe Dayan, "Israel's Border and Security Problems," *Foreign Affairs,* January, 1955.

42. M.J. Armitage, and R.A. Mason, 1983, *Air Power in the Nuclear Age,* Urbana and Chicago, University of Illinois Press, p. 124.

43. London *Sunday Times,* October 5, 1986.

44. "Israel Said to Deploy Jericho Missile," *Aerospace Daily,* May, 1981. Cited in Spector, *Going Nuclear,* op cit, pp. 131 and 139.

45. Daniel Ellsburg, "Call to Mutiny," in Joseph Gerson, ed., 1986. *The Deadly Connection,* Philadelphia, New Society Publishers; Barry M. Blechman and Stephen S. Kaplan, 1978. *Force Without War* Washington D.C., The Brookings Institution, p. 47.

46. *Ibid*

47. Robert W. Tucker, "Israel and the United States: From Dependence to Nuclear Weapons? in *Commentary,* November, 1975, p. 41.

48. London *Sunday Times.* October 12, 1986.

49. *Der Spiegel,* July, 1970.

50. *Time,* April 12, 1976, p, 39; also see Perlmutter, *Two Minutes,* op cit, p. 46.

51. Nadav Safran, 1978. *Israel: The Embattled Ally,* Cambridge, Mass., Belknap Press, p. 483.

52. Walter Pincus, "Nuclear Diplomacy Losing its Edge," *Washington Post,* July 26, 1985, p. A-I; also see Adams, op cit, p. 163.

53. In 1978 two Israeli officers published an article challenging the nuclear ship hypothesis. The authors presented evidence alleging that the Kissinger-Nixon White House fabricated the report in order to exert increased pressure on Israel during the crisis. The authors apparently convinced Shai Feldman. In my view the alternative version of events remains possible, though unlikely since the Israeli version cannot explain why the Soviet ship turned back. Major Yishai Kordova and Lt. Col. Avi-Shai, "Haiyum Hagarini Hasovieti Beshalhay Milhemet Yom Hakipurim" (The Soviet Nuclear Threat Towards the End of the Yom Kippur War), *Ma'archot* (Tel Aviv), No. 266, November, 1978, pp. 37-42.

54. Pincus, op cit. 55. Hart, op cit, p. 377.

56. Donald Neff's recently published study of the war suggests the popular Israeli impression was false. Neff claims that Israel continued to encounter stiff resistance from both Syria and Egyptian forces and made few gains in the last days of war. Moreover, according to Neff, the IDF's near-encirclement of the Egyptian Third Army was accomplished only after Israel violated the cease-fire. Donald Neff, 1988. *Warriors Against Israel,* Brattleboro, Vt., Amana Books, pp. 274-276 and 305-306.

57. The recent test of an up-graded Jericho II in the Mediterranean demonstrated a range of 500 miles, though it may be extended up to 900 miles. The cruise's range would be even greater (2500 km, or roughly 1500 miles), though scuttlebutt has it that the missile is years from maturity. "Soviets Warn Israel on Missiles," San Francisco *Chronicle,* July 30, 1987; "Three Nations Begin Cruise Missile Project," op cit.

58. Meir, op cit, p. 420. For a brilliant study of the Yom Kippur War see the London *Times* Insight Team, op cit.

59. Tucker, op cit, pp. 41-42.

60. *Davar,* November 13, 1981.

61. *Jerusalem Post,* November 13, 1981; *Ha'aretz,* August 10 1981; also see Norman Kempster, *Los Angeles Times - Boston Globe,* August 10, 1981.

62. *Ha'aretz,* November 13, 1981.

63. George Ball, 1984. *Error and Betrayal in Lebanon,* Washington D.C., Foundation for Middle East Peace, p. 48.

64. According to an in-depth CIA report, during the 1982 war Israel used nine different kinds of U.S.-supplied cluster bombs on at least 51 locations in Lebanon, including 19 in West Beirut. This constituted a series of flagrant violations of agreements made with Washington that these horrible weapons should be used only in defense of Israel, more explicitly, only if attacked "by the regular forces of a sovereign nation in which Israel is attacked by two or more of the nations Israel fought in 1967 and 1973." Other prohibitions banned the use of cluster bombs against areas "where civilians would be exposed." Apparently Israel's leaders believed that attacking refugee camps constituted defensive action. By this same logic, refugee camps apparently did not qualify as "civilian areas." Cited in *Ibid,* p. 48, and pp. 44-45.

U.S. complicity in the invasion also deserves condemnation. To begin with, the Israeli plans were no secret in Washington. Weeks before the invasion, on April 8, 1982, John Chancellor had described Israeli intentions in an NBC television report. So accurate was the report, in fact, that the principal chronicler of the war, Ze'ev Schiff, later claimed it had "amounted to a virtual exposure of the Israeli war plans." Secondly, as also reported by Schiff, none other than Secretary of State Alexander Haig gave Israel the 'green light' for the attack. Ze'ev Schiff and Ehud Ya'ari, 1984. *Israel's Lebanon War,* edited and translated by Ina Friedman, New York, Simon and Schuster, p. 31; also see Ze'ev Schiff, "Green Light, Lebanon," *Foreign Policy,* Spring, 1983, pp. 73-85.

Moreover, Pentagon spokesmen confirmed that shipments of U.S. war supplies, including cluster bombs, increased by at least 50% in the year before the war – amounting to a flood of U.S. aid in the months preceding the invasion. The same sources also confirmed that the shipments continued, even during the first weeks of fighting. Such was the destructive power of the U.S.-supplied weapons that some individual bombs reportedly killed hundreds of people. Claudia Wright, *New Statesman,* August 20, 1982; *In These Times,* September 8, 1982.

65. *Newsweek,* February 20, 1984, p. 47.

66. Ball, op cit, pp. 44-45.

67. From August, 1981, through May 1982, the IDF attempted to provoke the PLO into attacking northern Israel in order to elicit the needed pretext for the planned invasion. A total of 2125 violations of

Lebanese airspace and 652 violations of Lebanese territorial waters were documented by the UN. Wright, Robin, "Israeli 'provocations' in southern Lebanon fail to goad the PLO – so far," *Christian Science Monitor,* March 18, 1982; Alexander Cockburn and James Ridgeway, *Village Voice,* June 22, 1982.

The provocations failed. Arafat knew an Israeli invasion was possible and gave his ragged troops strict orders not to respond to Israeli border violations. Israel's foremost military journalist, Ze'ev Schiff, later admitted that the northern frontier had been quiet for nearly a year before the Israeli attack. In the end the declared pretext for the invasion was the London assassination attempt on Israel's chief diplomat in England, Ambassador Argov – carried out *not* by PLO, but by Abu Nidal, the PLO's hated enemy. Ze'ev Schiff and Yehud Ya'ari, *Israel's Lebanon War.* op cit, chapters one and two.

U.S. Ambassador to Lebanon Robert Dillon confirmed Schiff's analysis: "It was a good cease-fire, and it stuck. The Palestinian side so far as I know never violated it. That hardly surprises me. In situations like this, it's rarely the weaker side that violates these things. When you suddenly hear that weak country X has violated the airspace and borders of strong country Y, and has therefore forced Y to come in and beat the hell out of X, you can be a little skeptical that that was exactly how it happened. Yet we're asked to believe that over and over again." Green, *Sword,* op cit, p. 164.

68. Wolf Blitzer, "Opening salvos in Israel aid battle," *Jerusalem Post* March 4, 1983.

69. "Warning to Syria," *New York Times,* February 24, 1983.

70. *Christian Science Monitor,* March 17, 1983.

71. *Jerusalem Post,* March 3, 1983.

72. *Ibid*

73. The record of $4 billion was set in 1986. "Some See Shift in Basis of US-Israel Ties - Shared Values to Strategic Cooperation," *Los Angeles Times,* August 9, 1986, p. 16.

74. "Israel needs more US aid to spur economy and immigration, economist says," *Christian Science Monitor,* January 20, 1987.

Chapter Seven

"Cracks in the Defense Model"

We are strong enough to win...
– Prime Minister Yitzhak Shamir[1]

Arabs may have the oil,
but we have the matches.
– Ariel Sharon

Just as a dog returns to its vomit,
so the fool returns to his folly.
– Old Testament Proverb

As early as the mid-1950s, Israeli statesman Moshe Sharett noted with apprehension the drift of Israeli politics to the right.[2] The trend was fueled by the root contradiction of Zionism: commitment to democracy on the one hand, and the creation of an exclusively Jewish state on the other. Given the demographics of Palestine, the two were, quite simply, irreconcilable; thus was generated an unhappy dialectic whereupon moderates tended to be incapacitated by the very same events which strengthened the forces of reaction. The result was an increasingly polarized Israel, particularly after the occupation of Arab territories in June 1967.[3]

At the same time the role of the Knesset diminished – out of paralysis – resulting in a narrowing of democracy. By degrees the formulation of policy became the prerogative of a small inner circle within the cabinet – usually without significant input. Policy was effectively created also by the military, the other locus of power, whose function was to maintain security. The overall effect was a gradual but inexorable erosion of moderation, a downward spiral toward a *modus vivendi* emphasizing toughness, audacity, and contempt for liberalism and humanist values.

The net result of this process insured that foreign policy would be 'liberated' from the 'danger' of popular oversight. Almost any action, however repugnant – whether it be aid to the Nicaraguan dictator Anastasio Somoza or training for UNITA Contras in Angola – could be and was justified in the name of national security.[4] At the same time the balancing act between military independence and economic dependence, always tense under the best of circumstances, became an unforgiving tug-of-war between diplomatic 'perceptions' (image problems) on the one hand and an assortment of evils bred from expedience (apparent necessity) on the other.

Meanwhile, Israel's military prowess advanced on all fronts, impelling the country from crisis to crisis – or, as the Israeli writer Yoram Peri phrased it, from a status quo state toward regional hegemony.[5] Throughout this period, the greatest danger to Israel was not the Arab states, but the continuing 'threat of peace,' that is, increasing international pressure for Israel to accommodate Palestinian nationalism.[6] Moreover, even without announcing a clear nuclear doctrine, Israel meanwhile pressed forward with its nuclear agenda, guaranteeing that the future would brook no relenting of tension, no surcease from the past.

The ultimate dangers of these combined trends – in the context of an ambitious nuclear build-up – were accurately foreseen as early as the mid-1960s by the Israeli strategist Yisrael Ber. Those dangers were restated by Taysir Nashif in 1977, and reformulated again following the 1982 Lebanon war by Noam Chomsky in his *Fateful Triangle*.[7] Ber's analysis anticipated by a number of years the 'wild card' scenario that Nixon and Kissinger used against the Soviets in 1973. Ber believed an Israeli nuclear option would encourage mutiny against the superpowers and cause international nuclear anarchy. In 1983 Chomsky phrased it from the viewpoint of an American progressive – in terms of a frighteningly sudden evaporation of U.S. influence over Israel should a future U.S. President, or an awakened Congress, one day attempt a reassessment of U.S. policy.

Before outlining such a scenario, however, it must be admitted that at present – in 1988 – such a shift in U.S. policy appears highly unlikely, despite increasing Palestinian unrest in the West Bank and Gaza. For better or worse, Washington remains committed to viewing Israel as a strategic outpost. Still, if enough U.S. citizens became informed of the brutal realities of Israel's Iron Fist, increasing domestic support for recognition of Palestinian rights could force an historic end to Washington's foot-dragging on the central issue of Palestinian self-determination, and could create movement toward the only remaining possible option for a just resolution of the conflict: a two-state compromise settlement. This is the same formula supported today by the international consensus – in other words, by virtually the whole world (including the Soviet Union), excepting Israel and the United States. The plan would include recognized borders and security guarantees for both Israel and a Palestinian ministate.

Unfortunately, even if such a momentous shift in U.S. policy were to occur along the lines just described, it would not necessarily lead to a peace settlement. As already noted, Israel has never regarded a Palestinian state as a viable alternative.* Many Israelis would *not* view U.S. support for Palestinian self-determination as a positive development. Indeed, after years of U.S. complicity in Israel's occupation of Palestinian lands, many Israelis would probably interpret a U.S. reassessment as a breach of the 'special relationship.' Unfortunately, the negative Israeli reaction to such a development is extremely difficult to assess. In 1988 the key questions remain unanswerable: that is, would Israel resort to nuclear blackmail, as Francis Perrin warned, to make the United States back off from supporting such a peace initiative? At the very least, the spectacle of a nuclear-armed and desperate Israel prepared to drag the superpowers to the brink of Armageddon is a very real and sobering possibility that cannot be ruled out.

Over the years U.S. tax dollars helped build Israel's West Bank and Gaza settlements and forge the new political (and strategic) reality they represent. To a great extent it was U.S. aid that made possible the economic, political and cultural suppression of the Palestinians – which continues unabated today despite mounting resistance. Assuming a shift in U.S. policy were to occur, Israelis might conclude that a compromise solution was about to be imposed on them by a unified world community – something Israel's leaders have sworn they would never allow to happen.[8] In a nation deeply divided, and with a parliamentary government paralyzed short of a clear mandate for

---

* Though some of the leaders of Israel's small peace movement support the concept of a Palestinian state, the base of support in Israel for progressive change, while significant, remains small, no more than 10-15% of the population. Noam Chomsky, "Interview: Noam Chomsky," Interview by Burton Levine, *Schmate*, Summer, 1988.

peace, conditions would be ripe for the assumption of military rule. Nor would this necessarily involve a generals' coup in the usual sense of the word. At the conclusion of *Between Battles and Ballots,* the Israeli writer Yoram Peri presented credible scenarios suggesting that, faced with an imposed international solution, or alternatively, with mounting Palestinian unrest and violence, the Israeli government might invite the General Staff to declare martial law and 'rescue' the nation.

The Sharon Factor

A hint of other even darker possibilities was reported by former BBC journalist Alan Hart in his 1984 book *Arafat: Terrorist or Peacemaker?* In the book Hart recalled a 1980 conversation with one of Menachem Begin's senior ministers, who told him a terrifying story concerning the Israeli General Ariel Sharon, the man who might one day lead Likud – and possibly Israel:

> *I was sitting in the outer office of one of Begin's senior ministers....When he arrived he threw me his usual big smile of greeting, put his arm on my shoulder and propelled me to his inner sanctum....The minister sat back, put his feet on the desk, and was lost to me. He was very worried about something. There was a crisis of some sort but it was clearly not an emergency which demanded action by him. I knew the minister quite well and I had a great deal of respect for him. Eventually I said: "You've obviously got a problem....Do you want me to make another appointment?"*
>
> *For perhaps another full minute he said nothing....And I had the impression he was really frightened for probably the first time in...years. Finally he spoke. "I've just heard a terrible story. And it happens to be true. I've checked it."*
>
> *"Oh?" I said.*
>
> *"It concerns our famous General Sharon. Do you know what that lunatic has just done....He's sworn a secret oath. He's taken a vow that if this or any future government of Israel attempts to withdraw from the West Bank, he'll set up headquarters there and fight to the death to prevent a withdrawal."*
>
> *I said, "Do you think he's serious?"*
>
> *The minister looked hard at me. "Do you?"*

I said, "Yes."

*"So do I", the minister replied. "He's mad enough to
nuke the whole Arab world provided he can find a way to
protect this little country from the fallout!"*[9]

That Sharon had always been on record opposing nuclear
development did not prevent him on this or other occasions from
threatening the Arabs, or even the Soviet Union.[10] In fact, Sharon's
opposition to nuclear weapons did not follow from principle, but from
pessimism. Sharon doubted that the deterrent value of nuclear weapons
– even the fear of annihilation – could eliminate the danger of
escalation to their use, because he believed conventional war and
terrorism in the region were simply inevitable.[11] Sharon's belief that
deterrence could fail is certainly worrisome. If the Yom Kippur War,
the 1982 debacle in Lebanon, and the Iran-Iraq War have proved
anything, they demonstrate the great volatility of the Middle East,
suggesting that pessimism about the region may be well-founded.

General Sharon has matched the bluster of threats with personal
action. In 1987 he moved into an apartment in the middle of East
Jerusalem to create new 'facts' – that is, a conspicuous and highly
provocative Israeli military presence in that most Arab of all Arab
sectors of Palestine. Sharon's hatred of Arabs is well-known.
According to Noam Chomsky, in a meeting with a civilian
administrator Sharon once gave instructions on how to handle
Palestinian demonstrators: "cut off their testicles." (Sharon's Chief-of-
Staff, Raphael Eitan, went even further, telling IDF soldiers on the
northern front that "the only good Arab is a dead Arab," a generic
remark Americans will recognize from the dark days of the American
West.) On other occasions Sharon reportedly ordered his troops to beat
up Arab high school students on the West Bank.[12]

Sharon's overall intentions were revealed in a 1979 interview with
former Under Secretary of State George Ball. At the time the General
was Minister of Agriculture, in charge of the West Bank settlements
program. Ball described the conversation with Sharon in his published
study of the 1982 invasion of Lebanon:

*When he told me of his plan to settle a million Israelis in
the West Bank within the next thirty years, I asked him if that
meant that the government planned to push out the
Palestinians who lived there, forcing them to resettle in
Jordan or some other Arab country. He turned his back and*

walked away. According to a friend of mine, Sharon later
responded to the same question with the sardonic comment:
"Oh, we'll keep enough for labor."[13]

A similar account by Amos Perlmutter was reported in the *New York Times;* it alleged that Sharon "hopes to evict all Palestinians from the West Bank and Gaza and to drive them into Jordan."[14]

In an address made a few months before the 1982 war, Sharon candidly admitted that the eviction of Palestinians to Jordan would be only the first step of a greater plan. According to Sharon, the Palestinian exodus would undoubtedly precipitate the overthrow of Jordan's Hashemite Kingdom, providing the IDF with a pretext to intervene, leading to Israeli hegemony all the way to Saudi Arabia.[15]

George Ball interpreted the 1982 Lebanon invasion – which was engineered and led by Sharon – as an effort to solidify Israeli control over the occupied territories. Ball's logic was clear enough: dealing the PLO a crushing military defeat in the field would be followed by the decapitation of its leadership, the killing of Arafat, the dispersal of Fatah, etc. In this way the PLO's political grip over the West Bank Palestinians would be broken. Subsequent Palestinian demoralization would serve Israel's interests. As we know, despite nearly 20,000 fatalities in the war – mostly civilians – the failure of Sharon's plan could not have been more dramatic.[16]

The Litany of Israeli Pre-emption

As dangerous as movement toward a political compromise would surely be, those dangers are still preferable by far when compared with the near-certain consequences of present U.S. policy: a Middle East – possibly a world – cataclysm. By now, the pattern of U.S. support for Israel has become well-established. Time and again, the U.S. has armed Israel with sophisticated weapons systems, with the understanding that those technologies would be used for defensive purposes – only to have Israel turn and unleash them on its neighbors, sometimes within weeks of delivery. Washington policymakers seem unable to learn this most basic of lessons: namely, that Israeli military doctrine has always (the possible exception being the period between 1971-73) defined 'defense' in terms of waging so-called 'preventive' war. The military success of IDF campaigns in 1956, 1967, and 1982 was, in each case, based on the most advanced technology available, with an emphasis on superior leadership, tactics, and execution. But in each case the key element was pre-emptive attack.

In recent years the litany of Israeli military strikes and related actions has continued, sometimes with overt U.S. backing. A partial listing would include: the air war launched by the Israeli Air Force (IAF) against Lebanon during and after Camp David, active involvement in South Africa's efforts to destabilize the front-line African states, the 1981 bombing of an Iraqi nuclear research reactor, massive air attacks on PLO offices in Beirut and Tunis, the annexation of the Golan Heights, the 1982 invasion of Lebanon and the shelling of West Beirut, Israeli complicity in massacres of hundreds of Palestinians at the Sabra and Shatilla refugee camps, and continuing violations of Arab air space.

In the context of this study, the June 7, 1981 surprise air-attack on the Iraqi nuclear reactor is of particular interest. At the time of the strike by Israeli Air Force F-15 and F-16 fighter-bombers, the Osirak reactor, located near Baghdad, had been awaiting a second delivery of enriched uranium, in order to go on line. The day after the attack the Israeli government took responsibility for the raid in a public statement, and announced a new *casus belli*. Henceforth, Arab efforts to develop 'weapons of mass destruction' would not be tolerated.[17] Arab steps toward nuclear development would be resisted by whatever means necessary.

Nor was the 1981 raid the first instance of interdiction by Israel. A sabotage operation at La Seyne-sur-Mer on the French coast two years earlier succeeded in destroying 60% of the Osirak reactor's components, including the beehive-shaped pressure vessel designed to hold its atomic fuel rods. The Osirak components were being manufactured at the time under French contract; the reactor had been modeled on the French nuclear research facility at Saclay, near Paris. The commando attack reportedly set back the Iraqi nuclear program nearly two years.[18]

More recently, Israel's *casus belli* apparently has been extended to include non-Arab Pakistan, presumably because of Pakistan's Islamic ties with the Arab world. In 1987 the *Jerusalem Post* reported that the Israeli government had tried to persuade India to stage a joint raid on Pakistan's nuclear research center. Fortunately, India refused.[19] During the summer of 1987, two Israelis were arrested in Pakistan near Kahuta for allegedly photographing nuclear sites.[20] More recently, a West German television station carried a report detailing how a Mossad plot to kidnap West German scientists hired to work in Pakistan had been foiled.[21] These examples are indications of a trend already noted – the steady expansion of 'national security state' Israel. [22]

Given the record, how does one explain the blindness of American politicians in continuing the pipeline of ever-more advanced weapons to Israel? In his recent book, *Living by the Sword,* Stephen Green argues that the pattern is no mere coincidence, that U.S. policymakers have succumbed to the 'logic' of perpetual warfare. In short, the Middle East has become the 'combat laboratory' for the U.S. arms industry. As Green puts it, Israel's forays – as the U.S. proxy – into neighboring countries provide a ready-made crucible in which "to test advanced U.S. weapons systems against opposing Soviet and other Western systems in a variety of real conditions, on real roads, against real enemy emplacements, in real villages and cities, etc."[23]

The Arab Response

Not surprisingly, the Arab states have responded to the challenge of Israeli hegemony. As a result, in the period since the 1982 Lebanon war everything has changed. A vast military build-up has been underway throughout the region, featuring – for the first time ever – Arab deployment of advanced offensive missiles. All this was described by Green in September 1986 in a riveting article in *The Nation* – and amplified more recently in his new book.[24] If Green's analysis is correct, all the ingredients for a Middle East holocaust already exist, or will soon exist.

The Arab response has been led by Israel's principal adversary, Syria. In addition to a massive build-up of Soviet tanks, attack helicopters and other hardware, Syria has installed advanced SA-5 surface-to-air missiles (SAM), the first time that state-of-the-art Soviet air defenses have been deployed outside the Soviet bloc. More important, Syria has deployed another first: 12 batteries of the Soviet SS-21 tactical ballistic missile, an extremely accurate short-range offensive missile capable of targeting most Israeli cities from southern Syria.[25] According to Green's sources, Syria is also negotiating with Moscow for additional SS-22 and SS-23 intermediate range missiles, an even more potent combination.

While Syria's new SAM defense system probably does not pose a significant threat[26] – since the Israeli Air Force has repeatedly demonstrated its ability to outfox air defenses with high-tech countermeasures – the newly deployed SS-21 missiles are another matter. Because these powerful weapons (payload: 2200 lbs.) could be launched on warning, reaching targets in Israel in just three to five minutes, they represent an offensive threat not easily overcome, reducing Israel's chances for a successful surprise attack. No doubt, this is the Syrian strategy, one of deterrence: mutually assured destruction (MAD).

Today other Arab states are following Syria's lead. Iraq, Jordan and even Egypt may be in the process of acquiring similar missile technologies.

In addition, installation of Chinese intermediate range DF-3A ballistic missiles is known to be underway in Saudi Arabia.[27] Though the Saudis have stated that the new missiles are intended to deter Iranian aggression, their range (1500 miles) easily includes Israel. (Iran has repeatedly threatened Saudi Arabia because of its close relations with the West.) Apparently the Saudis turned to the Chinese when their requests for U.S. Lance missiles and F-15E aircraft were turned down by Washington. Though the deal with China had been in the works for more than two years – since July 1985 – the Saudis succeeded in keeping the acquisition secret through a variety of ruses.[28] It was only discovered by U.S. intelligence in January 1988. No doubt the Saudis feared – probably with justification – that an intelligence leak to Israel would result if Washington learned about the missiles. By the time the missiles *were* discovered, their installation in the Rub el-Khali (the Empty Quarter) desert region was already well-advanced.

Originally the Chinese-made DF-3A was designed to carry a nuclear payload. However, in a letter to President Reagan, King Fahd gave his personal assurance that the missiles had been modified to carry conventional warheads.[29] In fact, the remarkable case amounted to an instance of Israel shooting itself in the foot. As it turned out, the conversion of the Chinese missiles from nuclear to conventional had been carried out by a team of Israeli technicians. According to the *Washington Post,* the Israeli-engineered conversion was part of a larger arms deal between Peking and Jerusalem.[30] Obviously the Israelis were unaware the missiles would be sold to Saudi Arabia.

Nor was the missiles' non-nuclear status of much consolation. In March 1988 Yosi Ben Aharon, a close aide to Yitzhak Shamir, warned that "the possibility always exists" that Israel might strike at the Saudi missile sites. Aharon: "We have a reputation that we do not wait until a potential danger becomes an actual danger."[31] U.S. intelligence subsequently confirmed that the Israeli Air Force recently conducted "intensive low-level attack practice runs."[32] The Saudi response was to issue a threat of its own, delivered through Washington. Saudi diplomats let it be known that if Israel attempted to 'take out' the missiles, they would be fired at Israel.[33] Nor would taking out all the missiles in one surprise raid be easily accomplished. As many as half of the new missiles are being deployed on mobile launchers, making them elusive targets.

Israeli concerns about the DF-3A missiles is understandable in one respect. Their deployment at a considerable geographic distance from Israel would make them, potentially at least, a dangerous variable in a general war. On the other hand, aside from providing funds annually to the PLO, Saudi Arabia, a close U.S. ally, has for many years pursued a political agenda nearly as conservative as Israel's. Saudi Arabia's aid to Contra-style movements in Mozambique, Angola and Central America, in addition to its support for apartheid, are well-known.[34] For these reasons it is unlikely that the missiles represent a direct threat to Israel's security. More probably, they represent Saudi determination *not* to be intimidated. In the future, the Israeli Air Force is likely to think twice before staging overflights of Saudi airspace.

Of course, should the Arab states ever achieve a semblance of true military cooperation, the threat to Israel posed by the combined Arab missiles would indeed be formidable. Judging from the past record, however, this appears highly improbable. Today, as in the past, the Arab states distrust one another at least as much as they collectively distrust Israel.

Despite their new missile deployments, the Arab states have not achieved military superiority over Israel, or even parity – far from it. In Green's view, Israel could still defeat the new forces arrayed against it. What *has* changed, however, is the odds – reducing Israel's chances of a quick and easy victory. In fact, the new Arab missiles suggest that even a carefully orchestrated pre-emptive attack by Israel's most advanced aircraft, F-15 and F-16 fighter-bombers, could *not* with a high degree of assurance prevent an immediate retaliatory response.

That would come as a barrage of high-velocity, extremely accurate, conventionally-armed missiles, raining down a scale of destruction on Israel's cities comparable to the saturation bombing of West Beirut in 1982 – or worse, if Israeli reports of Syrian chemical weapons are accurate.[35] In such a battle the cost to Israel in lives alone would probably be greater – perhaps much greater – than losses in all previous wars. Probably Israel would prevail militarily in such a conflict. However, one can safely predict that the price of victory would be far too great to ever justify the risks of launching a pre-emptive strike. Consequently, the problem for Israel today is that the factors which made dramatic military successes possible in the past can no longer guarantee a repetition of that same pattern.

Shelving the Lavi

This grim new reality was the backdrop for the 1987 debate in Israel over the Lavi airplane. Initially slated to cost $800 million when first approved in 1979, by mid-1987 the controversial project had already topped $1.8 billion – almost all of which was covered by the United States. In other words, even before production had begun, the Lavi was a billion dollars overbudget, with additional cost overruns of $2.75 billion projected through 1993. After months of sometimes acrimonious cabinet debate, the project was finally scrapped in a close vote in early September.[36] American pressure played a large role in the decision: Washington made clear its unwillingness to continue supporting a fiscal white elephant. With hindsight, it appears the Lavi was not *simply* a financial nightmare. Quite possibly, it was also a conceptual anachronism. The Lavi had been billed as an all-purpose fighter-bomber, capable of meeting Israel's defense needs well into the next century. The plane was even referred to as "the crowning glory of Israel's armaments industry."[37] However, given the shift in the regional balance of power already described, the attempt to effect a technological 'fix' in the form of a new fighter-bomber was probably doomed from the start. In fact, the debate over affordability may have missed the point. The Lavi's rising costs, which no doubt were symptomatic of the new problems posed by a radically altered military environment, suggest a conclusion which, to my knowledge, no analyst thus far has dared to articulate, namely: that pre-emptive doctrines built around manned aircraft have reached – at least, in the Middle East – a wall of terminal exhaustion. Simply put, the former military equation has been altered forever by relatively cheap and easy-to-produce ground-to-ground missiles, weapons that cannot be countered by manned aircraft, even by a plane as advanced as the Lavi. Given all this, the implications for Israel should be unmistakable.[38]

The Nuclear Factor

In and of itself, the new reality of a Middle East stand-off might be reassuring, were it not for several factors that indicate just how high the stakes have become, the first being Israeli nuclear weapons proliferation. Thanks to Mordechai Vanunu, we now know that Israel's nuclear inventory is anything but small. Today Israel's nuclear arsenal numbers 100-200 warheads or more, and may well include thermonuclear weapons. For these reasons Israel's arsenal cannot be regarded as strictly defensive, over-turning a belief still held – no doubt passionately – by many decent but uninformed friends of Israel.

Dr. Frank Barnaby was one of the physicists who interviewed Vanunu and confirmed his authenticity. In the 1950s Barnaby worked with the British Atomic Weapons Research Establishment. He was also a director of the Stockholm International Peace Research Institute (SIPRI). Several months after the Vanunu interview, Barnaby expressed his concerns in a article in *Technology Review:*

> *Most commentators assume that Israel's nuclear weapons are intended as a last-ditch deterrent to military moves by Arab nations that would threaten Israel's existence. But this does not account for the size and quality of Israel's nuclear weapons. Israel could provide adequate deterrence by targeting ordinary fission weapons on major Arab cities – a dozen weapons the size of the Nagasaki bomb would suffice. No Arab city is big enough to "justify" a thermonuclear weapon.*[39]

According to Barnaby, atomic bombs (simple fission designs) become impractical for weapons over 50 kilotons – one kiloton equaling 1000 tons of TNT. (For sake of comparison, the Nagasaki and Hiroshima bombs were on the order of 20 kilotons.) Larger devices require thermonuclear designs. Of these there are two types, modified fission weapons 'boosted' in power many times by adding a secondary fusion charge, and the further-boosted hydrogen bomb – which has no theoretical upper limit in destructive power. Using advanced computers, 'boosted' weapons can be developed without testing, and are well within Israel's capability. On the other hand, development of hydrogen bombs was widely thought to require extensive testing because of the bombs' more complex "staged" design. In the aftermath of the Vanunu revelation, however, opinion began to shift. Thereafter at least one expert (Barnaby) began to speculate that Israel may have developed the hydrogen bomb.[40] Others such as Theodore Taylor have remained more skeptical, while still affirming that Israel could have developed simpler 'boosted' weapons, including neutron bombs.[41]

How, then, can one account for Israeli development of thermonuclear weapons? The most likely explanation is consistent with a strategy of 'polite blackmail.' Right or wrong, Israel's leaders may believe that their ability to apply political leverage where it counts – in Washington – will one day be directly related to deliverable megatonnage. In other words, the explanation is academic: the bigger the bombs, the greater the leverage.

An additional explanation is a possible Israeli commitment to deploy so-called 'enhanced radiation weapons,' i.e., the neutron bomb. Later in this chapter I will present a scenario of how a future Middle East crisis could trigger 'first use' of these weapons.

The Nuclear Black Market

A second factor which underscores the inherent instability of the present Middle East stand-off is the appearance of a black market for enriched uranium and plutonium. Although its existence was first reported on British television in October 1987, apparently the market has been operating for many years out of Khartoum, in the Sudan.[42] Its existence was verified by Sudanese Prime Minister Sadiq Al-Mahdi, and confirmed by other independent sources, including a Belgian arms dealer known only as "Eric," a retired IAEA inspector, Roger Richter, and former CIA Director Stansfield Turner. According to the British report, which was produced by 20-20 Vison, an independent television company, the black market was instigated in the mid-1960s to supply Israel with otherwise unobtainable – i.e., illegal – nuclear materials. Later other states, including South Africa, Argentina and Pakistan also entered into dealing.[43] In just the past year the market has further expanded to include Iran and Iraq. In fact, according to reports, in recent months Israel has been forced to buy highly enriched uranium at $3 million per kilogram simply to keep it out of the hands of potential enemies.[44] Assuming the reports are correct, words cannot describe the lunacy of Israel's early decision to encourage a black market: such folly can only be compared with Israel's nuclear alliance with South Africa.

The appearance of a nuclear black market is an alarming indicator that the unregulated spread of nuclear materials is already well advanced, validating the worst fears of anti-nuclear activists. Soon, if it has not *already* occurred, enriched uranium and plutonium will have passed to whoever can pay, ensuring the spread of nuclear weapons throughout the Middle East, and elsewhere.

The 1987 Internal Security Debate

The upshot of these combined developments is that Israel has reached an historic fork in the road. Its leaders face a clear choice with only two alternatives: abandon the concept of pre-emptive warfare while simultaneously laying the groundwork for a lasting regional peace by recognizing Palestinian rights – or else contemplate possibilities which border on the unthinkable.

A series of articles in *Ha'aretz* in August 1987 by Israel's foremost military correspondent, Ze'ev Schiff, suggests that a pivotal decision may be near, or has already been made. Schiff's articles described the fierce debate over defense strategy then underway within the ranks of Israel's military and political leaders. According to Schiff, the sometimes bitter debate – held behind closed doors – was the first of its kind in Israel in memory, and extended throughout the government. It raged in the Ministry of Economics, in a Knesset subcommittee, in the IDF, among Israel's military think tanks, and included prominent generals from the reserves. Partly as a result of the failed Lavi project, some leading figures had become painfully aware of the encroachment of an irreconcilable dilemma threatening to undermine Israel's present defense model, built around aerial supremacy and the doctrine of preventive war.

Background for the debate was the general recognition that "the party is over," as Schiff put it, that Israel can no longer afford the enormous financial costs of research aimed at maintaining conventional superiority, particularly when that research cannot guarantee results. Reading between the lines, it appears the debate turned on the key question of whether to incorporate Israel's nuclear arsenal into the IDF's war-fighting scenarios. It is interesting that Schiff's article mentioned 'the nuclear option' in a purely abstract sense: his discussion was framed in the general context of work already published by Shai Feldman – which probably explains why Schiff was able to discuss the nuclear question at all, that is, to evade government censorship. Israeli censors sometimes permit newspapers to print even 'sensitive' material if it has already been published outside Israel. In his final essay, Schiff referred to an integrated nuclear doctrine: "If one is to realize the nuclear option in the future, it will be combined with conventional forces which will be smaller and cheaper than they are today."[45]

Were it to occur, such a transformation of the IDF's 'defense model' would be unprecedented. Even though Israel has possessed nuclear weapons for many years, it seems that until now plans for their actual use – beyond posturing and threats – was regarded strictly as a last-resort option. Plans for actual deployment were held apart from the conventional battlefield. Apparently this continued to be the case in recent years despite many new advances.[46]

One of the precipitating causes of the debate was the army's deepening concern that the gulf between technology on the one hand and strategy on the other had dangerously widened. While technology surged ahead, the ramifications of technology were not always understood or assimilated – particularly by Israel's political leadership.* This helps to explain the bitterness of the debate, as noted by Schiff. In recent years, Israel's military men increasingly have tended to regard the government's failure to come to grips with the problem as irresponsible; hence their resentment of "the political echelons." The gulf between technology and strategy served to widen the gap between the army and the politicians.[47]

The Proposed Arrow Missile Defense

Besides the usual difficulties in assessing new weapons systems due to the rapid pace of technological 'progress,' the great complexity of the Middle East environment ensures that the synergetic effects of combined nuclear/non-nuclear technologies will not always be foreseeable. As a result, the potential dangers posed by certain non-nuclear developments are probably much greater than previously supposed. A prime example is the recently announced Arrow surface-to-air (SAM) missile project, presently in the proposal and evaluation stage.[48] According to the *Washington Post*, the Arrow's mission will be

---

* The problem was not new – nor unique to Israel. It had been described as early as 1966 by Yehoshafat Harkabi, a leading Israeli strategist: "Technological changes and new inventions are not always dictated by the needs of strategy, policy and diplomacy, for technological development has its own momentum. Technology probably influences diplomacy more than diplomacy influences technology. Diplomacy must strive to keep pace with technological change, adjusting to it and utilizing it both for its general needs and in solving the problems created by technology itself. ... Military doctrine lags behind weapon development by that period of time required for the mind to assimilate weapons innovations and envision their potentialities. The lag has increased with the appearance of nuclear weapons." Yehoshafat Harkabi, 1966. *Nuclear War and Nuclear Peace,* Jerusalem, Israel Program for Scientific Translations, pp. 3-4.

to protect Israel's Achille's heel – its airfields – from missile attack. That the new system was announced barely three months *after* the Lavi was abandoned suggests that Israel's strategic planners wasted little time responding in kind to the perceived threat posed by the new Arab missiles. Unfortunately, the decision to develop the Arrow will *not* make Israel more secure – much *less* so, in fact, given the frightening implications of ABM technology. Indeed, development of the Arrow represents a dramatic raising of the ante: if deployed, the Arrow system will blur the distinction between offense and defense to a matter of semantics, effectively obliterating deterrence. Notwithstanding the Arrow's stated defensive role, in practical application the only difference between *that* mission and offensive use – such as cover for a pre-emptive Israeli missile attack – would be a matter of timing. In fact, the difference between the two would be a matter of minutes – which just happens to be the weighty difference between a first-strike and counterforce (i.e., defense).

The Launch of the Horizon I

Do Israel's leaders actually believe that a pre-emptive missile attack could succeed in disarming the Arab states? Though it does not offer a clear-cut answer, the launch of an experimental spy satellite [*Ofek :* the Horizon I] by Israel on September 19, 1988 demonstrates that the Defense Ministry continues its elusive search for absolute security. When fully operational as early as 1991, *Ofek* will give Israel an unequalled intelligence capability, including the capacity to pinpoint Arab military targets, such as missile batteries, on an hourly basis. Assuming that Israel's leaders one day will have to decide whether or not to launch a pre-emptive missile attack, because of *Ofek* their fateful decision is unlikely to be determined by a shortfall of military intelligence.

The Consolidated Approach

Today the central unanswered question continues to be the possibility that Israel has integrated nuclear weapons with its conventional forces. Even before the 1987 security debate, such a move had been advocated for many years by one of Israel's leading strategists, the liberal Shai Feldman of the Center for Strategic Studies at Tel Aviv University. Mr. Feldman's views amounted to a curious combination of dovish politics and nuclear deterrence. Feldman advocated the so-called "consolidated approach," which essentially stated that Israel should 'go public' with its nuclear capability, relying for security on a declared strategy of nuclear deterrence, vis-à-vis the Arab states, while at the same time vigorously pursuing a liberal policy with respect to the Palestinians.[50] This would include withdrawal from the occupied territories and recognition of Palestinian rights.

However, it should be understood that Mr. Feldman's views were formulated *before* the evolution of the current dilemma. In fact, several of the conditions Feldman cited as crucial to the success of a "consolidated approach" have been nullified by contrary developments he warned against. For example, though Feldman explicitly warned against unnecessarily provoking the Soviets,[51] by the time his dissertation was published in 1980 Israel had *already* secretly embarked on the development of thermonuclear weapons, and the means for long-range delivery – which suggests that if Feldman's thesis was not wholly irrelevant from the day it appeared in print, it was, at very least, significantly compromised.[52]

In fact, the erosion of whatever security a nuclear deterrent might have afforded Israel was well underway within months of concluding the separate peace with Egypt in 1979. Henceforth Israel's leaders worked assiduously to undermine their own deterrent by undertaking a series of highly provocative military adventures, particularly on the northern frontier. This began with repeated air strikes aimed at alleged guerrilla bases in Lebanon, resulting in the destruction of a number of towns and villages.[53] The ill-conceived campaign raged on and off, reaching its unhappy culmination in Israel's 1982 invasion of Lebanon. Not only did Israel shell the Soviet embassy in West Beirut in that war, it also succeeded in devastating Syria's Soviet-supplied air defenses, violating an elemental principle of prudence: i.e., Israel humiliated a superpower.[54]

Israel's muscle-flexing continued in recent years, with development of a new intermediate range Jericho II missile, clearly designed to carry a nuclear payload, in addition to conventional warheads. Deployment of the new Jericho, in conjunction with the expanded nuclear arsenal already described, would give Israel the means to flatten every city of any consequence in the Middle East, and beyond. The new Jericho's potential range of 900 miles extended Israel's reach to the borders of the Soviet Union, including Soviet oil fields on the Caspian Sea, and Black Sea naval bases.[55] Perhaps this was what Ariel Sharon referred to when he spoke of Israeli military strength reaching "to the gates of Odessa."[56]

Needless to say, these developments did not pass unnoticed by Moscow. On at least three occasions in 1986-87 the Soviets warned Israel that continuation of the Jericho II project "will force the Soviet Union to carry out defensive and political steps." The most recent of these warnings was a Hebrew language commentary delivered over Radio Moscow.[57] Showing characteristic caution, the Soviets were taking no chances that Israel's leaders would misconstrue the gist of their message to Jerusalem – probably to head off the need for a more forceful response. *

The most recent Soviet warning occurred after Israel conducted a 500-mile live test of the Jericho II in the Mediterranean Sea. In order to appreciate the legitimacy of Soviet concern, the reader should try to imagine the White House reaction if the shoe were on the other foot: that is, if a country in our own hemisphere, such as Nicaragua, used the Caribbean for a missile range. In such a case, can there be *any* doubt that the U.S. response would be swift and deadly military intervention? In fact, the precedent for just such a response – consistent with the Monroe Doctrine – was established by President Kennedy during the 1962 Cuban missile crisis. Yet we take it for granted the Soviets will roll over like puppy dogs in *their* own hemisphere.

As important as the development of Israel's new Jericho surely is, even it was overshadowed by the shocking announcement in September 1988 of the successful launch of an Israeli experimental spy satellite, *Ofek:* the Horizon I, which I have already mentioned. The meaning of the launch is that Israel stands on the threshold of achieving not only a quantum leap in intelligence gathering capabilities, but an equally unprecedented breakthrough in missile technology. In this context the overriding cause for concern is not the satellite itself, but the powerful new rocket which catapulted it into orbit. In fact, launching satellites may ultimately turn out to be a purely secondary function for the new rocket, Israel's first truly intercontinental missile. Of immediate concern is the fact that, for the first time, Israel has achieved a missile with sufficient range (up to

---

* Noam Chomsky has suggested another reason: Soviet concern that the U.S. might circumvent the INF treaty by allowing Israel, the U.S. proxy to construct intermediate range missiles and target them on the Soviet Union. (Interestingly enough, Dr. Chomsky's suggestion was posted just days prior to Israel's first launch of an ICBM.) Letter from Noam Chomsky to the author, September 17, 1988.

4,500 miles, according to a recent Pentagon estimate) to target nukes directly on Moscow and other cities of the Soviet heartland.[58] If Israeli intermediate range missiles were already a cause of great concern in Moscow, one can imagine the alarm generated by the new Israeli ICBM. Shai Feldman's warning to Israeli policymakers about unnecessarily provoking the Soviets appears to have fallen on deaf ears, to say the least. In a subsequent discussion I will return again to speculate on the possible crucial role an Israeli ICBM could play in a future Middle East crisis.

Over this same period, the ties between Israel and the United States grew closer, moving ever-nearer to formal agreements of strategic cooperation.[59] So close had the relationship become by the mid-1980s that a former AIPAC lobbyist, Richard Straus, was quoted in an interview referring to Israel as "the 51st state." Others who were present countered – half-jokingly – that statehood would be a *disadvantage* since then Israel would have *only* two Senators instead of the current bloc of more than 50 who regularly look after Israeli interests.[60]

Taken together, these developments, including Israel's eager participation in SDI (Star Wars) research after May 1986, cannot have been viewed in Moscow as steps toward coexistence – just the opposite, in fact.[61] Symbolic of the trend was a 1986 agreement with the Reagan Administration to allow construction inside Israel of a giant Voice of America radio transmitter, to beam American broadcasts throughout the Soviet bloc – broadcasts certain to be regarded as hostile.[62] Had Israel's leaders consciously set out to fan the flames of reaction in Moscow, they could not have devised a better strategy.

Mr. Feldman also warned against "the adoption of a nuclear deterrent posture that seemed to be aimed at maintaining Israel's present hold over the West Bank, the Gaza Strip and the Golan Heights." With respect to the Palestinians, Feldman correctly saw that "as long as the issue...is, or appears to be, control over the territories, nuclear weapons [cannot provide] effective...deterrence."[63] In other words, even though Arab governments have been intimidated on occasion by Israel's nuclear arsenal, the Palestinians – with nothing to lose – might view things very differently. Judging from the recent Palestinian uprising, Feldman's assessment appears correct. The Palestinians have been anything but deterred. Months after their recent rebellion began in December 1987, strikes and demonstrations for self-determination continue in the territories on an almost daily basis.

Finally, Mr. Feldman's vote of confidence in nuclear weapons as a force for stability has been further undermined by the appearance of tactical nuclear weapons as a factor in the debate. Feldman's own 'consolidated' strategy advocated weapons of last resort – *not* battlefield weapons. In fact, in his dissertation Feldman explicitly warned against the deployment of tactical nuclear weapons because he quite rightly regarded them as destabilizing.[64] Unfortunately, Ze'ev Schiff's reference to a 'consolidated' nuclear strategy – in his coverage of the recent security debate – cannot refer to the same species of weapon intended by Feldman in 1980, just as the current meaning of SDI has moved far beyond President Reagan's original concept of a defensive shield.[65] The parallel reasoning in both cases is straightforward enough: technology surges ahead. In the case of Israel, confirmed development of thermonuclear weapons means, at very least, that today Israel has the capability of fielding advanced battlefield nuclear weapons, including neutron bombs.

For all these reasons the ongoing security debate reported by Ze'ev Schiff in 1987 is vital: whatever the outcome, it is certain to be a watershed for Israel and the Arabs – and possibly the Western world. If Israel's leaders correctly recognize the necessity of abandoning pre-emptive war, and act responsibly to stabilize the balance of terror while taking steps toward a just peace settlement, the Arab states are likely to respond positively. Is it not in the interest of the Arabs to avoid nuclear destruction? In fact, given the present conditions, it is hardly possible Israeli restraint would be perceived as weakness – the usual rationale offered by Israeli leaders in past years to justify their use of massive force. Indeed, these are compelling reasons for Israel to abandon the search for ultimate advantage. Thus far the build-up achieved by the Arab states is unambiguous. Non-nuclear, it is clearly designed to deter an Israeli conventional attack, *not* to disarm and destroy Israel. Arab leaders today undoubtedly realize that any attack on Israel would be suicidal – insuring their own destruction in the firestorm of Israeli nuclear retaliation.

Unfortunately, as the Sudanese nuclear black market demonstrates, time is rapidly running out. In an important sense the lessons which must be learned now are the lessons of the next war – which must never be fought. Can Israel learn these lessons beforehand? The answer remains very much in doubt. Despite Mr. Vanunu's courageous effort to sound a warning, Israeli progressives have been slow to appreciate the dangers. Yoram Nimrod, an activist and a former member of the original 1961 Committee for the Denuclearization of the Arab-Israeli Conflict, described the present lack of interest. "I've seen the same faces," Nimrod said recently, "Most are easily recognized. They are the same people committed to the idea [of nonproliferation] twenty years ago. There is no anti-nuclear movement [in Israel]. The public mind is empty. The public, uneducated about the nuclear issue, is thinking it is a weapon of last resort."[66] A writer for *Ha'aretz*, Dan Margalit, probably spoke for many Israelis in a recent debate on the issue when he stated: "Nuclear arms...are an umbrella under whose protection Israel can free itself of the historical memory of mass-destruction, a kind of safety-belt to deter any Arab ruler from fostering the hope of total destruction of the Jewish people."[67] Another Israeli writer, Tom Segev, summed up the mood in Israel: "What is there to discuss or argue about? The stronger we are the better."[68]

The Doctrine of Pre-emption

Few Israelis seem to appreciate that the IDF's own powerful logic constantly drives it toward pre-emption. An exception is *Jerusalem Post* Reporter Hirsh Goodman. As the national security debate was heating up in 1987, Goodman wrote: "The enemy is not going to be allowed to fire the first bullet. The armed forces can be built and trained to deal with these problems. The question is whether this country's political leadership will be capable of taking the right decisions at the right time."[69] The potentially deadly psychology implicit in Mr. Goodman's reference to "right decisions" – harkening back to Vanunu's warning – was accurately described by George Ball in his study of the 1982 Lebanon War:

> *Israel is still formally at war with all its neighbors except Egypt and its neuroses are now so far advanced that no amount of military power can provide it the "absolute security" it desires; thus it inevitably seeks "the neutralization" of its opponents as the only "sufficient guarantee."*[70]

Quite possibly, the currently deployed Arab missiles and chemical weapons will be regarded by Israeli policymakers as intolerable. From the Israeli standpoint, a stand-off may be regarded as unacceptable because, to paraphrase Moshe Dayan, it 'ties the IDF's hands.'[71] In a sense the new Arab missiles do represent a sort of *fait accompli,* precisely the sort of challenge Israel has always before met with superior force at the earliest opportune moment – usually with great success. Such was the case during the 1982 air war with Syria in Lebanon's Bekaa Valley. At the time, as reported by M.J. Armitage and R.A. Mason, the Syrian SA-2, -3, and -6 defensive missile batteries (SAMs) deployed there were not in position to interfere with the Israeli forces which had invaded Lebanon.[72] This, in addition to Israeli cabinet statements that Syria would not be touched if it stayed out of the conflict, probably accounted for the Syrians' great surprise when the Israeli attack came. It was surgically accomplished by a combination artillery-missile barrage, taking out the Syrian air defenses before they could respond. This was the same advanced S.R.C. 155-mm artillery – already described – used by Israel on the Golan Heights during the October 1973 War. The extremely accurate 75-mile-range Lance missiles also used in the attack had been supplied by the U.S. as well. With the SAMs removed, Israeli fighters swept in and completed the rout of the Syrian Air Force, using electronic countermeasures to jam the remaining Syrian radar. The result was a turkey-shoot. The final tally was a kill ratio almost unprecedented in the history of aerial combat: 86 or more Syrian Migs destroyed to one Israeli plane lost.

Such victories leave ineradicable impressions. Of course, whether or not Israel has followed through in the search for an 'optimal' configuration for battlefield nuclear weapons is pure conjecture in 1988. Nor does it necessarily follow that such weapons have been produced, even if achieved. *However, given the enormous stakes, can we afford to presume less?* Given the nature of the military dilemma Israel now faces, it is not difficult to imagine the features of such an 'optimal' weapon – the proverbial silver bullet – nor to speculate on how it might be used. The reader is asked to remember that the scenario which follows is largely speculation.

Raising the Ante Globally – Lowering the Risks Locally

The danger would come in a regional crisis, possibly precipitated by reports that an Arab government, as for example, Syria, was preparing to deploy a nuclear option, or a new chemical weapon. Whether confirmed or not, such reports could generate a precipitous rise in tensions. Israel's leaders might be tempted to pre-empt in an effort to disarm their Arab neighbor, to eliminate the 'imminent threat' to Israeli cities. In short, Israel would decide – fatefully – that the local threat was more tangible than the risks of triggering a wider war.

Furthermore, a variety of circumstances might 'compel' Israel's leaders to rule out sole reliance on conventional means. They might judge that a decisive advantage could be gained only by 'defensive escalation,' that is, limited use of nuclear weapons in concert with conventional forces. To be sure, such a move would raise the global ante beyond reckoning. But Israel's leaders might judge that they had little choice. Indeed, they might conclude that a 'window of opportunity' for complete success not only existed, but was achievable.

. Ultimately, they would bank on the Soviets' historical reluctance to intervene impulsively. In 1984, and again in 1985, Syrian Defense Minister Mustafa Tlas declared that the Soviet Union had "guaranteed" it would give Damascus nuclear weapons if Israel used nuclear weapons against Syria. Later, however, a Soviet spokesman denied Tlas' statement. To be sure, on other occasions Soviet officials told Western diplomats that the Soviet Union would assist its ally Syria should it be attacked.[73] However, the Israelis might discount the warnings, judging from the past Soviet record. On a number of occasions, in 1946 when threatened by President Truman, again during the Cuban missile crisis of 1962, at the time of the Yom Kippur War in 1973, and during the Israeli attack on Syria in 1982, the Soviets had backed down when confronted with Western military power.[74] The Israelis might judge that under certain conditions the odds again would be favorable. Those 'certain conditions' would be an application of technology so novel, and so unprecedented, that Israel would gamble with confidence on the element of surprise: i.e., if the IDF could gain but a few precious hours, perhaps a day, in which to achieve its objectives, the danger of a Soviet response would greatly recede.

Like the 1982 surprise attack on Syria's SAM missile batteries, Israeli strategy would rely on accurate intelligence gathering to pinpoint the location of the Arab positions.[75] In fact, military intelligence would be crucial to the success of the operation. As in 1982, the attack would commence with a carefully orchestrated salvo from Israel's 155-mm artillery and/or short-range missiles. However, instead of conventional warheads, Israel would fire tactical nuclear shells (low-yield 'clean' neutron bombs), arrayed as a barrage of aerial bursts thousands of feet above the Arab missile batteries and airfields.[76]

The primary objective of such an attack would *not* be the destruction of the Syrian troops manning the SAM and SS missiles. The explosions would be high enough that relatively few soldiers would be immediately affected. For similar reasons, destruction on the ground due to blast would be negligible. Instead, the objective would be the scrambling of electronic circuitry over a wide area by means of the electromagnetic pulse (EMP) generated by the nuclear bursts. In an instant the missiles and their launchers, airplanes, related metallic equipment, as well as the Syrian communications network, would individually and collectively become helpless passive antennae, gathering and amplifying the pulse, which would reach many thousands of volts per meter – with immediate and overwhelming results. Within a split second the Syrian missile and air defense system would simply cease to exist.[77]

Meanwhile, on the Israeli border, IDF-manned Arrow defensive missiles (supplied by the U.S.) would stand ready, on high alert, to sweep the skies over Israel should any Arab SS missile batteries survive to retaliate.[78] With fear and chaos spreading behind the Syrian lines, and with Israeli air supremacy unchallenged, the stage would be set for the *coup de grace*.

Within minutes, the Israeli Air Force (IAF) would sweep in with conventional air strikes, completing the destruction of the missile batteries and the Syrian air force. This accomplished, the IAF would turn its attention to the dismembering of Syrian ground forces, crushing whatever remained of their capacity to mount a counter-assault. Within a day, possibly within hours of the first attack, airborne IDF units would be lifted in, as needed, for the mop-up. Since little radiation would remain to contaminate the battlefield, Israeli soldiers would not worry about dangerous fallout.

In short, the most advanced weapon of destruction would be deployed in concert with conventional forces in a devastating assault carried out with near-surgical precision. Most significantly, it would be a case wherein the principles of warfare were exploited in such an ultimate manner that, in the words of former Israeli Chief-of-Staff Yigael Yadin, "...the fate of the battle [was] strategically determined before the fighting [even began] ."[79] For the first time in history, a major war would be launched, fought, and decisively won in a single day – making even the Six-Day War pale by comparison. In fact, the entire war would last a mere 14-18 hours, redefining the very meaning of the word 'audacity.' Once again Israel would vanquish its enemy. Once again, a humiliating defeat would be delivered – under the noses of the superpowers.

With the outcome on the battlefield already decided, the battle on the diplomatic front would be heating up. However, the advantage of initial surprise would still favor Israel. New 'facts' on the ground would already exist, nullifying the capacity of the superpowers to intervene effectively, making continued military escalation of dubious value. (Nobody likes to back a loser.) Even as the first wave of the IAF swept in to deliver the knockout punch, the Israeli Prime Minister would be issuing a stern warning to Moscow (and Washington), announcing that for all practical purposes the fighting had ceased, and urging restraint. In effect, the warning would convey a nuclear threat, backed up with several nuclear-tipped Israeli ICBMs targetted on Moscow, serving notice that Israel stood prepared to take whatever steps might be necessary to defend itself.

Under the circumstances, the threat would be taken seriously. Since the Soviet Union had not come under direct attack, Soviet leaders would be inclined to vent their outrage with verbal abuse and counterthreats rather than by taking overt military action. In short, Israel would count on superpower reluctance to commit world suicide. Indeed, this calculation had been the basis for the new equation: raising the ante globally to lower the risks locally. Despite the slaughter of thousands of Arab soldiers and civilians by Israel, in the end – after declaring a nuclear alert and exchanging heated words – the superpowers would step back from the brink together. Leaders on both sides would shake their heads in disbelief, wring their sweaty palms, and do nothing.

The U.S. Response

As usual, Israel would find itself alone before a seething United Nations. But this would not be unexpected. As always, Israel would rely on the United States' shield for protection. Of course, Israeli diplomats would have their work cut out for them, convincing the U.S. President of the defensive nature of the war. And this would be their approach: they would argue that there had been no time to consult Washington. They would claim they had acquired 'evidence' of an imminent Arab first-strike, leaving only minutes in which to respond before being overwhelmed themselves by chemical or nuclear weapons. Attack had been necessary to save Israel's urban population from destruction. And the decision to go nuclear? Again, they would claim it was justified on the basis of saving Israeli lives – a rationalization already familiar to Americans. (Was this not the reasoning used in 1945 to 'justify' dropping Little Boy and Fat Man on Hiroshima and Nagasaki? Those blasts – we are told – saved tens of thousands of American GIs.) In fact, the Israelis would explain that the IDF had used an absolute minimum of force to achieve its objectives. True, nuclear weapons had been used, but in a relatively benign manner, and only to regain a military advantage. Except for the initial salvo, Israel had relied exclusively on conventional means to disarm its enemies. What is more, every effort had been made to limit the attack to military targets; Arab cities and densely populated areas had been spared. (Of course, Arab reports would deny this.) The Israelis would point out that the level of death and destruction did not even begin to approach the dimensions of a holocaust. On the contrary, they would argue that, had Israel *not* moved pre-emptively, the imminent Arab attack would have dragged the superpowers into a full-scale world confrontation. Most important, due to the use of preferred 'clean' weapons, large numbers of subsequent radiation-induced deaths were not to be expected. Nor had the environment been appreciably damaged. (This claim would be hotly denied by environmentalists.)

On another level, the Israelis would point with a measure of pride to the new chapter in the annals of defensive warfare which had been written. 'Clean' nuclear weapons – neutron bombs – had made possible a lightning-fast victory, accomplished with amazingly light Israeli casualties. Finally, Israeli diplomats would point to the positive outcome: the sluggish Soviet ineptitude, the preservation of vital U.S. interests (OPEC oil continued to flow to the West), the elimination once-and-for-all of Syria as a military threat, and the highly favorable new balance of power in the region.

In the end, the U.S. President would swallow the hard new realities. Though initially he would condemn Israel in public, within hours he would release his 'truth squads' to effect 'damage control' at home. With a little packaging anything, even doublespeak, could be sold. Henceforth Americans would be asked to believe the unbelievable: that Israel's use of nuclear weapons had been necessary to prevent a wider nuclear war. Following the President's lead, key Senators and Congressmen would rally to Israel's cause, condemning the 'refusal of the Arab states to recognize Israel' as the principal cause of the tragedy. But what could the President and his men do in any case? The strategic alliance with Israel had for years been too pervasive to challenge in any fundamental way.[80] Because the U.S.

security establishment had become inextricable from Israel's, the 'special relationship' would, in the end, be preserved. Once again, the tail would wag the dog.

A Prayer and a Warning

If the frightful scenario described above sounds plausible – as indeed it is – it is no less insane. The fact that the U.S.S.R. has exercised great caution in the past is no guarantee it will back down in the future, particularly when confronted with yet another humiliation at the hands of Israel. Today the stakes are much greater. Though the Soviet technicians and advisors who initially manned the Syrian missile batteries were withdrawn after training Syrian replacements,[81] it is unlikely that the Soviets would stand idly by if Syria came under attack. Recent Soviet warnings should be taken to heart by Israel's leaders – and by Washington.[82]

Moreover, should Israel use neutron bombs, or other tactical nuclear weapons, the Soviets would be entirely justified in intervening on Syria's behalf. Under the terms of the Nonproliferation Treaty, which Syria – along with most of the Arab states – and the Soviet Union have ratified, signatories are obliged to come to one another's aid in the event of nuclear attack. It is difficult to escape the conclusion that IDF-initiated 'preventive war' on Syria would be regarded in Moscow as a precipitating cause for general war.

War or Peace?

Unfortunately, from the standpoint of the U.S. peace movement, there has been almost no recognition – let alone an outcry – concerning the crucial U.S. role in perpetuating conditions which make such a nightmare more likely. The reality is that the United States is pursuing a course which makes an already bad situation much worse. In addition to the obvious calamity of continuing U.S. materiel/financial support for Israel's Iron Fist, Washington's collusive silence regarding Israel's secret nuclear agenda, including its refusal to allow international inspections and its alliance with South Africa, all is having the effect of eroding the Nonproliferation Treaty, perhaps beyond salvation. Because of U.S. hypocrisy and the combined Israeli-South African challenge, Arab and African signatories soon may feel obliged to reconsider their commitment to nuclear regulation. All of this was pointedly summarized by Ken Coates of the Bertrand Russell Peace Foundation when he recently wrote that:

> *Now, in order to survive, the nonproliferation regime must discover how to disarm Israel and South Africa of their nuclear bludgeons....At stake is the whole question of the political will for peace and disarmament, as well as the deep-rooted problem of social justice.*[83]

Alternatives

In conclusion, the time has come for U.S. anti-nuclear activists to follow the selfless example of Mordechai Vanunu. If informed Americans in sufficient numbers organized around these issues, grassroots political pressure could be instrumental in implementing steps to lessen Middle East and world tensions. In addition to demanding enforcement of U.S. laws mandating a cut-off in aid to countries engaged in secret nuclear proliferation, peace advocates could lobby for concrete solutions, beginning at home. For one thing, the United States could take the lead in shutting off the flow of black market uranium/plutonium, *not* by following the Israeli example of commando-style raids, but by regaining international respect for U.S. integrity. A unilateral move to shut down commercial nuclear reactors in the United States would send an unambiguous message around the world that at last Washington really meant business, that nonproliferation rhetoric would finally be backed with action, that the tide had begun to turn against horizontal nuclear proliferation.* Such a move would also go a long way toward relieving Israel's insecurities.

It could be coupled with aggressive new programs to develop solar and other renewable energy resources – particularly photovoltaics – both at home and abroad. A major goal of one such program would be the formulation of a step-by-step plan for conversion of Israel's huge arms industry to the manufacture of solar technologies. Israel's present dependence on arms sales could then shift, with Israel rapidly becoming a world center for production, sales and distribution of solar know-how, a development certain to promote long-term peace in the Middle East.

---

* A proposal to shut down commercial reactors is hardly unprecedented. In early 1988 a report released by Public Citizen, a national non-profit consumer organization founded by Ralph Nader in 1971, claimed on the basis

Other unilateral moves could also be taken by the United States to defuse the risks of accidental war. For example, the U.S. Navy could pull back its forward deployment of nuclear weapons, reducing the temptation to use them. Such a move was proposed by a U.S. Navy Commander as early as 1983.[84]

However, without grassroots political pressure, these and other initiatives will never get off the ground. The reason? When it comes to the Middle East, Washington's capacity for making precisely the wrong move is almost boundless – the previously mentioned Arrow SAM missile project being an excellent case-in-point. According to reports, the U.S. will assume at least 80% of the costs of the new Arrow system, which will be designed specifically to defend Israel's air bases. That the system could also be used to cover an Israeli first strike is *undeniable,* yet the system's capacity for dual-use has been irresponsibly ignored by Congress – not to mention the academic community, the press, and the so-called peace movement. In fact, the conspicuous absence of debate or media commentary on the Arrow issue reveals the astonishing extent to which uncritical support for Israel has undercut free speech and unfettered exchange.[85]

The truth is that deployment of the Arrow system will directly contradict the spirit – if not the letter – of the SALT I ABM treaty signed by the United States and the U.S.S.R. in 1972. That logic is no less valid today, and can be simply stated: that anti-ballistic missile systems are destabilizing because they are inherently ambiguous; that is, they can be defensive, but they can also be used to cover a first strike. Because these 'defensive' systems invite pre-emptive attack, they must never be deployed. The U.S.-supplied Arrow missile could

---

of a two-year study that commercial power reactors in the United States cost taxpayers twice as much to operate as industry and government regulators will admit. The study also found that nuclear power currently supplies less than 5% of U.S. electric demand. In fact, if all commercial reactors had been shut down during 1986, the U.S. would still have had a 28% surplus of electricity, nationwide. The study claimed that conservation and energy efficiency improvements – alone – could more than make up for the loss of electricity supplied by the nuclear industry. The report concluded that government and industry have violated the public trust with false data and by using federal subsidies (taxpayer dollars) to prop up a technology that would otherwise collapse in a free market. *Too Costly to Continue: the Economic Feasibility of Phasing Out Nuclear Power,* Public Citizen, 215 Pennsylvania Avenue SE, Washington, DC 20003. ($20)

be the final ingredient in a recipe for a Middle East cataclysm.[86] This is one arrow which must never be unsheathed.

A Time to Choose

It is time to recognize – common sense dictates it – that the era of pre-emptive war is over in the Middle East. Yet, without skillful U.S. influence being brought to bear, is it really likely that Israel's leaders – old and without new ideas – will suddenly reverse a pattern they have cultivated for more than thirty years? Sadly, the U.S. role, wholly compromised by the continuing flow of advanced arms, cash, and materiel support to Israel – and elsewhere – has been anything but skillful. In fact, in the author's view, based on the facts outlined in this study, it is hard to escape the conclusion that U.S. involvement in the region has been and continues to be an unmitigated disaster. As regards the future, one thing alone is certain: if the familiar pattern is not reversed soon – for whatever reason – the deepening Middle East conflict could trigger a world conflagration. In that case the question posed as the title of this book will have been answered in the affirmative, though posthumously; for by then the United States will already have reaped, in an unimaginable whirlwind, the bitter fruit of its own sowing.

Notes to Chapter Seven

1. NBC News Nightline, April 27, 1988.

2. For references from Sharett see his diary entries for January 9, 10, 15, 25 and 26, October 1, 1955, and April 4, 1957 cited in Rokach, op cit, pp. 37, 49. (Also see note 28, chapter two of this study.) Note: the gradual erosion of Labor's base of support, and the rise of the Israeli right, is apparent form the following figures, which refer to the average number of Knesset members in each period:

	Labor	Nationalist-Religious *Herut*, et al
1949-51	61.7	42.0
1961-69	57.7	46.6
1973-84	43.5	60.7

The trend is also reflected by the relative percentage of the vote won by Labor in the country's key elections since independence: 1949, 50.4%; 1969, 46.2%; 1973, 39.6%; 1977, 24.6%. Figures from Gershom Schocken, "Israel in Election Year 1984," *Foreign Affairs,* Fall, 1984, p. 77.

3. For example, polls taken in Israel in late September, 1982 showed a strong trend toward both the hawkish and dovish ends of the spectrum at the expense of the center. Ronald J. Young, 1987. *Missed Opportunities for Peace,* Philadelphia, American Friends Service Committee (AFSC), p. 87.

4. For an abundance of source material on Israel's foreign policies, including destabilization, see Jane Hunter, 1987. *Israeli Foreign Policy. South Africa and Central America,* Boston, South End Press; also see Benjamin Beit-Hallahmi, 1987. *The Israeli Connection: Who Israel Arms and Why,* New York, Pantheon Books; Milton Jamail and Margo Gutierrez, 1987. *It's No Secret: Israel's Military Involvement In Central America,* Belmont, Mass., Association of Arab-American University Graduates; Bishara Bahbah, 1986. *Israel and Latin America: The Military Connection,* New York, St. Martin's Press; also see the 1987 documentary which explores the sincerity of Israel's promise to sign no new arms deals with South Africa: *A Farewell to Arms?,* Diverse Productions of London, available through *Israeli Foreign Affairs,* PO Box 19580, Sacramento, Ca 95819 (VHS/ $30.)

5. Yoram Peri, "From Coexistence to Hegemony," *Davar,* October 1, 1982.

6. Amos Elon, *Ha'aretz,* November 13, 1981.

7. Yisrael Ber, 1966. *Etmol-Hayom-Machar* (Israel's Security: Yesterday-Today-Tomorrow,) Tel-Aviv, Amikam, pp. 291-292; also see Nashif, op cit, p. 65; Chomsky, "The Road to Armageddon," *The Fateful Triangle,* op cit, pp. 441-469.

8. In a speech made on the West Bank in May 1981 Menachem Begin declared: "I, Menachem, son of Ze'ev and Hana Begin, do solemnly swear that as long as I serve the nation as Prime Minister, we will not leave any part of Judea, Samaria, the Gaza Strip or the Golan Heights." Carter, *Blood,* op cit, pp. 45 and 54.

A similar statement in the form of a warning to the United States was issued in a press release by Prime Minister Yitzhak Shamir in March 1988, and repeated again later in the month at the conclusion of the Prime Minister's visit to Washington. Shamir's statements amounted to a flat rejection of the latest American 'peace plan' presented by Secretary of State George Schultz – a plan which was more or less a rehash of the 1982 Reagan Plan. (In other words, it was a plan which offered nothing to the Palestinians.) Shamir's categorical rejection was qualified by an incidental remark which, incredibly, was interpreted by some in Washington as a sign of 'progress.' With a flourish Shamir declared that the only thing acceptable about Schultz's latest proposal was "Schultz's signature at the bottom." By early April, even Schultz had to admit publicly that his 'peace initiative' was dead. John M. Goshko, "Schultz Implies Shamir's Stance May Scuttle Peace Prospects," *Washington Post,* April 8, 1988.

More recently, Shamir threatened to crush any attempt to create an independent Palestinian state on the West Bank. Dan Fisher, "Shamir vows to crush creation of Arab state," *LA Times-Washington Post* Service, *The Oregonian,* August 11, 1988.

9. Hart, op cit, p. 391.

10. In an undelivered speech published in *Ma'ariv* in 1981 Sharon asserted that Israel's security interests stretched from Central America to "beyond the Arab countries in the Middle East." The role of the IDF, he said, was to defend "the area between Pakistan, Libya and Somalia against Soviet penetration." *Ma'ariv,* December 18, 1981, trans. in *Journal of Palestine Studies,* No. 43, Spring, 1982. As recently as 1986 Sharon has stated that Israel had the military strength to "reach the gates of Odessa." Gid'on Samet, "Superman Must Take it Easy," *Ha'aretz,* December 3, 1986, in *FBIS/Middle East and Africa,* pp.1-3-4.

11. *Yediot Aharonot,* January 28, 1977.

12. Cited in Chomsky, *Fateful Triangle,* op cit, pp 128-129.

13. Ball, op cit, p. 25.

14. Amos Perlmutter, *New York Times,* May 17, 1982.

15. Ariel Sharon, "Israel's Strategic Problems in the Eighties," an address prepared for a conference of the Institute of Strategic Studies, Tel Aviv University, December 14, 1981. For a critical analysis of Sharon's Philosophy see Yoram Peri, "From Coexistence to Hegemony," *Davar,* October 1, 1982.

16. Despite the inherent limitations of George Ball's analysis, his account of the war is well worth studying. Ball, op cit, pp 25-26. Note: the 20,000 casualty figure was announced by the Lebanese government, and has been cited in Israel – though it has been ridiculed by relief workers and reporters as a gross underestimate. See Chomsky, *Fateful Triangle,* op cit, pp 334 and 222-223.

17. For the complete text of the Israeli government statement, plus a detailed discussion/critical analysis of it and the raid, see "Operation Babylon: the Baghdad Reactor Raid," Green, *Sword,* op cit, pp. 135-152.

Similar warnings by Israeli officials have been reported in recent years. In a 1987 interview which aired on Australian television, former Israeli Chief-of-Staff Mordechai Gur stated: "As a result of the continuous threat by the Arab countries we have to survive and we have to take the [necessary] measures in order to survive. So that first of all we have to prevent any nuclear weapons in the Arab hands; that's a full support [sic] of the Israelis, and that we shall never be found weak by the Arabs. Every Israeli supports that policy. On top of that, no Israeli wants to know all the details. I mean, if you ask most Israelis, they don't have at all that feeling that they are being kept in secrecy." Couchman, op cit, p. 22.

18. Responsibility for the attack at La Seyne-sur-Mer was initially claimed by an "ecology group." The claim was quickly ruled out, due to the obvious professional nature of the operation. The deception does reveal something about Israeli propaganda, i.e., its readiness to manipulate and co-opt anti-nuclear sentiment. Ronald Koven, "Saboteurs Bomb French Plant Building Two Reactors for Iraq," *Washington Post,* April 7, 1979; also see *Ma'ariv,* April 8, 1979; "How Iraq Lost its Nuclear Option," *Foreign Report,* April 11, 1979, pp. 1-5.

19. David Horovitz, "Israel Reportedly Urged India to Join Attack on Pakistan Nuke Plant," *Jerusalem Post* Foreign Service, reprinted in *Northern California Jewish Bulletin,* February 27, 1987.

20. "Showdown on Israeli Nukes," *Israeli Foreign Affairs,* January, 1988.

21. *Jerusalem Post,* January 17, 1988.

22. To my knowledge, no evidence has been presented suggesting that Pakistan is likely to share its nuclear capability with other Islamic, or more specifically, with Arab states. In fact, all the evidence suggests just the opposite. No nuclear power to date is known to have supplied nuclear warheads to another nation. In fact, China and Pakistan are known to have categorically refused such requests made by Libya. Spector, *Going Nuclear,* op cit, pp. 146-155.

23. Green, *Sword,* op cit, p. 221.

24. Stephen Green, "Going MAD in the Middle East," *The Nation,* September 27, 1986; also see Green, *Sword,* op cit, pp. 219-234.

25. *Ibid*

26. The SA-5 surface-to-air missile has a range of 150 miles, sufficient to blanket the skies over Lebanon, Syria, northern Israel, and parts of the Mediterranean. Ned Tempko, "Moscow Warns Israel," *Christian Science Monitor,* March 17, 1983; Green, "Going MAD," op cit.

27. George C. Wilson and David B. Ottaway, "Saudi-Israeli Tensions Worry U.S.," *Washington Post,* March 25, 1988, p. A-1.

28. David Ottaway, "Saudis Hid Acquisition of Missiles," *Washington Post,* March 29, 1988, p. A-1.

29. Wilson, "Saudi-Israeli Tensions," op cit.

30. *Washington Post,* May 23, 1988.

31. *Ibid*

32. *Ibid;* also see *Newsweek,* April 4, 1988, p. 43.

33. *Ibid*

34. Beit-Hallahmi, op cit, p. 212; also see Marshall, Scott and Hunter, op cit, p. 13.

35. 1987 Middle East Military Balance Report, Jaffe Center for Strategic Studies, cited in *Tikkun,* January/February, 1988, p. 39; also see "Syria, Arab Countries Acquiring Chemical Weapons," *Jerusalem Domestic Service,* 1000 GMT, August 18, 1986, reprinted in *FBIS/Middle East and Africa,* August 19, 1986, p. 1-6, cited in Spector, *Going Nuclear,* op cit. p. 128, note #5.

36. *Time,* September 14, 1987, p. 51.

37. In a recent public workshop on the Lavi project, Major Orley Lahat, IAF, discussed the design and capabilities of the proposed new fighter-bomber. According to Lahat, the Lavi is the first 100%

computer-designed tailor-made aircraft. Another first: reliance on 25% composite materials. Top speed: Mach-2 (2000 km/hr) Also: because of its digital avionics, the Lavi's "low-rudder performance" makes it, in Lahat's words, "one of the most invulnerable planes in the world." Of course, given the Lavi's cost, by one estimate as much as $22,000,000 per plane, high survivability would be essential. Another of the Lavi's assets would be the ability to fly many sorties in a given period of time. "Beyond the Lavi Jet Fighter – Israel's Air Force and Security Needs," *Israel Education Day,* U.C. Berkeley, February 21, 1988.

38. If the Lavi could not meet the challenge of Arab SS missiles, what then was it's purpose? At least one commentator believes the plane was targeted for export. See Hunter, *Israeli Foreign Policy,* op cit, p. 45; also see "Decrease in U.S. Aid to Israel May Force a Halt in Lavi Program." *Aviation Week and Space Technology,* June 9, 1986.

Israel's economic dependence on arms exports is certainly no secret. In a recent public lecture on the Lavi airplane delivered at U.C. Berkeley, an Israeli Air Force officer, Major Orley Lahat, openly acknowledged Israel's need to export arms, and explicitly mentioned South Africa. (See note 37.) Furthermore, an in-house document prepared by Israeli Aircraft Industries in the early 1980's described ambitious plans to market the Lavi in Argentina, Chile, Taiwan – and South Africa. "The U.S. and Israel Are Closer Than Ever," *The Washington Post,* National Weekly Edition, August 18, 1986. In February 1987, the *New York Times* reprinted a report – originally appearing in *Davar* – that in 1980 Israeli Defense Minister Ezer Weizmann tried to interest the South African regime in the Lavi project. Israeli leaders continued to officially deny any such intentions. Dan Fisher, "Israeli Needs Time on S. Africa," *New York Times,* February 21, 1987.

A report also cited by Jane Hunter from *Jane's Defense Weekly* claimed that South Africa, with a different shopping list, may now itself – in the wake of the Lavi's demise in Israel – be trying to acquire the plans and sub-systems for the aircraft. Should Israel clandestinely arrange such a deal, it would be a flagrant violation of promises made to the United States, amounting to a billion-dollar U.S. subsidy of the SADF. Recently, the *Jerusalem Post* reported that many of the Israeli technicians laid off after cancellation of the Lavi, including aeronautical engineers and computer programmers, had been rehired in South Africa. "Aircraft to South Africa," *Israeli Foreign Affairs,* November 1987, p. 6; also see *Ha'aretz,* February 12, 1988; *Financial Times,* January 5, 1988; *Jerusalem Post,* March 7, 1988.

39. Barnaby, "The Nuclear Arsenal," op cit, p. 31.

40. *Ibid*, p. 30; also see Spector, *Going Nuclear*, op cit, pp. 130-141; Nordland, "Bombs in the Basement," op cit, p. 44.

41. Leonard S. Spector, "Nuclear Proliferation: Who's Next?" *Bulletin of the Atomic Scientists*, May, 1987, p. 18.

42. "Plutonium black market reported," *The Sacramento Bee*, October 31, 1987; also see David Horovitz "Israel alleged to have initiated black market in N-weapons material," *Jerusalem Post*, Nov. 1, 1987.

43. *Ibid*

44. *Ibid*

45. Ze'ev Schiff, "Cracks in the Security Outlook," *Ha'aretz*, August 7, 9, 10, 1987.

46. Another issue of contention may have been the Army's dissatisfaction with what they regarded as government complacency in the face of a growing Arab chemical weapons capability. According to reports already cited, both Iraq and Iran presently produce mustard and/or nerve gases, and Iraq has used them in the war with Iran. In a recent speech to the Knesset, MK and General (Res.) Matti Peled argued that the Israeli government had miscalculated in discounting the Arab chemical weapons threat. Peled claimed that chemical weapons, as weapons of mass destruction, constituted a danger to Israel no less real than nuclear arms. Speech reprinted in *Israel & Palestine*, April, 1988, p. 18.

47. Schiff, "Cracks," op cit.

48. "U.S. Israel to Collaborate on Tactical Missile Defense," *Washington Post*, January 1, 1988.

49. John Kifner, "Israel Launches Space Program and a Satellite," *New York Times*, September 20, 1988, p. A-1.

50. Feldman's views in 1980, summarized here, may already be an anachronism: "Nuclear weapons are particularly well suited for creating...stability. The increased stability of deterrence based on nuclear weapons results from their high cost-exchange ratio against answering or neutralizing [second strike] weapons.. They are relatively cheap and easy to make, to protect and to deliver. This means that an attempt to prevent nuclear weapons from doing their damage must cost vastly more than the nuclear weapons themselves and their delivery.

Nuclear deterrence increases the chances for peace primarily by increasing the overall level of security....Nuclear deterrence enhances the security of states primarily by strengthening their prospects for survival. Nuclear deterrence insures states against the worst and thus enhances security. By insuring the survival of states nuclear weapons reduce their incentives to wage war in the quest for security." Incidentally, these ideas were not new; they had been advanced for years to justify the balance of terror between the superpowers, a standoff usually referred to as Mutually Assured Destruction (MAD). Shai Feldman, 1980. *Israeli Nuclear Deterrence,* Doctoral Dissertation, U.C. Berkeley, pp. 22 and 33-34.

51. Feldman wrote: "Israel should refrain from developing a doctrine and capability for counter-Soviet nuclear deterrence. In order to avoid extreme Soviet responses resulting from unnecessary anxieties about Israel's nuclear capability, Israel should try to convince Moscow that her deterrent posture does not constitute a threat to Soviet security." *Ibid,* p. 265.

52. London *Sunday Times,* October 5, 1986; "Three Nations Begin," op cit, pp. 11-19.

53. Chomsky, *Fateful Triangle,* op cit, pp. 193-196; also see Young, op cit, pp. 11-19.

54. Israel's shelling of the Soviet compound in West Beirut was at least partly accomplished with the same 155-mm long-range artillery already discussed, which suggests – due to the weapon's accuracy – that the bombing was not accidental. *TASS,* June 21, 1982; also see "Soviet Embassy Heavily Damaged by Israeli Shells," *New York Times,* July 8, 1982. For a discussion of the surprise attack on the Syrian SAM batteries see Ball, op cit, pp. 41-43.

55. America's National Security Agency (NSA) monitored the recent Jericho II test, conducted in the Mediterranean. According to U.S. intelligence estimates, Israel currently possesses between 45 and 65 Jerichos. "Soviets Warn Israel on Missiles," San Francisco *Chronicle,* July 30, 1987. Note: a recent report also indicated South African involvement in the new Jericho II project. *Yediot Aharonot,* November 27, 1987, cited in-Israeli Foreign Affairs, March, 1988, p. 4.

56. "Superman Must Take It Easy," op cit (See note 10.)

57. "Soviets Warn Israel," op cit.

58. *Baltimore Sun,* November 23, 1988, cited in *Israeli Foreign Affairs,* December, 1988, p. 6.

59. For an extensive chronological review of successive "memoranda of understanding" between Israel and the United States during the 1980's which illustrate the deepening relationship, see Green, *Sword,* op cit, pp. 222-224; also see Beit-Hallahmi, op cit, p. 192.

60. The *Washington Post* National Weekly Edition, August 18,

1986. More recently during Israel's 40th birthday celebrations, Yitzhak Shamir and President Reagan signed a memorandum of agreement, formalizing for the first time the already intimate military/economic relationship. Glenn Frankel, "Security Alert Chills," San Francisco *Chronicle*, April 22, 1988.

61. Green, *Sword*, op cit, p. 224.

62. *Los Angeles Times*, August 9, 1986, p. 16.

63. Feldman, op cit, pp. 263-266, and 115.

64. *Ibid*, p. 110.

65. Dr. Robert M. Bowan (Lt. Col. USAF., ret.) 1985. *Star Wars: Defense or Death Star?*, Chesapeake Beach, MD., Institute for Space and Security Studies.

66. Quoted in David Newdorf, "Israeli anti-nuclear movement stagnates," *In These Times*, October 21-27, 1987.

67. Peretz Kidron, "Atoms for peace?" *Middle East International*, December 5, 1987.

68. Ian Black, "Israelis turn deaf ear to N-weapons controversy," *The Guardian*, November 17, 1986.

69. *Jerusalem Post*, October 5, 1987.

70. Ball, op cit, p. 97.

71. See quote by Dayan in the text of Chapter Six at note 41, p. 213.

72. In a series of articles after the war Israel's military journalist Ze'ev Schiff thoroughly refuted claims made by General Sharon that Syria had plans to attack Israel. Armitage, op cit, p. 141; also see Ball, op cit, pp. 41-43; Ze'ev Schiff, "An Excuse in Justification of the War," "Three Separate Wars," *Ha'aretz*, January 10, 11, 1983; Chomsky, *Fateful Triangle*, op cit, pp. 335-337.

73. Ned Temko, "Moscow Warns Israel," *Christian Science Monitor*, March 17, 1983; also see "War of Liberation," *New York Review of Books*, November 22, 1984, p. 36; Neil Roland, "Soviets Reportedly Offer Nuclear Help to Syria," UPI wire story, November 28, 1985, citing an interview with Tlas in Al-Ittihad, October 4, 1985, translated in *FBIS/Middle East and Africa*, October 7, 1985.

74. For a lucid discussion of past near-misses, see Ellsberg, "Mutiny," op cit, pp. 36-52.

75. In the weeks before the 1982 war Israel employed sophisticated unmanned drone aircraft to pinpoint the Syrian missile batteries. Reportedly the technology has since been used by South Africa. Armitage, op cit, p. 141; also see "A Farewell to Arms," Diverse Productions, op cit. More recently, these technologies have

been eclipsed by the launch of Israel's first *Ofek* (Horizon I) spy satellite.

76. According to James Adams, at the time of the 1973 war, the 30-50 km range of Israel's 155-mm artillery was far beyond anything possessed by the Syrians. Later, in the 1982 attack on Syrian SAM batteries its use sets a precedent. As Armitage put it: "This allocation of surface-to-surface firepower to eliminate air defenses marked a major change in priorities for artillery and set a new benchmark in land-air coordination." It is also quite possible that in recent years the cannon's range has been further extended by South African refinements. Adams, op cit, p. 42; Armitage, op cit, p. 140.

77. The plausibility of such a revolutionary application was confirmed to the author by Dr. Richard Muller, physicist at UC Berkeley and former blue-ribbon panelist. Conversation with Dr. Muller, May 3, 1988.

High altitude bursts apparently enhance the range and strength of EMP. For an early discussion of the discovery and effects of EMP, see Samuel Glasstone and Philip J. Dolan, Editors, 1977. *The Effects of Nuclear Weapons,* Washington D.C., U.S. Department of Defense and the Energy Research and Development Administration, pp. 514-540. For a more recent discussion see MIT Faculty, op cit, pp. 87 and 113; also see Amory B., and Hunter L. Lovins, 1982. *Brittle Power: Energy Strategy for National Security,* Andover, Brick House Publishing Company, pp. 72-74. For a brief history of EMP research, as well as a more technical analysis of EMP, see K.S.H. Lee, Editor, 1986. *EMP Interaction: Principles, Techniques, and Reference Data,* Washington, Hemisphere Publishing; also see, *EMP Threat and Protective Measures,* 1980, Federal Emergency Management Agency.

78. "US, Israel to Collaborate on Tactical Missile Defense," op cit.

79. Yigael Yadin, "For By Wise Counsel Thou Shalt Make Thy War" in B.H. Liddell Hart, 1967. *Strategy: the Indirect Approach,* London, Faber and Faber, appendix II, p. 397.

80. As reported by *Washington Post* writer Glenn Frankel, Prime Minister Shamir's reasoning, in pressing for formal military/economic ties recently, "was an attempt to make it more difficult for future Presidents to retreat from the special relationship with Israel," "Security Alert Chills," op cit.

81. Green, *Sword,* op cit, p. 229.

82. Tempko, "Moscow Warns Israel," op cit.

83. Spokesman, op cit, p. 30.

84. E.V. Ortlieb, Commander, U.S. Navy (Ret.), "Forward Deployments: Deterrent or Temptation?" *Proceedings,* U.S Naval Institute, December, 1983, p. 36.

85. In recent years military officers (such as General George S. Brown, former Chairman of the Joint Chiefs) and analysts (Andrew H. Cordesman) who dared to criticize the concept of "Israel as a strategic asset" have been effectively silenced with accusations of anti-Semitism, or, as in the case of General Brown, a personal reprimand from the President. Ball. op cit, pp. 126-128; Chomsky, *Fateful Triangle,* op cit, p. 464.

86 According to John Pike of the Federation of American Scientists, development of the Arrow missile is still in the early stages, flight testing being at least two years away. Conversation with Mr. Pike, April 26, 1988.

LIST OF ACRONYMS/TERMS

ABM	Anti-Ballistic Missile
AEC	Atomic Energy Commission (currently defunct)
AFSC	American Friends Service Committee
AIPAC	American-Israeli Public Affairs Committee (The Israel Lobby)
ANC	African National Congress
ERW	enhanced radiation weapon (neutron bomb)
FBIS	Foreign Broadcast Information Service
CIA	Central Intelligence Agency
DOE	Department of Energy
EMP	electromagnetic pulse
GAO	(US) Government Accounting Office
Haganah	forerunner of the IDF
Herut	forerunner of the Likud coalition
HEU	highly enriched uranium
IAEA	International Atomic Energy Agency (1957)
IAF	Israeli Air Force
IDF	Israeli Defense Forces
KMG	*Kirya-le-Mehekar Gariny* (Hebrew for NRCN)
MAD	Mutually Assured Destruction
MAPAI	Palestine Workers' Party (forerunner of the Labor coalition)
MAPAM	United Workers' Party (The Israeli left)
MK	Member of Knesset
Moodin	Israeli Military Intelligence
Mossad	Central Institute for Security Intelligence (the Israeli CIA)
NNPA	Nuclear Nonproliferation Act (1978)
NPT	Treaty on the Nonproliferation of Nuclear Weapons (1968)
NRC	Nuclear Regulatory Commission
NRCN	Nuclear Research Center of the Negev
NRL	Naval Research Lab
NSA	National Security Agency

NSC	National Security Council
NWFZ	Nuclear Weapon-Free Zone
NUMEC	Nuclear Materials and Equipment Corporation
OSTP	(White House) Office of Science and Technology Policy
SAAEB	South African Atomic Energy Board
SADF	South African Defense Forces
SALT	Strategic Arms Limitation Treaty (SALT I: 1972; SALT II: unratified)
SAM	surface to air missile
SDI	Strategic Defense Initiative (Star Wars)
Shabaq	formerly, *Shin Bet*
Shin Bet	Israeli Security Police (the Israeli FBI)
SIPRI	Stockholm International Peace Research Institute
SRC	Space Research Corporation
SSM	surface to surface missile
UNPCC	UN Palestine Conciliation Commission
UNTSO	UN Truce Supervision Organization
Yesh Gvul	in Hebrew, lit. there is a limit/border. *Yesh Gvul* progressives support a two-state settlement.

MAJOR DATES IN ISRAEL'S NUCLEAR PROGRAM

1949   Visit to Israel of French nuclear scientist Francis Perrin. Israel discovers uranium in the Negev desert.

1952   Creation of the Israeli Atomic Energy Commission (IAEC) under the authority of the Defense Ministry. Development of the Dostrovsky method for production of heavy water.

1953   Department of Nuclear Physics established at the Weizmann Institute. French-Israeli nuclear cooperation agreement.

1955   First discussion of nuclear cooperation with South Africa. Start of U.S.-Israeli nuclear cooperation.

1957   Secret agreement with France to build Dimona reactor and plutonium separation plant.

1958   Department of Nuclear Science established at the Israel Institute of Technology (Technion).

1960   Research reactor at Nahal Soreq goes on line. Ben Gurion tells Knesset about the Dimona reactor.

1963   Dimona reactor goes on line. Regular shipments of uranium from South Africa begin.

1966   Levi Eshkol reorganizes Israeli Atomic Energy Commission, Bergmann resigns as Chairman. Eshkol cuts a deal with President Johnson and freezes Israeli nuclear program. Israeli nuclear test in Negev.

1967   De Gaulle severs ties with Israel. Moshe Dayan launches plans to accelerate Israel's nuclear program.

1968   Cabinet capitulates to Dayan's nuclear agenda. CIA suspects Israel of having nuclear weapons.

1972   Technological breakthroughs made in uranium enrichment (laser method).

1973   Golda Meir gives the order to arm nuclear warheads during Yom Kippur War.

1976   South African President Vorster visits Israel; new nuclear agreement forged.

1977   Israeli-South African test in Kalahari desert detected by Soviet satellite and blocked by U.S. intervention.

1979   Israeli-South African test off South African coast.

1982   President Reagan sells advanced computers to South Africa.

APPENDICES

Appendix A. Letters to the Norwegian Nobel
Committee nominating Mordechai Vanunu for the
1988 Nobel Peace Prize.

The Bertrand Russell Peace Foundation Ltd.

Bertrand Russell House,
Gamble Street,
Nottingham NG7 4ET,
England (Reg. Office)
Reg. No. 891680 (England)
Telephone: 0602-784504
Cables: Russfound Nottingham

A LETTER TO THE NORWEGIAN NOBEL COMMITTEE

The Director,   July, 1987

The Norwegian Nobel Committee
Drammensvein 19,
N-0255 Oslo 2,
Norway

Dear Sir,

We wish to make a nomination for the Nobel Prize. As elected Members of the Parliament of the United Kingdom, we would like your Committee to consider the name of Mr. Mordechai Vanunu of Israel. The current address of Mr. Vanunu is care of Prison services, PO Box 2495, Jerusalem.

On the 5th October 1986, Mr. Vanunu published in the *Sunday Times* a detailed story about the Israeli government's nuclear bomb factory near Dimona in Southern Israel. In addition to a detailed description, Mr. Vanunu furnished the newspaper with photographs and diagrams, and his account of the plan was found to be "entirely authentic" by a number of international experts who subsequently examined it.

The threat of nuclear proliferation into various hot spots around the world is one of the major perils confronting the international community. It takes prodigious courage for a private citizen to confront his own Government on such a sensitive issue. Mr. Vanunu has paid a very heavy penalty. For revealing his knowledge, he was kidnapped in

Rome and secretly taken to Israel, where he has been locked in solitary confinement. Even his family have now been denied the right to visit him. Although he faces a death sentence, his trial is being conducted in secrecy.

World public opinion has reason for deep concern about the Israeli Government's preparation of nuclear weapons. This decision invites Arab states to follow on, and represents a terribly dangerous precedent. But Mr. Vanunu's kidnap is itself an illegal act, which has no justification in international conventions. We cannot doubt that the Italian government would have refused to extradite Mr. Vanunu for trial, on the evidence which is available. Vanunu's revelations serve to uphold the non-proliferation regime throughout the world, and are clearly a matter of conscience, quite unsuitable for criminal reprisals.

It is our opinion that the Nobel Committee can make a powerful contribution to justice and peace by publicly considering Mr. Vanunu for an award which he has richly earned.

Yours Sincerely, (MP's)

Kevin Barron
Tony Benn
Gerry Bermingham
Sydney Bidwell
Ron Brown
Richard Caborn
Dennis Canavan
Bob Clay
Clare Short
Dennis Skinner
Gavin Strang
Brian Wilson
Lord Brockway
Lord Jenkins of Putney
Lord Molloy of Ealing
Robin Cook
Frank Cook
Derek Fatchet
Martin Flannery
Maria Fyfe
Sam Galbraith

George Galloway
Nigel Griffiths
Stuart Holland
Doug Hoyle
Eric Illsley
Ron Leighton
Ken Livingstone
Eddie Loyden
Max Madden
Alice Mahon
Alan Meale
Chris Mullin
Calum A. MacDonald
Bob Parry

Also endorsed by:
Frank Allaun
Christopher J. Arthur
Gregory Blue
Claude Bourdet
Ken Coates

Professor Bernard Crick
Richard Eyre
Ken Fleet
Trevor Griffiths
Peter Hain
Royden Harrison
Geof Hodgson

Joseph Needham
Professor Jim Riordan
Mrs. K. Smith
Colin Stoneman
Tony Topham
J.H. Westergaard
Susannah York

PARLIMENT OF AUSTRALIA • **THE SENATE**

OLIVE ZAKHAROV
SENATOR FOR VICTORIA
597 GLENHUNTLY ROAD
ELSTERNWICK, VIC. 3185
TEL. 523 8844

1 June, 1987

The Norwegian Nobel Committee
Drammensvein 19
N - 0255 Oslo 2
Norway

Dear Sir/Madam,

Re: <u>Mr. Moredechai Vanunu - Proposed Candidate for the Nobel Peace Prize</u>

We, the undersigned, elected members of the Australian Parliament, hereby submit the following proposal for the award of the Nobel Peace Prize to Mr. MOREDECHAI VANUNU of ISRAEL for his effective contribution to nuclear disarmament and peace, in particular to nuclear disarmament in the Middle East.

On October 5 1986 the *Sunday Times* of London published a detailed report about a secret Israeli Government nuclear bomb factory (six storeys underground) attached to the 150 Megawatt reactor near the town of Dimona in Southern Israel. The report was based on information supplied to the paper by Mr. Moredechai Vanunu, a former employee of that plant, who is at risk of his life, (*sic*) photographed all six storeys of the secret plant. His photographs were examined by experts appointed by the newspaper, who confirmed the authenticity and accuracy of the information provided by Mr. Vanunu.

Whilst it is true that for many years rumours of Israel's production of nuclear weapons have been circulating around the world, Mr. Mordechai Vanunu's revelations have put an end to the ambiguity surrounding the danger. His service to world peace has been in providing the world with precise information which enables the international community to realistically assess the situation which lies behind Israel's refusal to sign the Nuclear Non Proliferation Treaty. Also amongst Mr. Moredechai Vanunu's revelations is that the Government of Israel has been secretly collaborating with the Government of South Africa in research, production, testing and deployment of nuclear weapons.

On September 30, 1986, Mr. Moredechai Vanunu was kidnapped from Rome airport by Israeli Government agents. He was taken to Israel, locked up in a secret prison, and kept in solitary confinement. For six weeks the Israeli Government denied any knowledge of Mr. Vanunu's whereabouts, whilst in fact he had been unlawfully imprisoned there. On November 9 1986, one day before the hearing of an application of Habeus Corpus on his behalf, he was brought to court for the first time to get a warrant for his arrest and further detention.

On December 28, 1986, his trial began, and he pleaded not guilty to the charges of "aggravated espionage and assisting the enemy in war" according to sections 99 and 113 (b) and (c) of the Israeli Penal Law 1977. The penalty for these charges is death. The court rejected a demand by the defense that the trial be open, and consequently all proceedings are in secrecy.

The courageous action which Moredechai Vanunu has taken for universal peace was the result of conscious decisions taken by him in complete selflessness, out of a sense of duty to humanity.

We believe that Moredechai Vanunu's action in revealing details of Israel's nuclear weapons arsenal to the world was motivated by a great and longstanding desire for world peace, and we believe that he deserves the world's recognition for his selfless action. The award of the Nobel Prize to him would be a timely and appropriate expression of such a recognition.

His postal address, since his abduction in September 1986, is

Moredechai Vanunu
c/o Prison Services
PO Box 2495
Jerusalem,
ISRAEL

Yours sincerely,

Senator Olive Zakharov
Allen Blanchard M.P
Senator Nick Bolkus
Lewis Kent M.P.
Harry Jenkins M.P.
Robert Tickner M.P.
Senator Margaret Reynolds
Peter Milton M.P.
Senator Jim McKiernan

Appendix B. Ad Hoc Panel Report on the September 22, 1979 event.

EXECUTIVE OFFICE OF THE PRESIDENT
OFFICE OF SCIENCE AND TECHNOLOGY POLICY
AD HOC PANEL REPORT ON THE SEPTEMBER 22 EVENT

July 15, 1980

Background

A panel of nongovernment scientists (listed in Appendix) was convened by Dr. Frank Press, Science Adviser to the President and Director of the Office of Science and Technology Policy, to assist in determining the likelihood that the light signal recorded by a VELA satellite over the South Atlantic on September 22, 1979, was from a nuclear explosion. Specifically, the panel was asked to (1) review all available data from both classified and unclassified sources that could help corroborate that the VELA signal originated from a nuclear explosion and suggest any additional sources of data that might be helpful in this regard; (2) evaluate the possibility that the signal in question was a "false alarm" resulting from technical malfunction such as interference from other electrical components on the VELA platform; and (3) investigate the possibility that the signal was of natural origin, possibly resulting from the coincidence of two or more natural phenomena and attempt to establish quantitative limits on the probability of such an occurrence.

The panel met three times; the last meeting was April 2-3, 1980. During the course of its work the panel (1) received numerous briefings by government agencies responsible for detecting non-U.S. nuclear explosions and collecting and analyzing data from such explosions. (2) studied performance data, circuitry and hardware involved in the VELA satellite program; (3) initiated and reviewed results of statistical analyses of the hundreds of thousands of light signals that have been recorded previously by VELA satellites and of computer modeling of natural phenomena that might have generated the September 22 signal; (4) reviewed all available data that might tend to corroborate whether that signal was generated by a nuclear explosion; and (5) reviewed analyses made by government agencies that bore on the question of whether the September 22 signal was of nuclear origin. In addition, a subgroup of the panel was briefed on available intelligence that related to the September 22 event.

The Office of Science and Technology Policy (OSTP) also requested the Naval Research Laboratory (NRL) to search worldwide for geophysical data that might bear on the origin of the September 22 event and do independent analyses of this data. NRL has not yet completed its task but has briefed the panel at its third meeting on its findings to date.

Summary of Conclusions

At its third meeting, the panel reviewed the most recently collected data and analyses. Its findings and conclusions are summarized as follows:

1. The light signal from the September 22 event strongly resembles those previously observed from nuclear explosions, but it was different from the others in a very significant way. The discrepancy suggests that the origin of the signal was close to the satellite rather than near the surface of the earth. In order to account for the September 22 VELA signal as coming from a nuclear explosion, one must hypothesize particularly anomalous functioning of the instruments (bhangmeters) that observed the event.

2. The bhangmeters on the VELA satellites have been triggered by and have recorded many previous nuclear explosions. They have also recorded hundreds of thousands of other signals, mostly from lightning and cosmic ray particles striking the light sensors. In addition they have been triggered several hundred times by signals of unknown origin, "zoo events." A few of these zoo events had some of the characteristics associated with signals from nuclear explosions, although they could be distinguished clearly from nuclear explosion signals upon examination of their complete time histories.

3. The search for nuclear debris and for geophysical evidence that might support the hypothesis that a nuclear explosion was the source of

the September 22 event has so far only produced data that is ambiguous and "noisy." At this date, there is no persuasive evidence to corroborate the occurrence of a nuclear explosion on September 22.

4. Based on the lack of persuasive evidence, the existence of other unexplained zoo events which have some of the characteristics of signals from nuclear explosions, and the discrepancies observed in the September 22 signal, the panel concludes that the signal was probably not from a nuclear explosion. Although we cannot rule out the possibility that this signal was of nuclear origin, the panel considers it more likely that the signal was one of the zoo events, possibly a consequence of the impact of a small meteoroid on the satellite.

Observed Bhangmeter Signals

Each VELA satellite carries two bhangmeters – devices that observe incident light and trigger a recording apparatus when light intensity changes rapidly. The two bhangmeters have different sensitivities so that a wide range of light intensities can be observed and recorded.

Many previous atmospheric nuclear explosions have been recorded by bhangmeters on VELA satellites. Overall, the VELA bhangmeters have been triggered hundreds of thousands of times, mostly by light from lightning and energetic cosmic particles both of which have identifiable short time duration signals. The bhangmeters have also been triggered by calibration signals from internal light sources or, recently, ground based lasers, direct sunlight and "other" sources (referred to as zoo events) which are not satisfactorily understood and which have great variation in signal character.

It had been though that the zoo events were due to passing meteoroids, but we have not been able to construct a satisfactory model to justify this explanation. More recently an explanation has been offered that these signals are from sun reflection from debris ejected from the satellite after a collision with a small meteoroid. This explanation seems more plausible to the panel but has yet to be fully developed.

Figures 1-4 show some bhangmeter records from different events:

* Figure 1 shows a typical low-yield nuclear explosion with its characteristic double-hump.

* Figure 2 shows the optical signature recorded by both the more sensitive (YC) and the less sensitive (YV) bhangmeter of the September 22 event.

* Figure 3 shows an example of one of the few zoo events in which a double-humped optical pulse is observed. However the detailed pulse shape is not consistent with what is observed from a nuclear explosion.

* Figure 4 shows an example of a long duration zoo signal which is obviously very different from a nuclear explosion signal.

Figure 1

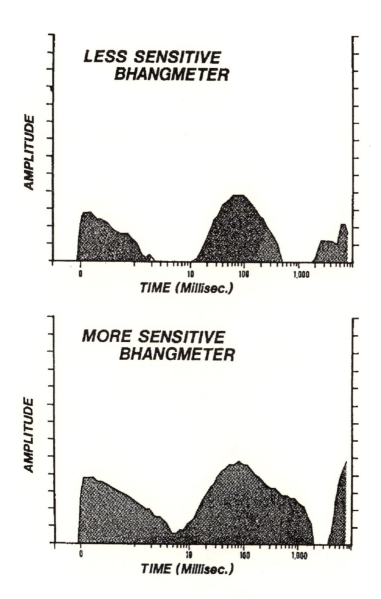

Figure 2

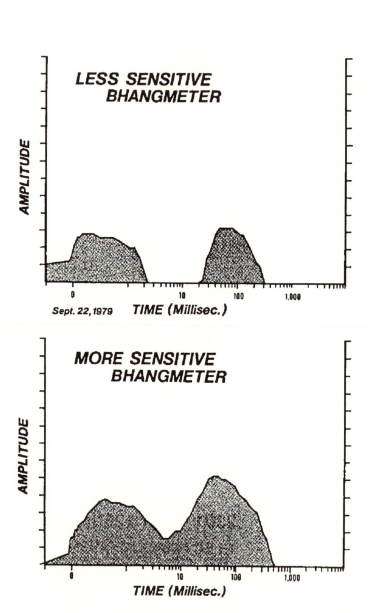

Figure 3

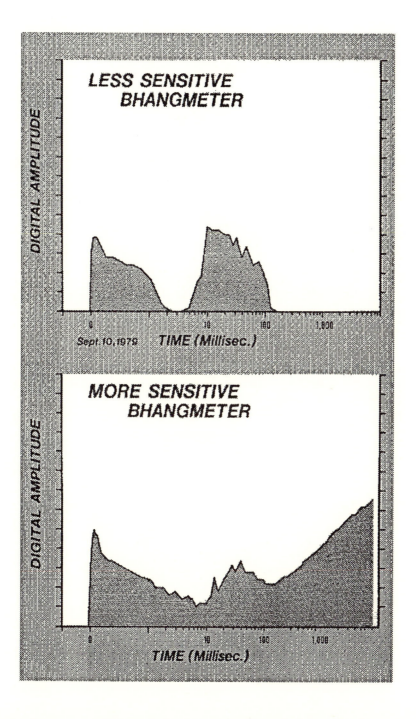

Figure 4

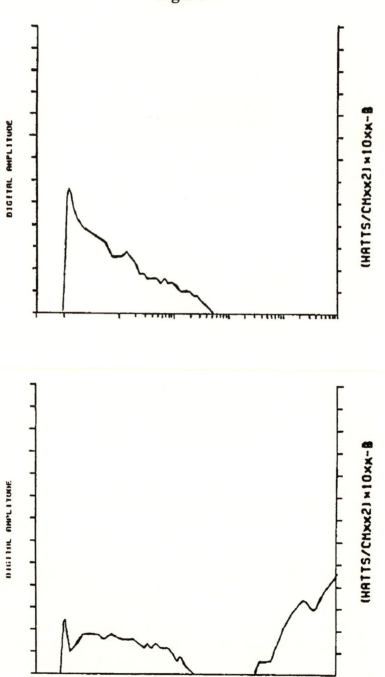

The September 22 Event

On September 22, 1979, the two "bhangmeters" on board a VELA satellite observed a flash of light consistent with that observed from a nuclear explosion on or near the earth's surface. Identical or very similar bhangmeters are also on board other satellites. However, these other satellites were looking at different parts of the earth and due to weather conditions had very little coverage overlap on the surface of the earth with the VELA satellite that observed the light flash. None of these others observed the light signal that was recorded by these bhangmeters.

The September 22 event has many of the features of signals from previously observed nuclear explosions. It has the right duration and the characteristic double-humped shape was recorded by both bhangmeters. The three separate yield determinations, which are normally derived from the time of the maximum and minimum of the pulse shape, are in rough agreement. (They agree about as well as one might expect, given experience with past low-yield events.) These results and the signal characteristics are consistent with a determination that the September 22 signal was from a nuclear explosion. But in making such a determination it is also necessary to show that the signal has no additional characteristics that rule out the nuclear origin hypothesis, or that there is not another class of signals for which it is more likely that the one of September 22 is a member.

Careful examination reveals a significant deviation in the light signature of the September 22 event that throws doubt on its interpretation as a nuclear event. The deviation is seen in the examination of the relative intensity of signals recorded in the two bhangmeters YC and YV. While the ratio of light recorded by YC and YV is not necessarily constant, it is expected to be reproducible, i.e., if at one time the bhangmeters recorded YC = 20, YV = 10 on a linear scale, then at a later time if YC = 20 again, one expects to see YV = 10 again, although YC may not be twice YV for other values. A "scatter plot" in which amplitude readings for the two bhangmeters are plotted against each other, should show a narrow locus for the recorded signals.

Actual data recorded for ground-based events does not completely conform to these ideal characteristics because of time differences between between triggering of the two channels and changes in background (termed "tailup" and "taildown") during data recording.

Figure 5 shows YC versus YV for twelve known nuclear events and the September 22 event, all recorded by the VELA satellite that observed the September 22 event. To obtain this plot small time-shift corrections to the original data have been made to compensate for the fact that the two bhangmeters operate independently and do not trigger at precisely the same time. In addition, each time history has been truncated at the onset of tailup or taildown effects.

In the resulting plot, the discrepant behavior of the September 22 event in relation to known nuclear events is evident. All of the nuclear events fall within a narrow band, but the second hump of the September 22 event causes it to fall distinctly outside the nuclear band. Qualitatively, this means that during the second hump, the ratio of the bhangmeter signals is significantly different from what would be expected from a nuclear explosion near the surface of the earth. Such anomalous behavior was never observed in bhangmeter recordings of previous nuclear explosions. Thus, although the September 22 event displays many of the characteristics of nuclear signals, it departs in an essential feature.

It is very difficult to account for such a departure if the source of the September 22 signal was at a great distance from the bhangmeters, ie., on the surface of the earth. On the other hand, if the source of the September 22 signal were close to the satellite sensors, the relative intensity of the light incident on the two bhangmeters could be quite different from cases where the source is far away. That is, an object passing near the satellite might be more in the field of view of one sensor than the other, whereas at a distance the field of view of both sensors is essentially the same.

If the September 22 event were a zoo member rather than a nuclear explosion, then the deviation from the nuclear signal region in the YC/YV scatter-plot is not surprising. Many zoo events show large deviations in the scatter-plot. Figure 6 illustrates this deviation.

These deviations are explainable by light reflections from material sufficiently close to the bhangmeter (within about 30 meters) so as to be out of the primary field-of-view of one or both of the optical sensors. In fact, the obvious discrepancy between the two bhangmeter signals was responsible for these events once being labelled "meteoroids." It is impossible to make the zoo events lie in the narrow range seen for earth-based signals (such as the known nuclear events shown in figure 5) by adjusting the time delay between the YC and the YV channels.

Figure 5

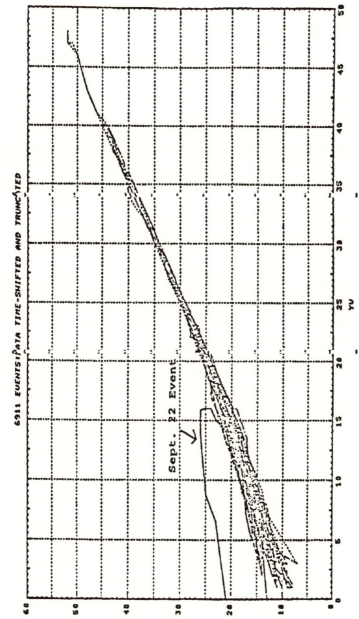

Figure 6

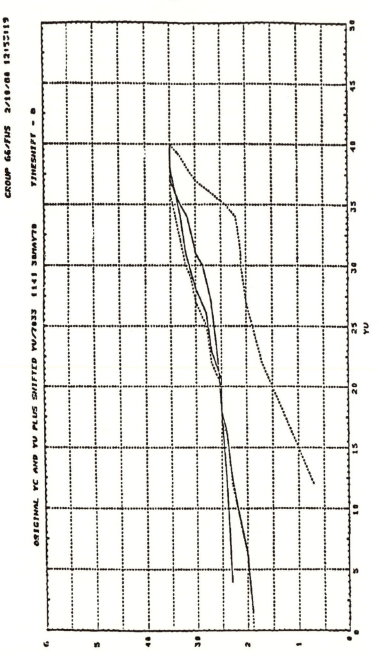

In light of the consistency of all known nuclear event data when presented in YC/YV parameter space, the discrepant behavior of the September 22 event assumes major significance. If it is a nuclear event, some source for the increase in YC signal (or decrease in YV signal) must be determined. VELA instrument malfunction has been examined as a possibility but remains highly unlikely. Background changes arising from spurious reflections from the optical detector baffling surfaces has been advanced as a cause; some evidence presented late in our meetings indicates that this possibility should be pursued (it may be testable experimentally) but it is unlikely that such a reflection can account for the discrepancy.

The alternative explanation is that the September 22 event is not of earth origin. Viewed only in terms of YC/YV ratios, the September 22 event more closely resembles the zoo events than it does the known nuclear events. If no other mechanism for the YC/YV discrepancy can be determined, a near-by origin for the event must be considered more likely than an earth-based nuclear origin.

Alternate Explanations of the September 22 Event

The panel has examined a number of possible alternative sources of the bhangmeter signals on September 22, including unusual astronomical events, ordinary lightning, superbolts of lightning, sunlight reflection from other satellites, sunlight reflections from meteoroids near the satellite, and sunlight reflected from particles ejected from collision of meteoroids upon impact with the spacecraft. Lightning and superbolts produce single light peaks and have rise times too short to be confused with nuclear events. Meteoroids of sufficient size are too rare and travel too rapidly through the field of view to generate the observed time sequences. Unusual astronomical signals would have been observed by other sensors. Other satellites are too distant to reflect enough light to trigger the VELA bhangmeters. For these reasons, except for meteoroid impacts, all of the above have been ruled out as likely causes of the September 22 signal.

At present a meteoroid impact with the VELA satellite appears to be the best candidate for a nonnuclear origin of the signal. Such an impact could generate secondary particles with a much greater mass than that of the meteoroid itself and moving with a low velocity relative to that of the satellite. The number of particles emitted can be quite large. These features provide a mechanism for generation of the complicated time histories seen in the unexplained zoo events as well as in the September 22 event. The short initial pulse could be accounted for by the entry of the first or first several particles from the ejecta into the field of view, and the long duration second-pulse from the large mass of ejecta which would soon follow. The event could be triggered by a meteoroid much smaller in size than would be required if the light signal had to be explained by reflection from the original meteoroid itself. Estimates show that such a collision can reasonably lead to the observed signal during the 10 years or so that the VELA system has been in operation.

There is additional indirect evidence from the Pioneer 10 spacecraft observations which supports this model. This spacecraft had both optical and impact sensors for meteoroid detection, but the frequency of signals recorded by the optical sensors on Pioneer 10 is two orders of magnitude greater than the detection rate recorded by its impact sensors. Interestingly, the Pioneer 10 optical observations are in reasonable agreement with the VELA zoo events, both being much more common than meteoroid impact measurements would suggest. By taking into account the much greater reflectivity of the large amount of material ejected from impact than that of the original meteoroid, one concludes that the satellite should observe large optical signals from the abundant small meteoroids that hit the satellite, rather than from close encounters with large meteoroids. Thus, the meteoroid impact model may account for both the zoo events and the high rate of optical observations of meteoroids by Pioneer 10.

Search for Supporting Data

Nuclear explosions produce fission products not otherwise found in the atmosphere and generate a variety of geophysical disturbances including hydroacoustic waves, acoustic waves, seismic signals, traveling ionospheric disturbances, electromagnetic pulses (EMP), and magnetic signals. Detection of radioactive fallout can immediately confirm a nuclear event. In contrast, geophysical signals from both natural and other artificial sources may resemble those from explosions. For low-yield explosions these geophysical signals are usually "noisy" and therefore by themselves cannot lead to unambiguous conclusions. At this time no data on EMP or magnetic disturbance that can be correlated with the September 22 signal are known to the panel. We describe below our assessment of the search for nuclear debris and data from the other geophysical sources.

a. Debris Collection

The efficiency of debris collection from a nuclear explosion is affected by the weather near the explosion site. Unstable weather and rain can significantly reduce the probability of debris collection due to rapid precipitation of debris. Weather data indicate broken clouds or overcast in much of the area of interest.

Vigorous attempts to locate debris were made. Background radiation is generally low in the Southern Hemisphere. A tentative positive result in New Zealand was subsequently shown to be erroneous. All other collections were negative, some of them indicating unusually low levels of background radiation.

Positive results from the debris collection effort would provide conclusive evidence of a nuclear explosion. However, the negative results actually obtained do not provide conclusive evidence that no nuclear explosion occurred.

b. Acoustic Data

An acoustic signal was recorded at a distant recording site in the northern hemisphere at an appropriate time. A second site in the same region had negative results for this event as did sensors in Australia. On the basis of expected propagation models for the season a better sound channel would be expected from the region of interest toward Australia than toward the northern hemisphere. Also, on the basis of statistics for low-yield nuclear explosions, no signal would be expected at any of the above sites. In addition, there is a substantial probability of an uncorrelated signal arriving within the large time frame window allowed, since the position of the signal's origin is unknown. Thus, the acoustic data available are considered unrelated to this event.

c. Hydroacoustic Data

In a very preliminary analysis, a search by NRL has shown weak signals at two sites. Signals a few decibels above background noise occur at these sites at times appropriate for direct arrivals from a source near Prince Edward Island and for rays reflected from the Antarctic ice shelf. These data were analyzed by a filtering procedure that is not normally used using a one cycle per second bandwidth in the region of 16 cycles per second.

In one case, 176 signals occurred above background during a 156-hour period. Similar information was not yet available for the other case. This entire study is still too incomplete to apply to the event because no determination of background signal amplitude and occurrence have been furnished to resolve the question of ambiguity in signal identification and source locations.

d. Traveling Ionospheric Disturbance (TID)

A TID consisting of a few aperiodic waves was observed by the Arecibo radar in Puerto Rico as traveling from SE to NW during several hours in the early morning of September 22. A S to N trace velocity of 1200 +/- 300 meters per second (m/s) was reported. The true velocity is a function of the direction of propagation which was reported to be such as to give a value of 500 to 750 m/s, which are values typical of large scale TIDs. Although a South-to-North propagation of large-scale TIDs from natural sources is considered unusual in low northern latitudes, only 120 hours of observation were available for this very sensitive instrument, providing a very weak data base. In this regard, weather satellite data of September 22 indicates that there was a tropical storm a few hundred miles from Arecibo at the time of interest and ionospheric disturbances are known to be generated by such storms. Longer observation at Arecibo may show such events more frequently. Also, a significant error in direction can reduce the true velocity to 150-200 m/s which is the realm of medium-scale TIDs. Arrival from the SE is not a rare event for the much more common medium-scale TIDs. In view of the inadequate data base, uncertainty in signal analysis, and alternative natural explanations, we do not at this time consider the Arecibo data as useful evidence related to the September 22 VELA signal.

Comments on the Nature of the Problem and Our Conclusions

The panel was charged with evaluating the significance of a single satellite observation combined with extensive additional data which were searched for and examined in consequence of that single observation. Specifically, the issue is to evaluate the likelihood that these observations provided persuasive evidence for the occurrence of a nuclear explosion. In concluding that it did not do so it is not necessary, and may in fact not be feasible, to provide a specific credible alternate explanation. This is not an unusual situation in ordinary scientific experience: many scientific investigations leave a residue of unexplained events. In particular, in approaching interpretations of a problem initiated by a single observation, the totality of available data may not provide a single persuasive explanation.

The preceding remark is intended to counter the concern that, "well if it is not a nuclear explosion, then what is it?" We consider the alternative explanation of the September 22 signal as light reflected from debris ejected from the spacecraft as reasonable, but we do not maintain that this particular explanation is necessarily correct.

We do in fact find that the VELA signal of September 22, 1979, contains sufficient internal inconsistency to cast serious doubt whether that signal originated from a nuclear explosion or in fact from any light source not in the proximity of the VELA satellite. Moreover, hundreds of signals exist which constitute a family of unexplained zoo events clearly not generated by nuclear explosions. The September 22, 1979, event may be considered as a possible member of that group.

As discussed elsewhere, the search for supplementary evidence on the nature of the September 22, 1979, event has provided extensive data of varying relevance to the problem. The panel recognizes that there is evidentiary value both in the paucity of such ancillary data as well as in the content of the data obtained. It is important to take into account öallò relevant information – e.g., data that conflicts with the hypothesis that a nuclear explosion occurred as well as the absence of data from certain sensors or locations. We surmise that had a search been made for corroborating data relevant to a nonexistent event chosen to occur at a random time, such a search would have provided "corroboratory data" of similar quantity and quality to that which has been found during analysis of the September 22 signal.

Although the panel is not able to compute the likelihood of the September 22, 1979, event being a nuclear explosion, it is our collective judgement that the September 22 signal was probably not from a nuclear explosion.

AD HOC PANEL ON THE SEPTEMBER 22 EVENT

Panel members:

Dr. Jack Ruina, Chairman, Dept. of Electrical Engineering, MIT

Dr. Louis Alvarez, Dept. of Physics, University of California, Berkeley

Dr. William Donn, Lamont-Doherty Geological Observatory, Columbia University

Dr. Richard Garwin, Thomas J. Watson Research Center, IBM

Dr. Riccardo Giacconi, Harvard/Smithsonian Center for Astrophysics, Harvard University

Dr. Richard Muller, Dept. of Physics, University of California, Berkeley

Dr. Wolfgang Panofsky, Stanford Linear Accelerator Center, Stanford University

Dr. Allen Petersen, Dept. of Electrical Engineering, Stanford University

Dr. F. Williams Sarles, Lincoln Laboratory, MIT

Appendix C. Report to Congress pursuant to section 508 (the Mathias Amendment) of the Comprehensive Anti-Apartheid Act of 1986. (Documenting those states violating the South African arms embargo.)

REPORT TO CONGRESS PURSUANT TO SECTION 508 OF THE
COMPREHENSIVE ANTI-APARTHEID ACT OF 1986:
COMPLIANCE WITH THE U.N. ARMS EMBARGO

Section 508 of the Comprehensive Anti-Apartheid Act of 1986 (P.L. 99-440) provides that the President shall conduct a study on the extent to which the international arms embargo on the sale and export of arms and military technology to South Africa is being violated. It also requires that a report be submitted to Congress setting forth the findings of the study, including an identification of the countries engaged in such sales and exports. In Executive Order 12571, the President directed the Secretary of State to implement the requirements relating to Section 508 of the Act.

The arms embargo referred to in the Comprehensive Anti-Apartheid Act was adopted by the Security Council on November 4, 1977. Resolution 418 on that date was adopted pursuant to Chapter VII of the U.N. Charter. Consequently, the requirements of the resolution are mandatory upon member states.

The Security Council determined that the acquisition of arms and related material by South Africa constitutes a threat to the maintenance of international peace and security. It therefore decided that all states must cease forthwith any provision to South Africa of arms and related materiel of all types. Resolution 418 provides that this includes the sale or transfer of weapons and ammunition, military vehicles and equipment, paramilitary police equipment, and spare parts. It also requires states to cease the provision of all types of equipment for such items and grants of licensing arrangements for the manufacture or maintenance of such items. The Security Council also decided that all states shall refrain from any cooperation in the manufacture and development of nuclear weapons.

The mandatory arms embargo is applicable to direct transfers by governments as well as private transfers of arms. States are required to take whatever measures are necessary to prohibit commercial exports of arms to South Africa.

In a separate paragraph, the Security Council called upon states to review all existing contractual arrangements and licenses involving South Africa relating to the manufacture and maintenance of arms, ammunition and military equipment and vehicles, with a view to terminating the arrangements. Unlike the other provisions referred to in the preceding paragraph, this particular provision does not constitute a binding decision of the Security Council.

It should be emphasized that this limited exception deals only with preexisting arrangements relating to the manufacture and maintenance of arms, ammunition, and military equipment. It does not authorize deliveries of arms under preexisting contracts. This interpretation of Security Council Resolution 418 was shared by the United States, the United Nations Legal Counsel, and all members of the Security Council at the time the resolution was adopted. It is, furthermore, the position of the United States that new agreements relating to the manufacture and maintenance of arms, ammunition, and military equipment (as well as extensions or renewals or preexisting agreements upon their termination) are subject to the mandatory ban. It appears, however, that some states may take a different view on the extension of preexisting contracts.

The United States has strictly enforced the mandatory arms embargo, and no exceptions have been authorized with respect to any prohibited sale or export. In addition, the U.S. also prohibits all exports from the U.S. to the military or police in South Africa (with two minor exceptions for medical supplies and devices to be used in preventing unlawful interferences with international civil aviation). This prohibition is based on significant U.S. policy considerations and prior statutory requirements, but is not required by Resolution 418. The U.S. is not required under the U.N. arms embargo or U.S. law to monitor compliance by other states.

The Key Judgements of the study conducted by the Department of State are:

1. South Africa has reacted to the international arms embargo by developing a large and sophisticated indigenous arms industry. It imports weapon systems and sub-systems when it cannot manufacture the item itself and cannot arrange a license-manufacturing arrangement in South Africa (or the cost of doing so would be extremely inefficient compared to the cost of available imports).

2. South African defense industries' clear preference is to maintain overall control of items manufactured in South Africa and to limit foreign involvement to technical advice and the provision of sub-systems either already complete or for licensed manufacture.

3. Most of the major weapon systems in the South African inventory were present prior to the 1977 arms embargo (French-designed armored vehicles, Israeli-designed patrol boats, Italian and French-designed combat aircraft). These items have been maintained and in many cases upgraded since the embargo, usually with the assistance of the original manufacturer.

4. Because most of the weapons systems that South Africa imports are small and difficult to detect, or are sub-systems, or are of licensed manufacture, we cannot estimate the volume or dollar value of the imports. Thus, we cannot assign a percentage of the market that originates with an individual nation.

5. Due to the nature of the South African imports and the efforts at concealment made by both importers and exporters, intelligence on non-compliance with the arms embargo is difficult to obtain. As a result, we have a partial, incomplete, and somewhat random picture. It is also difficult to substantiate through reliable intelligence means many of the allegations that are publicly made.

6. Given what we do know, we believe that South Africa obtains weapons systems and sub-systems from a wide variety of sources worldwide. There are three notable patterns in this worldwide supply network:

– We believe companies in France, Italy and Israel have continued to be involved in the maintenance and upgrade of major systems provided before the 1977 embargo.

– Prior to the Israeli government's decision on March 18 not to sign any new military contracts and to let existing contracts expire, Israel appears to have sold military systems and sub-systems and provided technical assistance on a regular basis. Although Israel does not require end-use certificates and some cut-outs may have been used, we believe that the Israeli government was fully aware of most or all of the trade. (There is no evidence that Israel has transferred U.S.

manufactured or licensed end-items, but in the absence of an inspection of Israeli made or licensed weapons in South African hands, we cannot say whether Israel has reverse-engineered U.S. weapons or transferred U.S. technology into Israeli weapons that are similar to U.S. systems.)

– Companies in Germany, the United Kingdom, the Netherlands, and Switzerland have on occasion exported articles covered by the embargo without government permission or have engaged in sales to South Africa in the gray area between civilian and military applications.

DATE DUE

The Library Store #47-0204